Contents

Preface

There are many books about how to conduct a job search and find a job but there are few books about how to successfully keep a job once you find it. This workbook was written to help people keep a job and advance their careers. The author has hired and supervised hundreds of employees throughout his career as a leader at workforce development agencies, entrepreneurial businesses, a Fortune 100 company, and higher education. Sharing personal experiences can help other people but this workbook is also based on research into what employers actually look for in the people who work for them and what employees must do to succeed.

Job Savvy is designed to help develop critical job-survival skills, increase productivity, and improve job satisfaction and success. Using a workbook approach, several activities are provided to reinforce key points and develop new job skills and career development plans. The narrative is easy to read and informative, and features good graphic design, many examples, checklists, case studies, and section summaries.

This is the sixth edition of *Job Savvy*. In the 27 years the workbook has been in print, more than 200,000 readers have been helped by the content and activities herein. Everything that made the first five editions so popular remains, so you get the best of the previous editions and many improvements.

This edition draws on the most recent research about job skills and career success. The major change in the sixth edition is the new insights from positive psychology, positive organizational development, and leadership studies. Studies from these areas have made significant contribution to our understanding of career success.

Why People Need to Improve Their Basic Job Skills

When the previous version of *Job Savvy* was released, the United States was just coming out of what has become known as the Great Recession. In the past eight years there has been a steady improvement in the job market and the country is now in one of the best employment outlooks in 30 years. Unemployment is now better than it has been since the beginning of the millennium. Indeed, consumer confidence in the economy is also at an 18-year high. All this data is good news for people who want to find a better job, obtain job promotions, and get raises.

As this book goes to press, the country is experiencing one of the lowest unemployment rates it has seen in almost 30 years. This makes it easier for people to find a job, but the need for skills to help a person to be competitive and keep a job is more critical than ever. The years ahead are projected to be a time of labor market opportunity as well as challenge for most workers. Some of these challenges and opportunities include the following:

- An increasing use of automation, artificial intelligence, and robots will result in more competition for jobs.
- Information technology will continue to change the way we work, and people must adapt to these changes.

- Many new and existing jobs will require higher levels of technical skills.
- The amount of education and training required for jobs will increase.
- Employers will expect their employees to be more productive and obtain better results in more complex jobs.

People frequently change jobs. A national research group found that people between the ages 18 and 48 held about 12 jobs. The reasons for leaving a job include being fired, lack of promotional opportunities, lack of raises, uninteresting work, and layoffs. Many labor experts predict the rate people change jobs will increase.

Workforce trends as well as individual changes in jobs will require people to have more diverse skills than in the past. The biggest need, according to most employers and labor market experts, is for employees to have technical skills and soft skills. Soft skills include dependability, reliability, good communication, problem solving, adaptability, good teamwork, and many others (that will be described in this workbook). In fact, there is strong evidence that these soft skills have been needed for the past century, but somehow soft skills are frequently not taught in career classes. This workbook is a tool to help change that situation. Here, you as well as schools, parents, government training programs, and employers receive a resource to learn and teach the soft skills that are critical for success in our world.

A Different Point of View

You will find numerous references in *Job Savvy* to the studies and research of psychologists, sociologists, economists, and other labor market professionals, yet this is not an academic book. Instead, this information has been used to form the basis for a practical and useful handbook for a working person—or one who soon plans to enter the world of work. Many employers have asked for such a book to give new workers the knowledge and skills to succeed on the job. And because the author has been both an employer and a trainer of new employees, he brings a unique and helpful point of view that will bridge the gap between an employer's and an employee's expectations. The result of this is increased job savvy that allows everyone to win.

A Parable

An explorer was once asked what he most disliked about the wilderness.
"Is it the wolves?"
"No," he replied. "It's the mosquitoes."

It is often not the big things that keep people from succeeding on the job but rather an accumulation of lots of small things. *Job Savvy* introduces you to both the big ideas as well as the many small ideas that help to succeed on the job.

How to Use This Workbook

This print workbook is designed to help you succeed in your job. You may fill in the activities with pencil or pen. Generally, you will work through each chapter like this:

1. Read the chapter in the workbook or ebook and watch the video presentation available in your ebook or from your instructor.
2. Complete in-workbook activities (including fill-in-the-blank questions, checklists, and games) and supplemental activities (referenced in the workbook margins) as you read through the print or ebook version of the workbook.
3. Review the concepts learned by using study tools available in the ebook or from your instructor.

Overview of Chapter Content

The following visual tour shows how to use the features in this program to develop the skills needed to succeed in your career.

CHAPTER 1

Your Employment Relationship

Objectives

- Identify strategies for dealing with changes in the workplace.
- Discuss and demonstrate how to understand an employer's point of view.

Did you know that most of us spend almost 95,000 hours of our lives working? Work is how we earn the money to pay for our material needs. Work satisfies many of our psychological needs. And work fulfills our needs for human interaction and friendship. Because work is such a major part of our lives, it's important to have a basic understanding of work in today's society.

In this chapter, you will closely examine employment relationships. When an employer hires and pays a worker for a full-time, 40-hour-a-week job, a traditional employment relationship is created. However, today it is common for many workers to look for flexible jobs, such as part-time, job-sharing, on-call, temporary, and contract jobs. In addition, people are working at home for an employer (often called "freelance," "remote," or "telecommute" work) or starting home-based businesses.[1] Regardless of the type of work, when two people enter into business together, an employment relationship forms, and it's important to your job success to understand what that means.

This chapter looks at the many influences on your employment relationships, including the labor force, the occupation types, the workplace, and the structure of work—all terms you will better understand after reading the chapter. Within each discussion, you will explore today's work expectations and what workplaces might look like in the future. For example, this chapter presents facts about diversity in the labor force that will help you appreciate your fellow employees.

Finally, in this chapter you'll learn what skills employers need from workers. A worker's skills, both technical and **soft skills**, determine how valuable an employee is to an **organization**. For example, technical skills required by auto mechanics include servicing vehicles and repairing mechanical parts, but employers also want mechanics to have soft skills, such as cooperation, **dependability**, and **self-control**.

Watch the Video
Your Employment Relationship

1

Workbook Chapters are divided into 13 topics that explore the key areas of interest to job seekers and employers.

Objectives define the concepts and skills you will demonstrate after successfully completing the chapter.

Video Presentations review the concepts in each chapter. You may access videos in the ebook.

Thinking about Your Education

What education is required for your job? _____

How much do you earn in a year? (If you're not sure, multiply your hourly wage by 2,080 if you work full-time. If you work part-time, multiply your hourly wage by the number of hours you work in an average week and multiply that by 52 weeks.)

_____
_____

How do your education and earnings compare with the national average for your occupation? (You can find this information in the *Occupational Outlook Handbook [OOH]* or online at https://www.bls.gov/ooh/.)

_____
_____

Are you planning to get a job in another occupation? _____

What are the educational requirements and average earnings for this occupation? (Again, you can find this information in the *OOH* or online.)

_____

What kind of training does your current job offer?

_____

How can this training help you advance in your current job?

_____

How can the training help prepare you for a future occupation?

_____
_____

Write some ways you can keep your education current and get the skills you need to be successful.

_____
_____
_____

The Structure of Work

The structure of work is changing, and that affects the way jobs are organized. Most organizations recognize the need to have a flexible workforce. This flexibility allows a business to keep its workforce as small as possible, thus saving money. Organizations use a combination of core employees and nontraditional workers to increase efficiency. People engaged in what the US Department of Labor identifies as "nontraditional work arrangements" help core employees achieve organizational goals. There are 15.8% workers in alternative work situations. This number is a 50% increase over the percent

Organizations and Work

In the US economy, most workers—81%, in fact—are employed by service-producing organizations.[5] As Table 1.1 shows, service organizations include a wide variety of businesses—not just fast-food franchises, which is what many people think when they hear the words **service economy**. The major areas of the service industry are in this table. The type of service industry is in the first column. The second column shows the percentage of workers employed by each industry group in 2016. The third column shows the projected employment for 2026.

The remaining portion of the workforce (the other 19%) is employed in goods-producing organizations, agriculture, and self-employment. This economic sector's share of employment has declined over the past several decades, and continued decline is expected. Table 1.2 shows current and projected employment for these businesses.

Most workers are employed in service-producing fields, and more than 50% work for smaller organizations—organizations with fewer than 500 employees.[6] A decline in an industry doesn't mean you won't be able to find a good job in that sector. But working in an industry with declining employment means you must continually develop your skills. And, to be safe, you also should develop skills that will help you get a job in another industry if it becomes necessary. Many people learned this lesson as a result of the corporate restructuring that has been a significant part of business in the last 40 years.

Smaller organizations are less likely than larger ones to provide their workers with **training**. This means that most workers must assess their own training needs and take control of their training and **education**. In other words, you are responsible for your own **employability** and competitiveness in today's workforce.

Journal Activity

Explore your job history. What industries have you worked in (service, product, producing)? Have you worked for small or large companies?

Journal Activity

What skills do you need to advance your career?

Table 1.1 Projected Employment Percentages in the Service Industry

Type of Service Industry	Percentage of 2016 Employment	Projected Percentage of 2026 Employment
Wholesale and retail trade	13.9%	13.1%
Federal, state, and local government	14.2%	13.7%
Educational, health care, and social assistance	14.5%	16.2%
Professional and business services	12.9%	13.3%
Leisure and hospitality	10.0%	10.1%
Information and financial activities	7.1%	6.9%
Transporting and warehousing	3.2%	3.2%
Other	4.1%	4.0%

Workbook Activities (including fill-in-the-blank questions, checklists, and games) are available in the print workbook, and in the ebook as PDFs that you can use to type in your answers using a computer.

Margin Activities reaffirm your understanding of concepts and give you real-life workplace communications practice. (Activities Supplements expand upon the margin activities and are available in the ebook.)

Tables provide a detailed look at important topics and statistical data that support the concepts taught.

Summing Up is a summary of the concepts you learned in each chapter.

Review and Assessment signifies the appropriate time to complete the chapter electronic or print Review Quiz, Review Activities, Activities Supplements handouts, and other resources and study tools available in the ebook or from your instructor.

What Should You Expect?

Most of us have several reasons for working. Your motivation and interest in a job depend on your reasons for working and how well the job satisfies your needs.

1. List your reasons for working. You might think of money first. That's fine, but also think of the other reasons you work.

   _____

   _____

   _____

2. Think about the jobs you've had. What did you like about each job? What did you dislike?

   _____

   _____

   _____

3. How do you expect an employer to treat you? What are things you want in return for the work you do?

   _____

   _____

   _____

Summing Up

The labor force, workplaces, and structure of jobs are changing. The US labor force is more diverse than ever before, with the addition of more women, people from ethnic and racial groups, older workers, and people with disabilities.

Most organizations provide customer services, and many service-related jobs require a high level of skill. Employers are restructuring jobs so that they can be done not only by traditional workers but also by contingent workers.

These changes demand higher skill levels. Workers need more education than ever before. Employers expect employees to have technical skills for a specific job, but they consider basic skills to be even more important.

Employers have expectations of employees. Workers also have expectations of their employers. Your relationship with an employer is built on these important points of understanding:

- The employer is in business to make a profit, not just to provide you with a job and paycheck.
- If you can identify the reasons you want to work and find a job that fulfills your needs, you will be happier and do a better job.

Review and Assessment

Take the Review Quiz posted to the ebook. See your instructor for additional resources.

Student Ebook

The ebook will provide you with direct access to video presentations, topical videos, study tools, review quizzes, and interactive PDFs that allow you to fill out the workbook activities electronically. You'll also find Activities Supplements handouts with guidance on how to complete the activities in the workbook margins. The following activities are provided in the workbook margins:

- **Journal Activity** allows you to privately reflect on topics learned by keeping a journal and answering/expanding on the questions in your journal.
- **Group Activity** allows you to explore concepts within small groups to further explore the concepts learned and add depth to your knowledge and interpretations while practicing how to professionally and effectively communicate in small groups or teamwork scenarios.
- **Discussion Activity** allows you to participate and share your knowledge, and ask questions in a large, formal setting—the full classroom—while practicing how to professionally and effectively communicate in large group settings.
- **Case Study** enhances your understanding of the concepts with real-life scenarios. Case Studies may be recorded in student journals, discussed in small groups, discussed in the classroom, or contemplated privately depending on classroom instruction.

Your Employment Relationship

Objectives

- Identify strategies for dealing with changes in the workplace.

- Discuss and demonstrate how to understand an employer's point of view.

D id you know that most of us spend almost 95,000 hours of our lives working? Work is how we earn the money to pay for our material needs. Work satisfies many of our psychological needs. And work fulfills our needs for human interaction and friendship. Because work is such a major part of our lives, it's important to have a basic understanding of work in today's society.

In this chapter, you will closely examine employment relationships. When an employer hires and pays a worker for a full-time, 40-hour-a-week job, a traditional employment relationship is created. However, today it is common for many workers to look for flexible jobs, such as part-time, job-sharing, on-call, temporary, and contract jobs. In addition, people are working at home for an employer (often called "freelance," "remote," or "telecommute" work) or starting home-based businesses.[1] Regardless of the type of work, when two people enter into business together, an employment relationship forms, and it's important to your job success to understand what that means.

This chapter looks at the many influences on your employment relationships, including the labor force, the occupation types, the workplace, and the structure of work—all terms you will better understand after reading the chapter. Within each discussion, you will explore today's work expectations and what workplaces might look like in the future. For example, this chapter presents facts about diversity in the labor force that will help you appreciate your fellow employees.

Finally, in this chapter you'll learn what skills employers need from workers. A worker's skills, both technical and **soft skills**, determine how valuable an employee is to an **organization**. For example, technical skills required by auto mechanics include servicing vehicles and repairing mechanical parts, but employers also want mechanics to have soft skills, such as cooperation, **dependability**, and **self-control**.

Watch the Video

Your Employment Relationship

The Changing Labor Force

The term **labor force** refers to the people who are available and want to work. Anyone who is looking for a job or working at a job is a member of the labor force. You'll be a better prepared worker if you understand some of the changes that are occurring in the United States labor force.[2]

Journal Activity

Why do you work?

1. **Labor force growth has slowed down.** Approximately 63% of the population participates in the labor force. Those not participating include children, students, retired persons, persons with disabilities, and those voluntarily not "working" (for example, stay-at-home parents or seasonal workers). Labor force participation is expected to decline between 2016 and 2026, though at a slower rate than during the previous decade. This decline is true for men and women.

   For several decades, the labor force's participation rate for women had increased. The rate peaked at 60% in 1999 but has since gradually decreased. Female participation in the labor force is projected to be about 56% in 2026. This is still a dramatic change from the end of World War II, when only 28% of the **workforce** was female. In more recent history, a similar decline in the male labor force has been seen. By the end of 2026, male participation in the labor force is projected to be 66%. At the same time, the number of job openings is expected to increase. This doesn't necessarily mean there will be a labor shortage. It does indicate that for people looking to work during the years from now until 2026, there will be many job opportunities.

   These labor market conditions have improved the pay offered for entry-level jobs in much of the economy. Most people (98.5% of full-time workers) are paid more than the federal minimum wage ($7.25). Even 90% of workers 25 and younger are paid more than the minimum wage.[3] This is good news for high school students and graduates looking for their first job.

2. **Women continue to impact the workplace.** Women's participation in the labor force has had an impact on how businesses operate. Employers now have policies and benefits specifically for child care, family leave, flexible schedules, job sharing, and sexual harassment thanks in part to women advocating for change in the workplace. Employees have found that these improvements benefit all. In fact, the shifting view of women in the workplace has changed the way many organizations view men's roles within the family. Both female and male workers now expect family-friendly employment practices. Many positive changes in the workplace have resulted from the increased participation of women, and this trend is likely to continue despite the slightly lower rate of participation by women in the labor force.

3. **Older generations continue to impact the workplace.** The number of workers ages 55 and over is expected to increase from 22.5% in 2016 to 24.8% in 2026. To put this in perspective, the number of workers in the 55-plus age group will grow three times faster than any other age group. This is the result of the baby boomer generation moving

Case Study

Angie is 20 years old. She is a receptionist at a dental office. Maureen is 52 years old. She was recently hired as a second receptionist. Angie has been instructed to train Maureen. What are the positive and negative reactions to this situation?

into this age group and staying in the workforce longer before retiring. By 2018, this age group included people 54 to 72 years old. The graying of the workforce likely will push businesses to rethink retirement policies and to find new ways to use workers regardless of age. The fact that this generation will be the healthiest and most vital group of older workers in history might also alter views about changing careers later in life.

4. **Ethnic and racial diversity is impacting the workplace.** The workforce will continue to change in racial and ethnic composition. Labor force participation from 2016 to 2026 is expected to grow two to three times faster for Asians and those of Hispanic origin than for blacks and whites. The composition of the labor force in 2026 is expected to be white (non-Hispanic) 58%, Hispanic 20%, black 12%, Asian 7%, and all others (including Native Americans) 3%.[4] Companies have responded to this trend by creating ethnic diversity programs to help workers of all **ethnic groups** understand and appreciate cultural differences. This mix of cultures in the workplace brings new perspectives to solving business problems. You can be a more effective (and valuable) employee if you can work well with others in a diverse workforce.

In summary, the workforce of the future will represent a broad range of gender, age, and racial and ethnic diversity. It's important for people entering the workforce to be aware of these changes and the need to work with all different kinds of people. Learning to appreciate differences isn't just a nicety anymore—it's a workplace necessity.

Case Study

Carlos and Mohammed work at a warehouse. Mohammed does not drink alcohol as part of his religious beliefs. Carlos invites him and other coworkers to the local bar at the end of the work day. What are the positive and negative reactions to this situation?

Group Activity

How do changes impact you at work?

What Does Your Workplace Look Like?

Following are descriptions of people in the workforce. Check all of the boxes that apply to people you currently work with. In the line after each group, write the number of people in your workplace who fall into that category.

Age

❑ 14 to 15 years old _____

❑ 16 to 19 years old _____

❑ 20 to 24 years old _____

❑ 25 to 34 years old _____

❑ 35 to 44 years old _____

❑ 45 to 54 years old _____

❑ 55 to 64 years old _____

❑ 65 and over _____

Gender

❑ Male _____

❑ Female _____

Ethnic and Racial Group

❑ White
(non-Hispanic origin) _____

❑ Black_____

❑ Hispanic _____

❑ Asian_____

❑ Native American_____

How would you rate diversity in your workplace?

❑ Low   ❑ Medium   ❑ High

Organizations and Work

In the US economy, most workers—81%, in fact—are employed by service-producing organizations.[5] As Table 1.1 shows, service organizations include a wide variety of businesses—not just fast-food franchises, which is what many people think when they hear the words **service economy**. The major areas of the service industry are in this table. The type of service industry is in the first column. The second column shows the percentage of workers employed by each industry group in 2016. The third column shows the projected employment for 2026.

The remaining portion of the workforce (the other 19%) is employed in goods-producing organizations, agriculture, and self-employment. This economic sector's share of employment has declined over the past several decades, and continued decline is expected. Table 1.2 shows current and projected employment for these businesses.

Most workers are employed in service-producing fields, and more than 50% work for smaller organizations—organizations with fewer than 500 employees.[6] A decline in an industry doesn't mean you won't be able to find a good job in that sector. But working in an industry with declining employment means you must continually develop your skills. And, to be safe, you also should develop skills that will help you get a job in another industry if it becomes necessary. Many people learned this lesson as a result of the corporate restructuring that has been a significant part of business in the last 40 years.

Smaller organizations are less likely than larger ones to provide their workers with **training**. This means that most workers must assess their own training needs and take control of their training and **education**. In other words, you are responsible for your own **employability** and competitiveness in today's workforce.

Journal Activity

Explore your job history. What industries have you worked in (service, product, producing)? Have you worked for small or large companies?

Journal Activity

What skills do you need to advance your career?

Table 1.1 Projected Employment Percentages in the Service Industry

Type of Service Industry	Percentage of 2016 Employment	Projected Percentage of 2026 Employment
Wholesale and retail trade	13.9%	13.1%
Federal, state, and local government	14.2%	13.7%
Educational, health care, and social assistance	14.5%	16.2%
Professional and business services	12.9%	13.3%
Leisure and hospitality	10.0%	10.1%
Information and financial activities	7.1%	6.9%
Transporting and warehousing	3.2%	3.2%
Other	4.1%	4.0%

Table 1.2 Projected Employment Percentages in the Business Industry

Type of Business	Percentage of 2016 Employment	Projected Percentage of 2026 Employment
Goods, production, mining, manufacturing, and construction	12.6%	11.9%
Agriculture	1.5%	1.4%
Self-employment	5.6%	5.7%

Educational Trends

The skills a person needs to obtain and keep a job are typically learned. Only 27.7% of all occupations require no education. Another 35.8% require at least a high school education. The other 36.5% require some education beyond high school.[7] Many jobs that do not require formal education or only a high school education require on-the-job training. As you can see, education plays an important role in an occupation. Workers sell their skills to an employer, so it is important to acquire good skills at the beginning of your career and to maintain your competitiveness with the help of continuing education and training.

The impact of education on earnings over a lifetime is staggering (see Table 1.3[8]). Take the example of a high school graduate who begins working full-time at 19 and retires 51 years later at age 70. Compare that person with a college graduate who begins working at age 25 and retires at age 70. The college graduate earns about $856,596 more in a lifetime than the average earnings of a high school graduate. Earnings and employment opportunities for less-educated workers declined significantly in the last decade. That trend is likely to continue. There's truth to the adage Education Pays.

Group Activity

How much education do you need to support your lifestyle and career goals?

Table 1.3 Education Pays

Level of Education	Average Annual Earnings	Percentage of High School Graduate's Earnings
No high school diploma	$27,040	73%
High school diploma	$37,024	100%
Some college, no degree	$40,248	109%
Associate degree	$43,472	117%
Bachelor's degree	$60,996	165%
Master's degree	$72,852	197%
Doctoral degree	$90,636	245%
Professional degree	$95,472	258%

Training and Continuing Education

It's also important—in fact, in today's economy, it's necessary—to continue learning once you're on the job. Although many businesses provide training, it's up to you to take charge of your continuing education. (Chapter 6 examines this topic.)

Thinking about Your Education

What education is required for your job? _____

How much do you earn in a year? (If you're not sure, multiply your hourly wage by 2,080 if you work full-time. If you work part-time, multiply your hourly wage by the number of hours you work in an average week and multiply that by 52 weeks.)

_____

_____

How do your education and earnings compare with the national average for your occupation? (You can find this information in the *Occupational Outlook Handbook [OOH]* or online at https://www.bls.gov/ooh/.)

_____

_____

Are you planning to get a job in another occupation? _____

What are the educational requirements and average earnings for this occupation? (Again, you can find this information in the *OOH* or online.)

_____

What kind of training does your current job offer?

_____

_____

How can this training help you advance in your current job?

_____

_____

How can the training help prepare you for a future occupation?

_____

_____

Write some ways you can keep your education current and get the skills you need to be successful.

_____

_____

The Structure of Work

The structure of work is changing, and that affects the way jobs are organized. Most organizations recognize the need to have a flexible workforce. This flexibility allows a business to keep its workforce as small as possible, thus saving money. Organizations use a combination of core employees and nontraditional workers to increase efficiency. People engaged in what the US Department of Labor identifies as "nontraditional work arrangements" help core employees achieve organizational goals. There are 15.8% workers in alternative work situations. This number is a 50% increase over the percent of nontraditional workers in 2005.[9] The following are explanations of the various work arrangements:

- **Core Employees** People with a traditional employment arrangement. Companies hire these full-time workers on a permanent basis—meaning that there is no planned end to the job. Core employees typically have some loyalty to the organization and understand both its short-term and long-term goals. They usually are provided with benefits such as vacation time, holiday pay, and health insurance. Core employees often coordinate or lead projects for an organization.

- **Independent Contractors** Self-employed individuals who provide services to an organization based on a contract signed by the employer and contractor. The service they provide might be computer programming, management consulting, cleaning, maintenance, payroll, accounting, security, telecommunications, editing, or printing. Contractors are paid a fee for completion of a task rather than a wage. Most independent contractors prefer their status to traditional employment, and these individuals comprise 8.4% of workers. This group makes up the largest group of contingent workers.

- **Contract Firms** Organizations that typically supply entry-level workers to an organization. The work is typically done at the employer's site. For example, electrical component assemblers might be employed by a contract firm rather than by the manufacturer. The manufacturer doesn't have to be concerned about performing all the management and administrative support functions involved in employing a large group of workers.

- **On-call Workers** Workers who are called to work when they are needed. They are paid for work only when they are called to perform a task. Employers might use this type of arrangement if they need workers to repair specialized manufacturing equipment, computers, or telecommunications equipment, or to install equipment when ordered.

- **Temporary Workers** Workers who are hired by an organization for a short time or whose services are obtained through a temporary employment service. Many organizations prefer to use a temp service because it reduces their paperwork, administrative tasks, and recruitment efforts. If temporary workers are hired to work on a specific project, their employment ends when the project ends. Temporary workers might be hired when an organization's workload increases beyond the capacity of its core employees. In that case, there might be no specific date when the work ends. Rather, the organization will stop using the workers' services when the workload decreases. Temporary employees often do not have benefits—unless the temp service provides them—and their work can be terminated without advance notice.

Journal Activity

Explore why companies need employees.

Group Activity

Chart your work experience as a group by using the five major structures of employment mentioned on this page.

Gig Economy

One form of nontraditional work is a gig (a temporary service, task, or function for which a person is paid). A **gig economy** is emerging that allows people to easily find nontraditional work opportunities.[10] The word *gig* has been around in different forms for a while. For example, lawn mowing, dog walking, and babysitting are gig jobs. The basic job skills reviewed in this chapter are even more important if you want to be successful at a gig job.

The way people find gig jobs and get paid for them has recently changed because of computers and smartphones. Today, it is much easier for someone who needs a small task done to find a gig worker and to be immediately connected with someone who will do the task. Examples of gig workers include Uber and Lyft drivers, Amazon Flex deliverers, and errand runners. A quick online search will reveal dozens of sites listing gig jobs.

Note: It's very important to be careful of scams. Check the website out with friends and family, social media, and the Better Business Bureau to ensure credibility.

So what does all this mean for you? It means that you are responsible for your own career. In today's economy, you simply cannot rely on an employer to provide a permanent job. When one job ends, you must be prepared to find another. It's important to develop as many skills as possible so that you can adapt to new tasks and projects, and to be prepared to work either as a core employee or contingent worker. Adaptability and a willingness to work in any structure allow you to take charge of your own career.

How Job Savvy Are You?

Alisha is a computer repair technician for a company with about 100 employees. She is paid by a temporary-service firm. Alisha earned her associate's degree from a community college three years ago. She earns about $850 a week but has no benefits.

1. What kind of worker is Alisha?

    _____

    _____

    _____

2. If you were Alisha, would you continue to work for this company? Give a reason for your answer.

    _____

    _____

    _____

Continues

3. What could Alisha do to increase her opportunities to work as a core employee?

_____

_____

_____

Jamal is employed full-time as a certified nursing assistant (CNA) orderly in a hospital and receives several benefits, such as paid holidays, paid vacation time, and health insurance. He earns about $500 per week. Jamal enjoys working in a medical environment but thinks he needs to earn more money. He graduated from high school, but he didn't like school and he doesn't want to go to college.

1. What kind of worker is Jamal?

_____

_____

_____

2. Would you be satisfied working in this situation? Explain your answer.

_____

_____

_____

3. What do you think Jamal could do to improve his salary and his work situation?

_____

_____

_____

Herschel is self-employed, so he pays for his own benefits and works from a home office. He spends most of his time working for a medium-sized business corporation, processing payroll checks for the company's employees, keeping time records, and filing employment-tax reports. He also does some work for smaller businesses. Herschel has a bachelor's degree in accounting. His business earns about $70,000 a year, but he would like to earn much more money.

1. What kind of worker is Herschel?

_____

_____

2. Would you be satisfied with a work situation like Herschel's?

_____

_____

3. What do you think Herschel can do to make more money?

_____

_____

Your Work Experience

In the following space, briefly describe your last three jobs. Were you employed full-time or part-time? Did the company hire you or were you assigned by a temporary agency? How large was the company in terms of numbers of employees and customers, amount of sales, and locations? What types of technology did you use on the job?

1. _____

_____

_____

_____

2. _____

_____

_____

_____

3. _____

_____

_____

_____

21st-Century Skills

Employers need employees with technical skills, such as computer coding, bridge designing, and CPR administration. These more technical skills are sometimes referred to as "hard skills." Workers who have good technical skills are still sometimes unsuccessful at their jobs because they don't possess soft skills (also considered basic skills), like communicating professionally and working well in teams. Soft skills are also important to job success.

Many studies provide insight into the basic skills that employers expect their workers to have to succeed on the job. Having a better understanding of what it takes to do well on a job will help you achieve personal success. This book can help you acquire many of the basic skills you need to do well at any occupation. Probably the most interesting aspect of studies about workplace skills is that their results have been consistent during the past 100 years. However, they have become even more important during the 21st century as workers in the United States are competing with workers around the world.

Workplace Basics

The US Secretary of Labor created a commission to "define the know-how needed in the workplace." The Secretary's Commission on Achieving Necessary Skills (SCANS) was made up of people from business, education, and government who identified the skills needed to succeed in high-skilled, high-paid jobs. They listed three foundational skills and five workplace competencies. The foundational skills include the following:

- **Basic Skills**   Reading, writing, mathematics, speaking, and listening
- **Thinking Skills**   The ability to learn, reason, think creatively, make decisions, and solve problems
- **Personal Qualities**   Individual **responsibility**, self-esteem, self-management, sociability, and **integrity**

Workplace competencies are the skills workers need to be productive. The commission listed the following:

- **Resources Skills**   The ability to allocate time, money, materials, space, and staff
- **Interpersonal Skills**   The ability to work on teams, teach others, and serve customers, as well as to lead, negotiate with, and work with people from diverse cultural backgrounds
- **Information Skills**   The ability to acquire and evaluate data, organize and maintain files, interpret and communicate information, and use computers to process information
- **Systems Skills**   The ability to understand social, organizational, and technological systems; monitor and correct performance; and design or improve systems
- **Technology Skills**   The ability to select equipment and tools, apply technology to specific tasks, and maintain and troubleshoot equipment

Discussion

How has technology at work changed?

The SCANS report demonstrates an important fact: Different, higher-level skills are needed in today's labor market as compared to the skills required 20 years ago. This report is supported by the Workplace Basics study, which was conducted by the American Society for Training and Development (ASTD).[11]

ASTD asked employers throughout the United States what basic skills their employees need. The study found that most employers want their employees to possess the workplace basics, including these skills:

Group Activity

What skills are in demand that you'd like to explore?

- **Knowing How to Learn**   The concept of lifelong learning is common in the business community. Employees who don't have good learning skills will be unable to take advantage of training and might soon find their skills obsolete.
- **Reading, Writing, and Computation**   People who are weak in these skills will have trouble in most jobs. The average number of years of education required for jobs in the early part of the 21st century is approximately 13.5 years.
- **Listening and Oral Communication**   The average person spends 8.4% of communication time writing, 13.3% reading, 23% speaking, and 55% listening. Communication is as critical to success on the job as the three Rs (reading, 'riting, and 'rithmetic).
- **Adaptability**   Organizations must be flexible to adapt and keep pace with advances in technology, changes in the marketplace, and new management practices. Employees who are creative problem solvers are essential to today's businesses.

Journal Activity

How flexible are you when it comes to learning new skills?

- **Management**   Self-management covers self-esteem, goal setting and motivation, and personal and career development. For businesses to succeed, employees must take pride in their work and be able to formulate and achieve goals. Finally, employees must know how to advance within an organization and how to transfer skills to another business. As more businesses engage in participative management, these skills will become increasingly necessary.
- **Effectiveness**   Individualism is a thing of the past in most jobs. It is far more important that workers understand and practice **teamwork**, negotiation, and interpersonal skills. People who understand how to work effectively in groups are the foundations of successful enterprises.
- **Influence**   Each employee must establish his or her own influence in order to successfully contribute ideas to an organization. Employees must understand the organizational structure and informal networks in order to implement new ideas or to complete some tasks.

Who Needs These Skills?

In 2006, the ASTD conducted an online survey that asked its members to identify the skills most lacking by employees in their organizations.[12] Because employees lack these skills, the organizations end up with the responsibility of developing these skills in their employees. The results of this survey are shown in Table 1.4.

Table 1.4 Skills Most Needed

Skill	Percentage Who Say It's Most Needed
Managerial/supervisory	55%
Communication/interpersonal	51%
Leadership	45%
Process and project management	27%
Technical/systems	24%
Customer service	20%
Professional or industry specific	19%
Sales	17%

It is interesting that employers considered many basic skills to be more important than technical skills needed for a job. This is different from the perception most people have. That might be why job seekers promoting their abilities often overlook and downplay their more basic skills. It is also a reason to use this book to develop these skills.

The Public's View About 21st-Century Skills

In 2010, the Partnership for 21st Century Skills—a group of major corporate and educational organizations—cooperated with the American Management Association and surveyed more than 2,100 managers and executives on their attitudes about the most important skills needed to succeed in the modern workforce.[13]

The survey defined the four skills as follows:

- **Critical Thinking and Problem Solving**   The ability to make decisions, solve problems, and take action as appropriate
- **Effective Communication**   The ability to synthesize and transmit ideas both in written and oral formats
- **Collaboration and Team Building**   The ability to work effectively with others, including those from diverse groups and with opposing points of view
- **Creativity and Innovation**   The ability to see what's *not* there and make something happen

Managers and executives were asked how they believed the four skills would be viewed by their organization in the next three to five years. They responded as noted in Table 1.5.

Table 1.5 Future Importance of Top Skills[14]

Statement About Skills	Percentage Agreeing with Statement
Skills will become more important.	75.7%
Skills will remain the same.	22.5%
Skills will become less important.	0.6%
No opinion.	1.1%

Almost 98% of executives and managers indicated that critical thinking, effective communication, team building, and creativity will remain or become more important skills for workers in their organization.

Best Jobs for the 21st-Century Skills

One of the earliest studies that discussed basic skills was published in 1918.[15] The Carnegie Foundation employed Professor Charles Mann to study what engineering professors should teach students so they would be successful at work. Professor Mann discovered many ideas about the hard skills that engineering students needed to learn. A surprising outcome of the study was how important soft skills are for an engineer's success at work. A survey of 1,500 engineers found that the engineers' self-identified soft skills were needed seven times more than their hard skills.

A recent study by Google was similar to the one done by Professor Mann, except the Google study asked what skills were needed to be a good leader (the ultimate goal of job success).[16] Table 1.6 compares the skills identified for job success by Professor Mann to those identified by Google. As you can see, the skills needed for succeeding on the job have remained the same over the past century even though the words describing the skills have changed with the times.

Table 1.6 Skills Then vs. Now

1918 Skills	2011 Skills*
Common Sense	Good Coach
Resourcefulness	Resourceful (Empowers Team)
Initiative	Clear Vision/Strategy for Team
Tact	Listens and Shares Information
Thoroughness	Results-oriented
Accuracy	Productive
Efficiency	Does Not Micromanage
Understanding of People	Expresses Interest/Concern for Team Members

*Adapted from Google Leader Skills.

The various studies described in this chapter, along with others, are nicely summarized in a study funded by the United States Agency for International Development (USAID) Education titled *Key "Soft Skills" that Foster Youth Workforce Success: Toward a Consensus across Fields.*[17] This study looked at 380 sources about the relationship between soft skills and success on the job. The essential skills discovered in the study are shown in the Skills Checklist exercise (on the next page). To help you better understand some of these key skills, each chapter in this book focuses on a specific skill. The chapters and the featured skill in each are shown in Table 1.7.

This book helps you be better prepared for the workforce by focusing on most of the essential soft skills. It also helps you understand how to learn and apply these skills in an effective manner in the workplace.

Table 1.7 Essential Skills Explored in *Job Savvy*

Chapter Number	Chapter Title	Skill
2	Avoiding the New-Job Blues	Self-control, **Self-motivation**
3	Making a Good Impression	**Self-concept**
4	Being There . . . On Time!	Dependability, Responsibility
5	Communicating in the Workplace	Communication
6	Learning—What It's All About	Self-motivation, **Critical Thinking**
7	Knowing Yourself	Positive Self-concept, Self-motivation
8	Getting Along with Your Supervisor	Hardworking, **Social Skills Dependability**, Responsibility
9	Getting Along with Other Workers	Teamwork, Social Skills
10	Meeting the Customer's Expectations	Social Skills, Responsibility
11	Problem-Solving Skills	**Problem-solving, Decision-making**
12	Doing the Right Thing	Critical Thinking, Integrity
13	Getting Ahead on the Job	**Positive Attitude**, Hardworking, Dependability

Journal Activity

Give an example of how you use each of the major skills used in the workplace (refer to the Skills Checklist on the next page).

Skills Checklist

Using this scale, rate how successfully you practice each of the following skills at work: 1) Very Well, 2) Somewhat Well, 3) Unsure, 4) Somewhat Poorly, 5) Very Poorly.

Social Skills (Respecting Others, Resolving Conflict) _____

Problem-solving _____

Critical Thinking _____

Decision-making _____

Self-control _____

Positive Self-concept _____

Communication _____

Hardworking, Dependability _____

Self-motivation _____

Teamwork _____

Responsibility _____

Positive Attitude _____

Integrity/Ethical _____

Dependability vs. Responsibility

The dictionary definitions of these words are similar. But when they are used in the world of work, they have slightly different meanings. Dependability means being on time and at work every day and notifying your supervisor when you are unable to be there. Responsibility means following through with a job. When the boss asks you to do a job, you prove your responsibility by completing the assigned task and then looking for other things to do. Both of these skills fall into the general area of personal management skills, but employers often cite them as the most essential skills employees need.

How Your Skills Help Your Employer

Employers are looking for workers with the skills that can help make an organization successful. There are three essentials needed for an organization to be a success.

1. **Provide a product or service of high quality.** Consumers want whatever they buy to be of high quality, so organizations place great emphasis on quality. The US government even recognizes companies for their emphasis on quality by giving them the Malcolm Baldrige National Quality Award.
2. **Satisfy the customer's needs and wants.** An organization depends on the goodwill of its customers. If customers are pleased with products they've purchased or services they've received, they will continue to do business with an organization and even recommend it to friends. Conversely, people talk about a bad experience with friends, family members, acquaintances, coworkers, and even complete strangers.
3. **Make a profit.** Product quality and customer satisfaction have to be provided at a cost that allows a business to make a profit. There's no reason for the owners or stockholders to continue the business if they could invest their money elsewhere and receive a higher rate of return.

Group Activity

How do you produce quality work?

Group Activity

Plan a summer program for children. What expenses might be involved? How much will you charge each student? What factors might affect your profit? How many employees will you have? What salaries will you pay them?

An employer expects all employees to help the organization accomplish the three essentials of a successful operation. Employees are expected to work hard, help when asked, and please customers for a wage that allows the organization to make a **profit** and stay in business.

Journal Activity

How can you improve self-management?

Profit

The money an organization earns through sales or services is income. All bills the organization pays are expenses. Profit is the amount of money an organization has left after paying all its expenses. Profit belongs to the owners, partners, or stockholders of an organization; profit is the compensation business owners receive for risking their money in a commercial venture. Often owners take money from their profit and reinvest it in the organization by buying new equipment, opening new facilities, or hiring new workers. This creates a healthy economy. Some business owners have profit-sharing programs that distribute a share of the profit to all employees as a reward for their hard work.

Even government and nonprofit agencies must stay within a budget. Nonprofit agencies must earn enough money to pay all their expenses. And, although they can't distribute earnings greater than their expenses to stockholders, government and nonprofit agencies are expected to operate as efficiently as profit-making businesses.

How Job Savvy Are You?

Tom takes orders at a fast-food restaurant. He has worked at the restaurant for three weeks and believes that he deserves a raise. After his shift, Tom talks with his supervisor, Janet, and tells her that he feels he deserves a raise.

1. If you were Janet, what would you tell Tom?

    _____

    _____

    _____

2. Why?

    _____

    _____

    _____

You are a supervisor in a large insurance company. This morning, you asked Angel, a file clerk, to go to the supply room for a box of new file folders. Later, you found Angel sitting at her desk, filing her nails. When you asked, "Why aren't you working?" Angel replied, "I ran out of file folders."

1. What would you say to Angel?

    _____

    _____

    _____

Continues

2. What skill(s) does she need to improve?

_____

_____

_____

Your Reasons for Working

You can't expect every job to satisfy all of your expectations and values. Many people work at jobs they don't want until they can get the education or experience necessary to start the career they do want. Sometimes you have to make sacrifices while you work toward the job you want. You must determine your most important expectations and values and then evaluate what each job offers.

Many studies have asked what American workers consider their most important job values and expectations. A study conducted by the Society for Human Resource Management in 2017 identified why employees leave or stay with their employers.[18] Table 1.8 shows the reasons people stay or go.

Group Discussion

How can you increase your job satisfaction?

Table 1.8 Reasons Workers Stay at/Leave a Job

Reason	Stay	Leave
Compensation/Pay	44%	56%
Flexibility to Balance Work/Life Issues	34%	18%
Benefits	32%	29%
Job Security	29%	25%
Meaningful Work	29%	14%
Location (e.g., Convenient, Accessible)	22%	13%
Challenging Work	13%	8%
Relationship with Immediate Supervisor	12%	7%
Manageable Workplace Stress	11%	16%
Overall Organizational Culture	7%	7%
Career Advancement Opportunities	6%	21%
Training/Development Opportunities	3%	5%

To a large degree, *you* are responsible for how satisfied you feel about a job. Select a job that will fulfill most of your expectations, but accept that no job can fulfill all your expectations. Then work with your supervisor and coworkers to make the job an even more pleasant experience. You can increase your job satisfaction even more by focusing on internal rewards—positive thoughts and compliments that you give yourself.

What Should You Expect?

Most of us have several reasons for working. Your motivation and interest in a job depend on your reasons for working and how well the job satisfies your needs.

1. List your reasons for working. You might think of money first. That's fine, but also think of the other reasons you work.

   _____

   _____

   _____

2. Think about the jobs you've had. What did you like about each job? What did you dislike?

   _____

   _____

   _____

3. How do you expect an employer to treat you? What are things you want in return for the work you do?

   _____

   _____

   _____

Summing Up

The labor force, workplaces, and structure of jobs are changing. The US labor force is more diverse than ever before, with the addition of more women, people from ethnic and racial groups, older workers, and people with disabilities.

Most organizations provide customer services, and many service-related jobs require a high level of skill. Employers are restructuring jobs so that they can be done not only by traditional workers but also by contingent workers.

These changes demand higher skill levels. Workers need more education than ever before. Employers expect employees to have technical skills for a specific job, but they consider basic skills to be even more important.

Employers have expectations of employees. Workers also have expectations of their employers. Your relationship with an employer is built on these important points of understanding:

Review and Assessment

Take the Review Quiz posted to the ebook. See your instructor for additional resources.

- The employer is in business to make a profit, not just to provide you with a job and paycheck.
- If you can identify the reasons you want to work and find a job that fulfills your needs, you will be happier and do a better job.

CHAPTER 2

Avoiding the New-Job Blues

Objectives

- Prepare for a typical first day on the job.

- Demonstrate personal accountability and effective work habits.

- Explain basic decisions that employees need to make when they start a job.

The first day on the job can be confusing and difficult because you have a great deal to remember. Where do I go? What are the policies for lunch, coffee, and bathroom breaks? Who are my coworkers? What work am I expected to do? It can be confusing until you have these and many other questions answered. But you can reduce your confusion by knowing what to expect on the first day and being prepared.

Your first day on a job will differ from one organization to another, but some things are the same. Here are some typical first-day activities:

- **Report to Work**   In large organizations, you probably will report to the **human resources (HR)** office. Smaller companies might have you report to the office manager or directly to your supervisor.
- **Attend Orientation**   Organizations usually provide **orientation** training for new employees to introduce them to the organization, take care of necessary paperwork, and review policies and **benefits**.
- **Job Introduction and Workplace Tour**   A supervisor will probably introduce you to the job that you have been hired to do. In most cases, the supervisor will show you around the work area and other parts of the facility. During this tour, you will be introduced to people who are important to know in order to do your job effectively.

This chapter reviews what you can expect during these first-day activities. It also helps you understand the process called "onboarding."[1] **Onboarding** is a series of ongoing activities to help new employees learn to do their job well and feel as though they are part of the organization. When you finish this chapter, you will be better prepared to start a job.

Watch the Video

Avoiding the New-Job Blues

Reporting to Work

It is important to make a good impression on your first day on the job. Contacting your new supervisor a day or two before you are scheduled to start helps make the transition to a new job easier. Ask your supervisor about topics that require your attention before you arrive at the new job. You might ask these questions:

- What is appropriate clothing to wear for this job?
- When I arrive, where should I go and who will meet me?
- Should I bring identification or any other documents?
- Are there tools, equipment, or other items I'm expected to furnish?

The following sections contain some checklists to help you prepare for your first day at work. Get the information you need to complete the checklists by asking the human resources department or your supervisor.

Dress Appropriately

It's embarrassing to show up for work dressed the wrong way. You stand out like a sore thumb, and people remember you for weeks (or even months) because of how you looked that first day. You should ask your supervisor what type of clothing is suitable or required for the job. Think about any specific clothing types that might be necessary for your job.

Your employer might require you to wear a uniform. If so, find out whether it will be issued on your first day or if you are to arrive in uniform on the first day. You also should ask whether you are expected to buy the uniform or if the company provides it.

Certain jobs require special safety clothing. Working with chemicals demands a variety of clothing, depending on how toxic the chemicals are. Hardhats and steel-toed safety shoes are required on some jobs to avoid injury. If you work near machinery, you might need to avoid wearing jewelry or loose clothing that could get caught in mechanical parts. Learn your organization's safety requirements and obey them. (See Chapter 3 for a more thorough discussion of employer policies regarding safety clothing and equipment.)

Organizations for which no special clothing is required still have expectations about the way you dress. When you visit an organization for interviews, notice how the workers dress. After you are hired, ask your supervisor to advise you on what is appropriate to wear on your first day at work.

Dress for Success Checklist

Examine this dress checklist. If a uniform is required, be prepared to ask the questions listed about uniforms. Pay special attention to the items you might need to wear on your first day.

Uniform

- ❏ Does my employer provide a uniform?
- ❏ When do I need it?
- ❏ Where do I pick it up?

- ❏ What items make up the uniform?
- ❏ How many of each item do I receive?

- ❏ What are my responsibilities for care and for returning the uniform when I leave the job?

Safety Clothing

- ❏ Hard Hat
- ❏ Safety Goggles
- ❏ Hearing Protection

- ❏ Safety Mask
- ❏ Apron
- ❏ Gloves

- ❏ Steel-toed Boots
- ❏ Other Protective Clothing

Work Clothes

- ❏ Suits
- ❏ Shirts/Blouses
- ❏ Pants/Slacks

- ❏ Jeans
- ❏ Dresses
- ❏ Skirts/Jackets

- ❏ Jewelry
- ❏ Ties

Starting the Day

Talk with your supervisor or the HR department before your first day on the job and ask exactly when you should arrive, where you should go, and who you should contact. At some companies, employees report at a different time and location on their first day at work than they do on other workdays.

First-Day Checklist

Check off each item as you answer the question.

- ❏ What time should I arrive? _____
- ❏ Where should I report? _____
- ❏ Who should I meet? _____
- ❏ What documentation should I bring? _____
- ❏ What special equipment do I need? _____
- ❏ What will I be expected to do? _____
- ❏ What do people usually do for lunch? _____

Paperwork

Your employer might ask you to bring specific documents on your first day of work. Find out which documents you will need and check them off as you collect them.

Paperwork Checklist

❑ Birth Certificate or Passport

❑ Driver's License or ID Card

❑ Social Security Card

❑ Work Permit (for Workers Under 18)

❑ Immigrant Work Authorization (for Noncitizens)

❑ Medical Records (for example, Physical Exam Results)

❑ Occupational License (for example, for Realtors, Truck Drivers, Bartenders, or Others)

❑ Other Documents

Be Prepared

Some employers expect workers to furnish tools, equipment, or other items. This isn't common, but you should determine whether this expectation exists. Find out which items you will need and check them off as you collect them.

Miscellaneous Items Checklist

❑ Cell Phone

❑ Construction Tools

❑ Electronic Diagnostic Equipment

❑ Electronic Repair Tools

❑ Excavation Tools

❑ Flashlight

❑ Laptop

❑ Mechanical Tools

❑ Notebook and Pen/Pencil

❑ Padlock for Locker

❑ Reference Books

❑ Other

Onboarding

Many employers conduct onboarding for new employees. Onboarding is a series of activities that organizations provide to help new employees feel comfortable in their new job. It begins with an orientation to the organization on the first day of work. Then there may be classroom training, on-the-job training, lunches with fellow employees, social activities, meetings with key people/leaders, and other activities to help you feel like a member of the organization. The onboarding process differs from one company to the next. Onboarding may last several days, a few weeks, or even months. Cheerfully taking part in these activities will make your new job more engaging and easier to perform. Onboarding often leads to making new friends. Typically,

Job Savvy: How to Be a Success at Work

the activities will be led by HR or your supervisor. You will share a lot of important information at this time, including:

- **Personal Information**   You must provide proof that you are legally allowed to work in the United States permanently or temporarily. Be prepared to provide this information when asked.
- **Payroll Requirements**   You need to complete payroll withholdings forms.
- **Benefits and Policies**   You will learn about the company benefits and be given a chance to discuss them. Also, you will learn about your employer's important policies and practices. This includes information about vacations, holidays, and other days approved for excused absences.
- **Employer Expectations**   You will learn what the employer expects. Many of the points reviewed in Chapter 1 will be discussed at this time.
- **Workplace Introduction**   You will learn what the organization does, how it is structured, and who the key people are.

The following sections explain common benefits and HR policies in greater detail.[2] Not all organizations offer the same benefits or follow the same procedures, yet the explanations here will help you understand the onboarding process in general.

Personal Information

Employers need documents/tests to verify information about new employees. You provide these documents on or before your first day of work.

- **Citizenship/Immigration Verification**   Federal law requires employers to demonstrate that all workers are legally entitled to work in the United States. Employers must have proof of citizenship or an immigrant work authorization permit for each employee. You will be asked to fill out Form I-9 Section 1 and provide documentation of your work eligibility. A copy of your birth certificate and your driver's license are usually enough to document your citizenship. If you are not a US citizen, check the acceptable documents listed in Form I-9 (see Figure 2.1 on pages 25–26).
- **Work Authorization Number**   To withhold taxes, employers need your Social Security number or USCIS number, foreign passport number, Form I-94 admission number, or other identification that shows you are legally allowed to work in the United States.
- **Licenses/Identification Cards**   Some occupations require an identification card issued by the state government. If this is the case in your occupation, your employer will need to see the card and make a copy for company records. Card application and payment are usually the worker's responsibility.
- **Health Forms**   Your employer might require you to have a physical exam. Most employers pay for the exam, and the results go directly to them. Alternatively, you might be asked to bring in the results when you report to work.

Group Activity

Complete the Paperwork Checklist on the previous page. Identify the reasons an employer might need each document.

Discussion Activity

Share your answers to the *How Job Savvy Are You?* exercise on the following page. What other first-day mishaps could happen?

- **Drug Tests** Employees who abuse drugs have a tremendously harmful effect on the workplace—they are more likely to have extended absences from work, show up late, and be involved in workplace accidents and file workers' compensation claims.[3] Consequently, your employer might require you to take a drug test. If you are taking prescription medication, you should notify the drug test administrators. If you test positive but have not been taking drugs, you should ask to be retested.

How Job Savvy Are You?

Chad arrived at Merlin Controls at 6:45 a.m., ready for his first day at work. He was stopped at the guard's gate because he didn't have an identification badge, which was needed to enter the plant. Chad explained to the guard that it was his first day and provided the name of his supervisor, Linda. The guard called Linda and then asked Chad to wait until she came to escort him into the plant. Linda arrived at the gate 45 minutes later. She apologized for not coming sooner but said she had problems to take care of first. Linda then told Chad that he should report to the Human Resources office when it opened at 8:00 a.m. Chad waited in the reception area until the office opened.

1. How would you feel if you were Chad?

   _____

   _____

2. How could Chad have avoided this situation?

   _____

   _____

Felicia was excited about her first day as a claims processor trainee at Adams National Insurance Company, and she wanted to make a good first impression. She even took an early bus to make sure she arrived on time. When Felicia got to work, she was asked to show her Social Security card and driver's license for identification purposes. Felicia did not have them. The HR director told her that she could start training that day, but she would have to bring the documents tomorrow.

1. If you were Felicia, how would this make you feel?

   _____

   _____

2. How could Felicia have avoided this situation?

   _____

   _____

Following is the US Citizenship and Immigration Services Form I-9 Employment Eligibility Verification (pages 1 and 3). Federal law requires employers to keep this form on file for every employee. Practice filling out the form by completing section 1, Employee Information and Attestation. The employer is required to fill out page 2 of the form, which is not shown here. (To avoid identify fraud, do not write your Social Security number or information in section 4 on the form here.)

Figure 2.1 Form I-9

Employment Eligibility Verification	USCIS
Department of Homeland Security	**Form I-9**
U.S. Citizenship and Immigration Services	OMB No. 1615-0047
	Expires 08/31/2019

▶ **START HERE:** Read instructions carefully before completing this form. The instructions must be available, either in paper or electronically, during completion of this form. Employers are liable for errors in the completion of this form.

ANTI-DISCRIMINATION NOTICE: It is illegal to discriminate against work-authorized individuals. Employers **CANNOT** specify which document(s) an employee may present to establish employment authorization and identity. The refusal to hire or continue to employ an individual because the documentation presented has a future expiration date may also constitute illegal discrimination.

Section 1. Employee Information and Attestation *(Employees must complete and sign Section 1 of Form I-9 no later than the **first day of employment**, but not before accepting a job offer.)*

| Last Name *(Family Name)* | First Name *(Given Name)* | Middle Initial | Other Last Names Used *(if any)* |

| Address *(Street Number and Name)* | Apt. Number | City or Town | State | ZIP Code |

| Date of Birth *(mm/dd/yyyy)* | U.S. Social Security Number | Employee's E-mail Address | Employee's Telephone Number |

I am aware that federal law provides for imprisonment and/or fines for false statements or use of false documents in connection with the completion of this form.

I attest, under penalty of perjury, that I am (check one of the following boxes):

☐ 1. A citizen of the United States

☐ 2. A noncitizen national of the United States *(See instructions)*

☐ 3. A lawful permanent resident   (Alien Registration Number/USCIS Number): _____

☐ 4. An alien authorized to work   until (expiration date, if applicable, mm/dd/yyyy): _____
      Some aliens may write "N/A" in the expiration date field. *(See instructions)*

Aliens authorized to work must provide only one of the following document numbers to complete Form I-9:
An Alien Registration Number/USCIS Number OR Form I-94 Admission Number OR Foreign Passport Number.

1. Alien Registration Number/USCIS Number: _____

OR

2. Form I-94 Admission Number: _____

OR

3. Foreign Passport Number: _____

    Country of Issuance: _____

| QR Code - Section 1 |
| Do Not Write In This Space |

| Signature of Employee | Today's Date *(mm/dd/yyyy)* |

Preparer and/or Translator Certification (check one):
☐ I did not use a preparer or translator.   ☐ A preparer(s) and/or translator(s) assisted the employee in completing Section 1.
(Fields below must be completed and signed when preparers and/or translators assist an employee in completing Section 1.)

I attest, under penalty of perjury, that I have assisted in the completion of Section 1 of this form and that to the best of my knowledge the information is true and correct.

| Signature of Preparer or Translator | Today's Date *(mm/dd/yyyy)* |

| Last Name *(Family Name)* | First Name *(Given Name)* |

| Address *(Street Number and Name)* | City or Town | State | ZIP Code |

🛑 *Employer Completes Next Page* 🛑

Form I-9 07/17/17 N

Page 1 of 3

Continues

LISTS OF ACCEPTABLE DOCUMENTS
All documents must be UNEXPIRED

Employees may present one selection from List A
or a combination of one selection from List B and one selection from List C.

LIST A		LIST B		LIST C
Documents that Establish Both Identity and Employment Authorization	**OR**	**Documents that Establish Identity**	**AND**	**Documents that Establish Employment Authorization**

LIST A	LIST B	LIST C
1. U.S. Passport or U.S. Passport Card	1. Driver's license or ID card issued by a State or outlying possession of the United States provided it contains a photograph or information such as name, date of birth, gender, height, eye color, and address	1. A Social Security Account Number card, unless the card includes one of the following restrictions: (1) NOT VALID FOR EMPLOYMENT (2) VALID FOR WORK ONLY WITH INS AUTHORIZATION (3) VALID FOR WORK ONLY WITH DHS AUTHORIZATION
2. Permanent Resident Card or Alien Registration Receipt Card (Form I-551)		
3. Foreign passport that contains a temporary I-551 stamp or temporary I-551 printed notation on a machine-readable immigrant visa	2. ID card issued by federal, state or local government agencies or entities, provided it contains a photograph or information such as name, date of birth, gender, height, eye color, and address	2. Certification of report of birth issued by the Department of State (Forms DS-1350, FS-545, FS-240)
4. Employment Authorization Document that contains a photograph (Form I-766)	3. School ID card with a photograph	3. Original or certified copy of birth certificate issued by a State, county, municipal authority, or territory of the United States bearing an official seal
	4. Voter's registration card	
5. For a nonimmigrant alien authorized to work for a specific employer because of his or her status:	5. U.S. Military card or draft record	
a. Foreign passport; and	6. Military dependent's ID card	4. Native American tribal document
b. Form I-94 or Form I-94A that has the following:	7. U.S. Coast Guard Merchant Mariner Card	5. U.S. Citizen ID Card (Form I-197)
(1) The same name as the passport; and	8. Native American tribal document	6. Identification Card for Use of Resident Citizen in the United States (Form I-179)
(2) An endorsement of the alien's nonimmigrant status as long as that period of endorsement has not yet expired and the proposed employment is not in conflict with any restrictions or limitations identified on the form.	9. Driver's license issued by a Canadian government authority	
	For persons under age 18 who are unable to present a document listed above:	7. Employment authorization document issued by the Department of Homeland Security
6. Passport from the Federated States of Micronesia (FSM) or the Republic of the Marshall Islands (RMI) with Form I-94 or Form I-94A indicating nonimmigrant admission under the Compact of Free Association Between the United States and the FSM or RMI	10. School record or report card 11. Clinic, doctor, or hospital record 12. Daycare or nursery school record	

Examples of many of these documents appear in Part 13 of the Handbook for Employers (M-274).

Refer to the instructions for more information about acceptable receipts.

Form I-9 07/17/17 N

Page 3 of 3

Payroll Requirements

Most employers will ask you to complete payroll information on your first day at work. This section explains the information your employer will require and why they need it.

Withholding Taxes

In addition to Form I-9, all new employees typically complete two tax forms before they are added to the payroll: Form W-4 for federal withholding taxes and a withholding form for state taxes. These tax-withholding forms are used for the following purposes:

- **Federal Income Taxes**   Your employer will automatically withhold federal income taxes from your **paycheck**. The amount of taxes withheld is based on the number of personal allowances you claim. All taxpayers automatically get one personal allowance. You may claim more than one personal allowance if others are dependent on your income. Or you can claim zero allowances if you want more taxes withheld (for example, if you earn income on the side that does not have taxes taken out). You need to complete a W-4 form so that your employer can calculate the correct amount to withhold.

- **State and Local Income Taxes**   Most states and some cities and counties have income taxes. You must complete withholding forms for these taxes. Your employer uses the information you provide on the state withholding form to deduct the correct amount from your pay.

- **Federal Insurance Contributions Act (FICA)**   This is a Social Security tax. Your employer must withhold a set percentage of your paycheck and contribute a similar amount to your FICA account. This money funds retirement benefits and is credited to your personal account. Your account number is the same as your Social Security number.

- **Medicare Contributions**   Medicare provides health-care insurance to workers who have retired or are disabled. Similar to Social Security withholding, a set percentage of your pay is deducted from each paycheck for this service.

Group Activity

Choose one of the following topics to define and discuss: common types of taxes withheld, benefits, voluntary deductions, or employee services.

IRS Withholding Calculator

Income tax laws for the federal government allow for **deductions** and adjustments in a worker's paycheck. The backside of Form W-4 has instructions to help you calculate the personal allowances you can take to reduce the amount of tax withheld from each paycheck. You may also visit https://JobSavvy6.JIST.com/WithholdingCalculator and follow the suggestion the calculator provides. Typically, you want to withhold enough taxes so you do not owe additional taxes at the end of the year. The average refund check from the IRS is $2,800.[4] You probably don't want too much money to be taken out of each check because this allows the federal government to use your money rather than letting you save or spend it for an entire year. Every year, you can make adjustments to have the correct amount of money withheld from your paycheck.

Pay Information

Typically, information is provided about when and how you will be paid when you complete the payroll forms. You should review the following information:

- **Payment Method**   Many companies offer employees the choice of being paid by check, **direct deposit**, or **payroll card**. The payroll department can give you details if your employer offers these services. Be prepared to tell your employer which method you prefer. If you want to be paid by check, you will need to deposit the check into your bank account. Alternatively, you could bring the check to a check cashing service place to convert it into cash, but you will typically pay a fee. Direct deposit places the money you earn directly into your checking or savings account. You receive an electronic form showing the amount of money your employer deposited. This saves you a trip to the bank, makes the money available to you quickly, and may fulfill some bank requirements to prevent fees or penalties. The latest way employers are paying workers is through payroll cards. With this payment method, employees do not need to have a bank account. Payroll cards are similar to debit cards or prepaid credit cards and can be used in a similar way. Most state laws require that cardholders are allowed to make one payment for free each pay period. However, pay cards can charge other types of fees, so be sure you understand the way your card works and the fees involved.

- **Payday Schedule**   Find out when you will receive your first paycheck. New employees are not always eligible for a paycheck on the first payday after they start work. You should also ask about the regular payday schedule. Some organizations distribute paychecks only at specific times. If your employer has such a policy and you are not scheduled to work during that time, you need to make arrangements to pick up your paycheck.

- **Withholding Amount**   You can expect 15% or more of your check to be withheld for taxes and other deductions (unless you are self-employed or an independent contractor, then you will be responsible for paying more). Check the calculations for withholdings and deductions after you receive your first paycheck. If you don't understand how the calculations were made, talk to the payroll department.

How Job Savvy Are You?

Janelle, a recent college graduate, has been hired as a paralegal at a large law firm in the city. Her new position pays $45,000 per year, but her supervisor has told her that if she is willing to work overtime, she may be able to earn an additional $5,000–$7,000 this year. Janelle is single, has no children, and has just signed an apartment lease.

1.   Look at Figure 2.2 Form W-4. How many personal allowances should Janelle claim?

_____

Continues

2. Why should Janelle claim this number of personal allowances?

_____

Tonya earns $68,500 annually doing computer programming. She and her husband have two preschool-aged children. Cal, her husband, cares for the children during the day and works part-time at a retail store in the evening. Last year he earned $22,900. Tonya and Cal are filing jointly.

1. Look at Figure 2.2 Form W-4. How many personal allowances should Jade claim?

_____

2. How many personal allowances should her husband claim?

_____

3. Why should Jade and her husband claim this number of personal allowances?

_____

_____

Following is Figure 2.2 Form W-4 of the Internal Revenue Service (slightly modified). The form may change slightly from one year to the next, but this sample will be useful for practice. Complete the form with your personal information to determine your tax withholding. (To avoid identify fraud, do not write your Social Security number on the practice form.)

Figure 2.2 Form W-4

Form W-4 (2018)

Future developments. For the latest information about any future developments related to Form W-4, such as legislation enacted after it was published, go to *www.irs.gov/FormW4*.

Purpose. Complete Form W-4 so that your employer can withhold the correct federal income tax from your pay. Consider completing a new Form W-4 each year and when your personal or financial situation changes.

Exemption from withholding. You may claim exemption from withholding for 2018 if **both** of the following apply.

• For 2017 you had a right to a refund of **all** federal income tax withheld because you had **no** tax liability, **and**

• For 2018 you expect a refund of **all** federal income tax withheld because you expect to have **no** tax liability.

If you're exempt, complete **only** lines 1, 2, 3, 4, and 7 and sign the form to validate it. Your exemption for 2018 expires February 15, 2019. See Pub. 505, Tax Withholding and Estimated Tax, to learn more about whether you qualify for exemption from withholding.

General Instructions

If you aren't exempt, follow the rest of these instructions to determine the number of withholding allowances you should claim for withholding for 2018 and any additional amount of tax to have withheld. For regular wages, withholding must be based on allowances you claimed and may not be a flat amount or percentage of wages.

You can also use the calculator at *www.irs.gov/W4App* to determine your tax withholding more accurately. Consider using this calculator if you have a more complicated tax situation, such as if you have a working spouse, more than one job, or a large amount of nonwage income outside of your job. After your Form W-4 takes effect, you can also use this calculator to see how the amount of tax you're having withheld compares to your projected total tax for 2018. If you use the calculator, you don't need to complete any of the worksheets for Form W-4.

Note that if you have too much tax withheld, you will receive a refund when you file your tax return. If you have too little tax withheld, you will owe tax when you file your tax return, and you might owe a penalty.

Filers with multiple jobs or working spouses. If you have more than one job at a time, or if you're married and your spouse is also working, read all of the instructions including the instructions for the Two-Earners/Multiple Jobs Worksheet before beginning.

Nonwage income. If you have a large amount of nonwage income, such as interest or dividends, consider making estimated tax payments using Form 1040-ES, Estimated Tax for Individuals. Otherwise, you might owe additional tax. Or, you can use the Deductions, Adjustments, and Other Income Worksheet on page 3 or the calculator at *www.irs.gov/W4App* to make sure you have enough tax withheld from your paycheck. If you have pension or annuity income, see Pub. 505 or use the calculator at *www.irs.gov/W4App* to find out if you should adjust your withholding on Form W-4 or W-4P.

Nonresident alien. If you're a nonresident alien, see Notice 1392, Supplemental Form W-4 Instructions for Nonresident Aliens, before completing this form.

Specific Instructions

Personal Allowances Worksheet

Complete this worksheet on page 3 first to determine the number of withholding allowances to claim.

Line C. *Head of household please note:* Generally, you can claim head of household filing status on your tax return only if you're unmarried and pay more than 50% of the costs of keeping up a home for yourself and a qualifying individual. See Pub. 501 for more information about filing status.

Line E. Child tax credit. When you file your tax return, you might be eligible to claim a credit for each of your qualifying children. To qualify, the child must be under age 17 as of December 31 and must be your dependent who lives with you for more than half the year. To learn more about this credit, see Pub. 972, Child Tax Credit. To reduce the tax withheld from your pay by taking this credit into account, follow the instructions on line E of the worksheet. On the worksheet you will be asked about your total income. For this purpose, total income includes all of your wages and other income, including income earned by a spouse, during the year.

Line F. Credit for other dependents. When you file your tax return, you might be eligible to claim a credit for each of your dependents that don't qualify for the child tax credit, such as any dependent children age 17 and older. To learn more about this credit, see Pub. 505. To reduce the tax withheld from your pay by taking this credit into account, follow the instructions on line F of the worksheet. On the worksheet, you will be asked about your total income. For this purpose, total income includes all of

Continues

Continued

Figure 2.2 Form W-4

Form **W-4**	**Employee's Withholding Allowance Certificate**	OMB No. 1545-0074
Department of the Treasury Internal Revenue Service	▶ Whether you're entitled to claim a certain number of allowances or exemption from withholding is subject to review by the IRS. Your employer may be required to send a copy of this form to the IRS.	2018

1 Your first name and middle initial	Last name	2 Your social security number

Home address (number and street or rural route)	3 ☐ Single ☐ Married ☐ Married, but withhold at higher Single rate.
	Note: If married filing separately, check "Married, but withhold at higher Single rate."
City or town, state, and ZIP code	4 If your last name differs from that shown on your social security card, check here. You must call 800-772-1213 for a replacement card. ▶ ☐

5 Total number of allowances you're claiming (from the applicable worksheet on the following pages) . . . | **5** |

6 Additional amount, if any, you want withheld from each paycheck . . . . | **6** $ |

7 I claim exemption from withholding for 2018, and I certify that I meet **both** of the following conditions for exemption.
 • Last year I had a right to a refund of **all** federal income tax withheld because I had **no** tax liability, **and**
 • This year I expect a refund of **all** federal income tax withheld because I expect to have **no** tax liability.
 If you meet both conditions, write "Exempt" here . . . . ▶ | **7** |

Under penalties of perjury, I declare that I have examined this certificate and, to the best of my knowledge and belief, it is true, correct, and complete.

Employee's signature
(This form is not valid unless you sign it.) ▶ _____ Date ▶ _____

8 Employer's name and address (**Employer:** Complete boxes 8 and 10 if sending to IRS and complete boxes 8, 9, and 10 if sending to State Directory of New Hires.)	9 First date of employment	10 Employer identification number (EIN)

For Privacy Act and Paperwork Reduction Act Notice, see page 4. | Cat. No. 10220Q | Form **W-4** (2018)

Form W-4 (2018) | Page **3**

Personal Allowances Worksheet (Keep for your records.)

A Enter "1" for yourself . . . . **A** _____

B Enter "1" if you will file as married filing jointly . . . . **B** _____

C Enter "1" if you will file as head of household . . . . **C** _____

D Enter "1" if:
 • You're single, or married filing separately, and have only one job; or
 • You're married filing jointly, have only one job, and your spouse doesn't work; or
 • Your wages from a second job or your spouse's wages (or the total of both) are $1,500 or less.
 D _____

E **Child tax credit.** See Pub. 972, Child Tax Credit, for more information.
 • If your total income will be less than $69,801 ($101,401 if married filing jointly), enter "4" for each eligible child.
 • If your total income will be from $69,801 to $175,550 ($101,401 to $339,000 if married filing jointly), enter "2" for each eligible child.
 • If your total income will be from $175,551 to $200,000 ($339,001 to $400,000 if married filing jointly), enter "1" for each eligible child.
 • If your total income will be higher than $200,000 ($400,000 if married filing jointly), enter "-0-" . . . . **E** _____

F **Credit for other dependents.**
 • If your total income will be less than $69,801 ($101,401 if married filing jointly), enter "1" for each eligible dependent.
 • If your total income will be from $69,801 to $175,550 ($101,401 to $339,000 if married filing jointly), enter "1" for every two dependents (for example, "-0-" for one dependent, "1" if you have two or three dependents, and "2" if you have four dependents).
 • If your total income will be higher than $175,550 ($339,000 if married filing jointly), enter "-0-" . . . . **F** _____

G **Other credits.** If you have other credits, see Worksheet 1-6 of Pub. 505 and enter the amount from that worksheet here . . **G** _____

H Add lines A through G and enter the total here . . . . ▶ **H** _____

For accuracy, complete all worksheets that apply.
 • If you plan to **itemize** or **claim adjustments to income** and want to reduce your withholding, or if you have a large amount of nonwage income and want to increase your withholding, see the **Deductions, Adjustments, and Additional Income Worksheet** below.
 • If you **have more than one job at a time** or are **married filing jointly and you and your spouse both work**, and the combined earnings from all jobs exceed $52,000 ($24,000 if married filing jointly), see the **Two-Earners/Multiple Jobs Worksheet** on page 4 to avoid having too little tax withheld.
 • If **neither** of the above situations applies, **stop here** and enter the number from line H on line 5 of Form W-4 above.

Benefits and Policies

Employers can attract workers with the type of benefits they offer their employees. Not all employers offer benefits, though, and typically, benefits are available only to full-time employees. But some surveys show that benefits are a major reason people work.

Your employer might fully pay for some of your benefits; however, most employers now require employees to make partial contributions to their benefits. Some employers offer "cafeteria" plans, giving you the choice of which benefits you want (see the "Cafeteria Plans" box on the next page). The following benefits are commonly offered to employees:

- **Health Insurance** A percentage of doctor and hospital expenses is paid for by health insurance. Most health insurance has a standard deductible—that is, the amount of medical expense you must pay before the insurance company will pay your medical bills. Some health plans cover the cost of prescription drugs, vision, and dental work. Today, 70% of workers have access to health insurance through their employers, and workers are often required to pay some of the health insurance cost.[5]

  Health Savings Accounts (HSAs) are another method of providing health coverage to workers. These accounts may be used to supplement high-deductible health insurance. You do not have to pay tax on the money in the account.

  Currently, everyone in the United States is required to have health insurance; those who don't, must pay a penalty to the federal government. Healthcare services can cost a person thousands of dollars per year and health insurance helps defray much of those costs. In general, there are four primary costs that you should be aware of:

  - **Premium** This is the monthly or yearly cost of your insurance policy.
  - **Deductible** This is how much you must spend for covered health services before your insurance company pays anything. Insurance won't kick in until you've paid this amount out of your own pocket.
  - **Copayments** These are payments you make every time you get a medical service (often after reaching your deductible). These tend to be small ($10 to $25 per visit).
  - **Out-of-pocket Maximum** This amount is the most you must spend for covered services in a year. Once you reach this amount, the insurance company covers all remaining expenses.

  Employer-sponsored health insurance plans are the way to go for most people. They often offer the least expensive premium options, the company provides guidance in choosing a plan, and the premiums are deducted automatically from your paycheck pretax.

- **Disability Insurance** If you are sick or injured for several weeks or more, disability insurance pays part or all of your salary. These payments usually begin after you have used all of your paid sick leave.
- **Life Insurance** This is particularly important if you have dependents because you can designate a person (the beneficiary) to receive a payment from the insurance company if you die. Some employers pay for a life insurance policy equal to one year's salary and offer plans (for a fee) that pay out higher amounts.
- **Dependent Care** This comes in several forms. Some companies run childcare centers that provide low-cost care for their employees' children. Organizations that don't run daycare facilities might reimburse

Discussion Activity

What types of benefits are most valuable to you? What factors must you consider?

employees for a portion of the employees' childcare costs. As the workforce ages, many employees need care for elderly parents. Many businesses partner with adult daycare centers to offer this benefit to employees with elderly parents.

Here are rules of thumb for choosing benefits:

- If the employer provides the benefit free of charge, you should sign up for it.
- If the employer requires you to pay part or all of the benefit costs, sign up only for those you really need and those that you can not buy on your own in the open market for less money.

Cafeteria Plans

This is an increasingly popular type of benefit plan in which an employer provides a wide variety of choices and a set amount of money to cover individual employees' benefits. Employees can choose which benefits to "buy." The use of cafeteria plans saves money for both the organization and the employee.[5] Benefits are adjusted as workers move through life stages. For example, a young worker starting a family might want to use the plan for child care. Later in life, the same worker might want to put that money into a disability plan.

Paid Time Off

Your employer might offer paid time off for one or several of the following circumstances. This benefit varies greatly from one employer to another, so it's important to understand your employer's policies.

Journal Activity

How will your benefit needs change in 5 and 10 years?

- **Holiday Pay**   The organization designates holidays. On these days, you may not be required to work and you may still receive pay.
- **Paid Sick Leave**   Employers normally establish a limited number of paid days that you can use for sick days. If you exceed the limit, you won't be paid for days you can't work due to illness. There are many different methods of accumulating sick time.
- **Vacation Leave**   This is time off paid for by your employer. As a general rule, the amount of vacation time increases with the number of years you work for an organization.
- **Personal Leave**   The definition of a personal day differs from one employer to another. For example, you might be able to use it only for medical appointments or family illnesses, or you might be able to use it as an additional vacation day.
- **Paid-time-off Bank**   A paid-time-off bank allows employees to choose how time-off days will be used. Employees are given a certain number of days off, without having to explain how they will use the time off (vacation, sick, or personal).
- **Jury Duty Leave**   Some states require employers to pay employees for time served on a jury. Some employers do so voluntarily because they feel it is a community responsibility.

Case Study

Enzo is 46 years old. He is unmarried and has one child. He cares for an aging parent with dementia. He also works full-time. Identify the benefits he may want.

- **Funeral (or Bereavement) Leave**   This leave, usually limited to one to three days, is given when a member of your immediate family dies. Various organizations define *immediate family* differently. Ask about your employer's policy.
- **Military Leave**   Members of the reserve or national guard are required to attend active-duty training for at least two weeks each year. Although they are not required to do so, some employers pay for the time that an employee is on active military leave or pay the difference in salary. When an employee is deployed for an extended time period, an employer must guarantee that a job is available when the person returns from duty. The rules are complicated, so get advice on how they apply to you through your chain of command.
- **Maternity, Paternity, and Adoption Leave**   This is time off for your child's birth or adoption. The Family and Medical Leave Act (FMLA) requires that a company with more than 50 employees provide maternity, paternity, and adoption leave. A company does not have to pay the employee during the leave, but it does have to keep the employee's job (or a similar job) open for him or her. Smaller companies must treat maternity leave like sick leave.

Benefits and Deductions You Want

In the following list, place a check mark beside the benefits or deductions you want, even if you must pay a portion of the cost. Write your reasons for selecting or not selecting each item.

❏ Health Insurance _____

❏ Dental Insurance _____

❏ Prescription Drugs _____

❏ Life Insurance _____

❏ Disability Insurance _____

❏ Child Care/Adult Day Care _____

❏ Child Support _____

❏ Retirement Program _____

❏ Union Dues _____

❏ Savings Plan _____

❏ Charity Donation _____

❏ Stock Options _____

Required Benefits
Federal and state laws require some employee benefits. Some of the most important laws are the following:

- **Federal Insurance Contributions Act (FICA)**   An employer must match your contribution to the Social Security fund. Upon your death, this fund pays benefits to your children who are under age 18. Depending on your situation, the fund may pay you, your spouse, and your dependents if you are disabled. It also pays you a pension when you reach retirement age.
- **Unemployment Insurance**   Your employer must contribute to an unemployment insurance fund administered by your state or agree to pay your unemployment claims. If you are laid off or dismissed from your job, you can file a claim with your state employment agency. Eligibility requirements vary from state to state. The reasons for unemployment also are taken into consideration. A state's employment office determines eligibility, and the state establishes the amount and length of time you receive unemployment benefit payments.
- **Worker's Compensation Insurance**   Most states require employers to carry this insurance, which pays for injuries that occur to workers on the job. In addition, you receive partial payment for time off the job caused by work-related injuries.

Voluntary Deductions
In addition to benefit deductions, your employer can deduct other withholdings from your paycheck with your approval. Some deductions, such as federal and state taxes, are required. Others are voluntary, such as the following:

Discussion Activity

Discuss the difference between required and voluntary deductions. Why would an employee elect voluntary deductions?

- **Child Support**   You might want to have monthly child support payments automatically deducted from your paycheck. Check with your lawyer or court representative to find out how this is done. Also, a court may order your employer to make deductions for child support.
- **Savings Plan Payments**   You might have a portion of your pay sent directly to your bank or credit union savings account. This will help you save automatically, yet the money is there if and when you need it.
- **Charity Donations**   You can arrange for a deduction to a charity. Check with your company to see what charities are approved.
- **Union Dues**   Most unions make arrangements with employers to withhold dues from your paycheck. In some areas, unions have agreements with employers requiring them to withhold dues *even if you are not a union member*. Laws related to the withholding of union dues are complicated because they differ from state to state.
- **Retirement Fund Contributions**   The US Bureau of Labor Statistics reports that 70% of employers offer some type of retirement plan.[6] The IRS lists over a dozen retirement plans employers can establish. Many books have been written to help people understand how to make wise decisions about retirement plans. In trying to summarize this advice, there are basically three questions to consider when deciding whether you should enroll in a retirement plan offered by your employer. Does

the plan allow you to make contributions from pretax earnings? Does the employer match your contribution to the plan? Does the plan allow you to delay paying taxes on money earned from the investments until you retire? If the answer to these questions is yes, then you should seriously consider enrolling in the retirement plan. Network with family and friends and identify professional advisors if you are confused.

- **Stock Options**   You might be able to have pretax deductions withheld from your paycheck to purchase company stock. This is a unique benefit typically offered at start-up companies or at traditional companies for upper-level management positions.

Employee Services

Employers provide many different services for their employees. Many organizations feel that the more they do for their employees, the more the employees will do for them. Here is a partial listing of services your employer might provide:

- **Educational Assistance Plans**   Employers sometimes reimburse college or technical school tuition for employees who are working toward a degree or taking work-related courses. They also might reimburse employees for textbooks.
- **Employee Assistance Programs**   Employees might receive counseling for personal or work-related problems, including treatment for drug or alcohol abuse.
- **Financial Services**   Employers sometimes offer financial services for employees, usually at a lower cost than banks or savings-and-loan institutions. Such services may include free accounts at credit unions or member-only institutions.
- **Other Employee Services**   These can include legal assistance, health services, an on-site cafeteria or food service, financial planning, reimbursement of housing and moving expenses, transportation, purchase discounts, and recreational services.

Table 2.1 shows the percentage of employees in the US workforce who receive typical benefits.[7]

Table 2.1 Typical US Workforce Benefits

Benefit	Recipients by Percentage of US Workforce
Paid Vacations	74%
Paid Sick Leave	72%
Paid Holidays	76%
Life Insurance	58%
Medical Care	71%
Retirement Plan	70%
Unpaid Family Leave	88%

Case Study

Asha has received two job offers, one with higher pay but few benefits and one with lower pay but many good benefits. Which job should she choose, and why? Which benefits do you think should be the deciding factors?

Check the Benefits Your Employer Provides

Check the paid time off and employee assistance benefits your employer provides. If you aren't currently employed, check those that you think are important for an employer to provide.

- ❑ Holiday Leave
- ❑ Vacation Leave
- ❑ Personal Leave
- ❑ Jury Duty Leave
- ❑ Sick Leave

- ❑ Funeral (or Bereavement) Leave
- ❑ Military Leave
- ❑ Family Leave
- ❑ Medical Leave (Long-term)

- ❑ Educational Assistance
- ❑ Employee Assistance Plan
- ❑ Credit Union
- ❑ Others (Specify)

How Job Savvy Are You?

Steve and his wife have a seven-year-old daughter and three-year-old son. Steve is a carpenter for a construction firm and is working on a construction technology degree at a local community college. During the past year, the children have been sick several times. Steve and his wife just purchased a new home.

1. List six employee benefits or services that Steve needs.

   _____

   _____

   _____

   _____

2. Explain why each benefit is important to Steve.

   _____

   _____

   _____

   _____

Pilar is the branch manager of a bank. She is divorced and has a four-year-old daughter. Pilar is active in the Naval Reserve. During the past year, she has been mildly depressed about her divorce and has been drinking more than she would like.

1. What benefits would be the most helpful for Pilar?

   _____

   _____

   _____

2. Explain why these benefits are important.

   _____

   _____

   _____

Introduction to the Job

After orientation, your supervisor is likely to take you on a tour of the job site or work area. If you do not receive the following information, be prepared to ask your supervisor for it.

Work Instructions

It's important that you understand how to do your job. Your supervisor should show and tell you how to do the tasks that make up the job. Here are a few guidelines to follow as you're learning the job:

- **Don't Panic**   You won't be expected to learn everything at once. And you aren't expected to do everything right the first time.
- **Listen Carefully and Watch Closely**   You may get only one chance to have tasks demonstrated for you.
- **Ask Questions**   When you don't understand something you've been told or shown, be sure to ask for clarification.
- **Take Notes**   Review these notes as you need them. You may want to ask if you can record (audio or video) orientation/demonstrations with your cell phone.
- **Learn What is Expected**   Make sure you know exactly what the supervisor expects of you.

Supplies and Equipment

You need to know how and where to get the supplies and equipment you need to do your job. If you do not know the answers to the following questions, be sure to ask your supervisor for help:

- Where are the supplies kept?
- What are the procedures for checking out supplies and equipment? Many industries and construction sites have tool bins or sheds where employees check out tools or supplies. Some large offices have a person who provides supplies to employees. This is sometimes done for theft protection and sometimes for inventory control so supplies are always stocked.
- Who is in charge of supply ordering and distribution?

Communication Systems

All businesses rely on communication. In addition to the specialized tools your company uses, you'll need to know your employer's expectations and policies for using the following common communication systems:

- **Phone System**   Office phone systems can be incredibly complex and intimidating, with rows of buttons, lights, and dozens of features. Ask your supervisor to show you how to use the most common features of the phone system. Also, know the general telephone policy. Who answers your phone if you're away from your desk? What should you say when you answer the phone? Can you make/receive personal calls? Is there an access code you must enter when making long-distance calls?
- **Voicemail**   Get the instructions for setting up your voicemail account. Find out the phone number you must dial to access your account

when you're in your office and from remote locations. Provide a password that you can easily remember.

- **Cell Phones**   If your job requires travel or work outside the workplace, you may be given a cell phone. How does your employer expect the cell phone to be used? Can you make or receive personal calls? What about personal texts? What about personal data streaming (music, video, etc.)? What is the organization's policy concerning cell phone use while driving?
- **Pagers**   Another method of contacting employees who are working away from the office continues to be the pager, particularly for hospital and emergency workers who must be in contact when cell phone/wireless communication systems are down (e.g., in a crisis or during bad weather). If you are given a pager, learn how to use it. Find out how your employer expects you to respond.

Computer Systems

Many businesses have a computer for every employee. These are often used for improving communication between employees through email, messaging, and collaboration apps. Computers are also used for common tasks that might be a part of your job, such as entering data for customer orders, writing documents with word-processing software, or creating a spreadsheet. Employees responsible for administering computer systems are called system administrators, system managers, or some variation of these job titles. If you do not receive the following information, ask your supervisor for it:

- **User Name(s) and Password(s)**   Accessing a network that links computers together requires entering a user name and password. This information comes from your company's system administrator (some organizations might use a variation of this job title). The email system will likely require a user name and password that are different from the ones you use for the overall system. Request all log-in directions and credentials from your supervisor, unless otherwise directed.
- **Instant Messaging**   If the organization uses instant messaging, get help setting up an account. For security purposes, the company might use a customized instant messaging program.
- **System and Email Policies**   Most organizations have policies on the use of the computer system, email, and instant messaging. These policies define how you can use the system and what restrictions on access to information there are. Common issues addressed in most organizations' policies include:
  - **Privacy**   Communication that happens over email is often considered to be the property of the organization. That means that managers and supervisors might be able to read email that you send to another employee or someone outside the company.
  - **Confidentiality**   Information that you find on the system about customers, business practices, pricing, inventory, employees, and so on is considered confidential. Normally, employees are blocked from accessing information that isn't necessary to their jobs.

Discussion Activity

What communications equipment information is least and most important for you to know on your first day?

However, you should not share any information that you can access with other employees or any person outside the organization.

- **Personal Use**   Many computer systems are connected to the Internet. You should find out restrictions that the organization might place on accessing and using the Internet. Organizations vary on whether employees can use the Internet during breaks and before/after work. You should find out whether employees are allowed to send email to friends and relatives. Keep in mind that most organizations have software that allows them to monitor the websites you visit and all email communication.

Building Security

Organizations are concerned about maintaining a secure workplace. It is important to follow policies and procedures to ensure the security of everyone—including yourself. Consider the following:

- **Keys/Keycards**   You might be issued a key or keycard to enter a building or restricted area. Always keep these in your possession, and don't loan them to someone else—even another employee. Keys should not be duplicated. Always return keys or keycards to the employer when you resign from a job. Other mechanical methods for unlocking doors include key fobs and wrist bands. High-security buildings sometimes use biometric methods, such as fingerprints.
- **Visitors**   Most companies have procedures for screening anyone who enters their buildings. That means you shouldn't admit a person into the building without following the procedure. For example, someone at a rear/side entrance should be directed to the proper entry for visitors (usually the front door). Visitors often must sign in and get a visitor badge before being allowed into the building. Also, don't leave doors propped open.
- **Restricted Areas**   Many offices have restricted areas, even businesses open to the general public such as retail stores and restaurants. Keep doors to restricted areas closed. When you find someone who isn't an employee in a restricted area, ask the person to leave and then notify a manager. Access to some areas, including the main entrance, is often restricted by use of a coded keypad. Never share the password to these keypads with anyone.
- **Weapon Restrictions**   Most organizations prohibit employees from having knives, guns, martial-arts weapons, or other weapons in the workplace. There may even be restrictions on having these in a car parked in the organization's parking lot. Immediately report to your supervisor or to security any person who acts suspiciously or any objects that might be weapons.
- **Security Monitoring**   Some businesses, particularly retail stores and restaurants, monitor buildings with security cameras. Keep in mind that these cameras track your actions as well as those of visitors and customers.

Breaks

Companies have policies for taking breaks. You might be able to take your breaks whenever you want as long as you're responsible about them. Or you might have to take your breaks only at specified times. Many organizations prohibit smoking on the job. Others may allow it outside buildings or off company premises. If you intend to smoke during your break, you need to know where it's allowed. Here are some of the types of breaks employers may offer:

Case Study

Raphael is the supervisor that is giving a tour of the work facilities. Where should he start? What do you think is most important to show new employees?

- **Personal Breaks**   In some jobs you must find a worker to take over your job post before taking a break. The Occupational Health and Safety Administration (OSHA) requires employers to provide restroom facilities and allow employees to take restroom breaks. However, there are no specific rules about how long or how often restroom breaks must be. Also, the federal government requires employers to provide breaks for a nursing mother for up to one year after the baby's birth. The employer must also provide a room, other than a restroom, that offers privacy for nursing mothers.
- **Rest Breaks**   Employers often provide two 15-minute breaks (in addition to a meal break) in an eight-hour shift. Find out when you can take a break and if there is a break room.
- **Meal Breaks**   You will probably be allowed a meal break around the middle of your workday, if you work an eight-hour shift. Ask when you can take a meal break and how much time is allowed.

Organizations may have one or multiple locations for you to enjoy your lunch/meal breaks, including cafeterias, outdoor patios, break rooms, or your desk. In addition to knowing where you can eat, find out whether your employer provides a kitchen with a refrigerator or microwave for employee use.

Your supervisor should explain what you need to know about work tasks, supplies, telephone systems, and breaks. If he or she forgets, don't be afraid to ask. This is important information to learn during the first few days on the job.

Off to a Good Start

After your supervisor shows you around, you'll be on your own, and you'll start your new job in the same way everyone else does. You won't know much about the job. You may not know your coworkers. You might wonder whether you can do the job and whether you'll like it. Here are some suggestions to help you adjust during the first few weeks:

- **Be Positive**   Expect good things to happen. Starting a new job gives you an opportunity to prove yourself to your supervisor and coworkers.
- **Ask for Help**   Your supervisor and coworkers expect you to ask questions. They are willing to help when you ask. Listen carefully so that you don't have to ask the same question more than once.
- **Don't Be a Know-it-All**   You are new on the job. No matter how much you know and how skilled you are, you don't know everything about this particular job. Take the first few weeks to learn. Gain the

respect of your coworkers and supervisor by demonstrating your ability to do your job well, then you can begin making suggestions to improve the way things are done. Your coworkers seldom appreciate the phrase, "At the last place I worked, we did it this way."

- **Have a Sense of Humor**   Other workers might test new workers. Some want to see how you respond to teasing and practical jokes. Try your best to accept good-natured teasing, but if you feel unfairly treated, harassed, or abused, talk with your supervisor about the situation. Also, immediately report to your supervisor and HR any bullying, harassment, or discrimination.

- **Find a Friend**   Look for someone who seems to know the job well and ask him or her to help you if you need it. Sometimes your supervisor will assign someone to help you during the first few days.

- **Follow Instructions**   Your supervisor is the most important person in your work life. Supervisors decide whether an employee stays on the job, gets promoted, is given interesting assignments, and receives raises. Follow the leader's instructions, be helpful, and do your best.

- **Read Company Policies**   If your company has a booklet or website explaining policies and procedures, read through it carefully. Ignorance is not an excuse for doing something wrong or not knowing what to do.

- **Determine Evaluation Policies**   Find out what is expected of you in the first few days, weeks, and months; what standards are used to measure your success; and who does the evaluation.

Discussion Activity

What can you do to welcome a new employee to a job?

The first few days on the job are important, and they often determine the way you feel about the job. Staying positive, asking questions, and listening will help make your first few days on the job a positive experience.

How Job Savvy Are You?

On Craig's first day as a stock clerk, his supervisor, Sharon, introduced him to the other workers. She walked him around the store and explained how the shelves should be stocked, when to stock the products, where to get new items, and how to price the items. Sharon then left Craig on his own. Everything went fine until he came to a brand that he wasn't sure how to price. Craig didn't want to appear as though he didn't know what he was doing, so he went ahead and marked the prices the same as another brand.

1. What would you have done if you were Craig?

     _____

     _____

     _____

2. What problems do you think Craig might have caused?

     _____

     _____

     _____

Continues

Continued

Vicky is a new administrative assistant for a law firm. Her supervisor gave her a tour of the office, introduced her to other workers, and told her what tasks she would be doing. She then told Vicky to contact her if she had questions. List three questions Vicky should ask her supervisor.

1. _____
2. _____
3. _____

Active Listening

From your first day on the job to the last, active listening is a useful job skill. Active listening will make adjusting to your new work environment less stressful. Practice active listening every workday to increase your value as an employee. A new job orientation is a good place to practice active listening.

When a staff member listens without interrupting and concentrates on the customer's words, active listening is taking place. An **active listener** is defined as a person who practices the following behaviors:

- **Focusing Your Attention on the Trainer**   Look at the trainer. Make eye contact. Do more listening than speaking.
- **Listening to Learn**   Take time to understand the points being made. Recognize that you need to learn. Take notes, photos, or videos (if approved) to help you remember.
- **Asking Questions**   As appropriate, make sure you understand what has been said. Summarize what you have learned.
- **Listening Patiently**   Do not interrupt others at inappropriate times. Avoid finishing someone's sentences. Listen for clues (such as, "Are there any questions?") or wait for a pause before you ask questions.
- **Reacting to What is Said**   Do react to what is being said: smile, nod your head, verbally agree, and answer questions.[8]

As an active listener, you will be rewarded. When you start really working, you will remember more of your training. Also, you will have laid the foundation of a positive relationship with your trainer, coworkers, and supervisors.

Summing Up

Preparing for a new job is the key to creating a positive first impression. Of course, you can't prepare for every situation, but the more issues you're aware of and the more questions you ask before you start work, the better you'll do on the job.

Approach your job in a businesslike manner. Be willing to learn. Expect to succeed. Remember that your supervisor and all of your coworkers once experienced their first day on the job, too.

Review and Assessment

Take the Review Quiz. See your instructor or reference your student files in the ebook for additional resources.

CHAPTER 3

Making a Good Impression

Objectives

- Demonstrate your self-worth and a positive view of self.

- Make a good impression on the job by demonstrating appropriate dress, personal hygiene, mannerisms, and attitude.

- Recognize nonverbal messages and other cues that may mean you're giving a poor impression, and then identify strategies to make a positive impression on others.

People form impressions based on looks and actions.[1] In this chapter, you will learn how to dress and groom for confidence and success. It's a natural human reaction that our impressions about people affect the way we treat them. Because your physical appearance often determines what kind of first impression you make, it's important that you look and feel as good as possible to make that first impression positive.

Hygiene (personal body care) also influences the impression you make on people. Messy hair, bad breath, and body odor make a poor impression.

Some behavioral experts have found that the way you dress affects the attitudes and behavior of other people toward you. Employees who dress neatly and appropriately are perceived in a positive way. The implication is that you will care about your job the same way you care about yourself.

When the first edition of this book was written in 1990, society had more standards for appearance than it does today. Most companies followed a business formal or business casual dress code—but today there are more dress exceptions than hard rules. Exceptions and relaxed standards make it tricky to give advice about appearance in the workplace.

The best advice for making a good impression is to learn what the formal and informal appearance standards are for your specific workplace. Topics like dress and hygiene might seem basic, but they are critical elements for work success. This chapter will also help you better understand how other factors, like a positive attitude and confidence, can help you make a good impression on the job.

Watch the Video

Making a Good Impression

Dress for Success

What to wear on the job is often a difficult decision, unless the employer provides a uniform. About 15% of workers are employed in manufacturing, construction, and agricultural jobs, and most of these jobs require employees to wear either uniforms or clothes that comply with safety regulations, like jeans or cargo pants. The remaining 85% of workers are employed in jobs that allow a wider variety of clothing types. Many service jobs, such as retail stores, restaurants, and medical facilities, still require employees to wear uniforms; however, those uniforms may not require special fabric for safety. By and large, most jobs are located in offices where employees have flexibility in how they dress at work.

It's valuable to understand the corporate culture of any particular workplace. Corporate culture refers to the beliefs and behaviors of a company's employees. The best way to understand a company's corporate culture is by observing its employees. How do they dress at work? What seems to be acceptable among the majority of employees? You can also ask HR to define the corporate culture for you. The corporate culture may define the dress codes and influence the parameters of what is considered appropriate dress. For example, the company handbook may define the dress code as business casual, but that could look very different in a Los Angeles, San Francisco, or New York City office compared to a midwest office. It's always good to observe others and take cues based on the corporate culture.

Even with personal choice, many employers have dress guidelines or codes that help guide your choices. According to surveys, employer dress codes often align with what employees like most—and according to one survey, 64% of workers prefer casual dress in the workplace.[2]

A search on the Internet using the term **business attire** will provide examples of dress styles matching each type of dress code. The descriptions that follow here are based on the definitions of dress codes supplied by the Society for Human Resource Management.[3]

- **Business Formal**   Typically in offices where highly paid professionals work the dress style is business formal, and all office and support staff is usually expected to follow the same dress code. Business formal tends to stick to one or two colors, with the predominant color being black or dark gray. A typical outfit for men may include a pressed suit, vest, tucked-in and starched dress shirt, and tie. For women, a typical outfit may include a suit or a pantsuit. Formal shoes (black or dark-gray oxfords, loafers, or low heels) and other accessories like belts and cuff links are expected. Open-toed shoes are not acceptable in most dress codes (even casual). There is also a category for "business professional." This dress style is common at professional services offices where employees do not typically interact with high-profile clients at the office. The style uses the same limited color options as business formal and may include a sports coat, dress pants, a shirt with tie, a pantsuit, knee-length skirt with blouse, or a conservative dress. Dress shoes are still expected.

- **Business Casual**   This dress style is often found in corporate offices and government workplaces. Business casual accepts color variety and may include khakis, button-down shirts, polo shirts, cardigans/sweaters, knee- or ankle-length skirts, and dress shoes.
- **Casual/Street Clothes**   This dress is typically worn in small businesses and entrepreneurial companies where there is often little personal contact with customers. Casual clothing includes jeans, open-button shirts (like flannels), T-shirts, leggings, gypsy or wrap skirts, and sneakers. There is also a category for "smart casual." This includes, for example, pairing jeans with a sports coat and tie, or a blouse/button-down shirt with a suit jacket, cardigan, or dressy sweater.
- **Uniforms**   Employers may provide uniforms to you and/or instructions on what types of clothing are accepted as the uniform (for example, Target Corp. requires employees to wear red shirts and khaki pants/skirts). Uniforms are typically used in businesses providing health care, automotive services, groceries, and fast food. In addition, many franchise operations, such as restaurants, have some type of uniform. Today, a personal style uniform is popular because of leaders such as Steve Jobs (remember the turtlenecks?) and Mark Zuckerberg. A personal uniform often consists of wearing a variation of the same outfit style while working. The idea is that a personal style helps build yourself into your own brand while also freeing up your mind to innovate rather than reinvent your outfits every day before work.

General Dress Guidelines

Even if the dress code in your workplace is more casual, it's important to remember that clothes influence the way people perceive you. Here are some general guidelines for what to wear, or avoid wearing, on the job:

- **Follow Dress Codes**   The best way to know how to dress is to ask. Your supervisor and coworkers know about official and unofficial dress codes for the workplace. For example, many "casual" dress codes still don't allow workers to wear jeans or shorts to the office. Clothes worn by employees in the workplace and the attire of workers in the field may differ. Unofficial dress codes can affect work assignments, pay raises, and promotions, so if in doubt—ask!
- **Fashion to Avoid**   You probably have some very nice clothes that are not suitable for the workplace. For example, clothes you would wear for a night on the town probably aren't appropriate work clothes, and neither are tight-fitting clothes, low-cut dresses, unbuttoned shirts, short skirts, and neon-hued or metallic outfits. If you are unsure about the appropriateness of your clothing, just don't wear it. When you pay attention to the atmosphere of the workplace, you may be able to more clearly determine if your personal clothing is also appropriate workplace clothing.

    Items to avoid wearing to work are frequently listed in business magazines and newspapers. They include flip-flops, shorts, tank tops,

Case Study

Chris works at a telemarketing company with a business casual dress code. Describe the appropriate kind of dress for Chris.

Group Activity

What is your personal style? How might you change your personal style for the workplace?

Discussion Activity

Write a list of jobs that require uniforms, and then discuss why some businesses require employees to wear uniforms.

transparent fabric, T-shirts with nonbusiness logos/slogans, yoga pants, workout clothes, and anything that shows too much skin.[4]

- **Dress Neatly** Make sure the clothes you wear are neat and clean. Press them, if necessary. Even casual dress must be tidy. Your clothes should be in good shape, with no tears or stains. Save that expensive pair of ripped jeans for your day off. Your shoes should be clean, in good condition, and polished if they are leather.
- **Know the Uniform Rules** Uniforms vary depending on the type of work being done. Hats, scrubs, aprons, and/or specially designed shirts may be required. Here are some questions you need to ask your supervisor or HR representative about uniforms:

  - Who is responsible for keeping uniforms clean and pressed? Some employers have a cleaning service; others expect you to keep your uniform clean and in good shape.
  - How many uniforms do you need?
  - Who pays for repairing or replacing damaged uniforms?
  - How should the uniform be worn? (Do you need special shoes or blouses with it? Should you wear only certain colors?)

- **Follow Safety Protocol** Some jobs present possible safety hazards, and you might be required to wear certain clothing as a result. Always follow company safety protocol. Here are some common safety considerations:

  - Loose clothing or dangling jewelry can get caught by and pull you into moving equipment. Avoid wearing such items if you work around moving equipment.
  - Hard leather shoes and steel-toed boots are a must if something heavy could drop on your feet.
  - Jeans and heavy-duty cargo pants help protect you from scrapes and cuts that can happen on some jobs.

Personal Protective Equipment

Certain jobs require protective dress considerations.[5] Find out what **safety equipment** is required on the job, *and then wear it*. Safety equipment can be slightly uncomfortable, but if you don't wear it, you could lose your job (or get hurt). An employer is responsible for your safety and will not tolerate safety infractions. The following is a list of common safety equipment:

- **Safety Glasses** Safety glasses are required for jobs in which small particles could strike or lodge in your eyes. For example, workers drilling into metal parts wear safety glasses.
- **Ear Protectors** If your job exposes you to continuous or loud noise, which can cause hearing problems, ear protectors are needed. Ground personnel who work around jet airplanes wear ear protectors.
- **Hard hats** A hard hat might not protect you from all injuries, but it can reduce the seriousness of an injury. Most construction workers are required to wear hard hats.

Group Activity

Discuss whether very expensive, fashionable torn jeans are acceptable in a business casual work environment? Are athletic shoes acceptable at a construction site?

Journal Activity

Identify various jobs and types of clothing or grooming practices that may not be safe for those jobs.

- **Masks**   Wearing a mask is a must if you work where exposure to fumes from dangerous chemicals is unavoidable. Failure to wear a mask in some jobs could result in serious injury or even death. A painter in a body and trim shop typically wears a mask.
- **Gloves**   Protect against the frostbite, blisters, or rope burns that are hazards of some jobs by wearing gloves. A person stacking hay bales or working in the frozen-food section of a grocery store wears gloves.
- **Protective Clothing**   If you work with hazardous materials, your employer must provide protective clothing and teach you how to prevent injury. This clothing includes specialized protective gloves, aprons, coveralls, boots, or protective suits. People who work with or near hazardous materials wear protective clothing.

Discussion Activity

Discuss each personal protective equipment item listed here and what it is used for. What might happen if the equipment was not used?

How Job Savvy Are You?

Jill is a salesperson at a life insurance company. The office regularly has clients in the office. Clients are typically families. Check the items you think would be acceptable for her to wear to work.

❑ Blouse	❑ Skirt	❑ Sweater	❑ Sweat pants
❑ Boots	❑ Capris	❑ Jacket	❑ Running shoes
❑ Khakis	❑ Slacks	❑ T-shirt	❑ Sandals
❑ Polo shirt	❑ Dress	❑ Jeans	
❑ Shorts	❑ Socks	❑ Tie	
❑ Business suit	❑ Dress shirt	❑ Jewelry	

Why did you select these items?

_____

_____

_____

Tyler is a counter attendant in a dry-cleaning shop. Check the items you think he could wear to work.

❑ Sports jersey	❑ Kilt	❑ Sweater	❑ Sweat pants
❑ Boots	❑ Capris	❑ Jacket	❑ Leather shoes
❑ Khakis	❑ Slacks	❑ T-shirt	❑ Running shoes
❑ Polo shirt	❑ Trousers	❑ Jeans	❑ Oversized jewelry
❑ Shorts	❑ Socks	❑ Tie	❑ Sandals
❑ Business suit	❑ Dress shirt	❑ Jewelry	❑ Baseball cap

Why did you select these items?

_____

_____

_____

Continues

Cal is a production worker in an automotive parts factory. Check the items you think he could wear to work.

❏ Tank-top	❏ Thobe	❏ Sweater	❏ Sweat pants
❏ Boots	❏ Capris	❏ Jacket	❏ Leather shoes
❏ Khakis	❏ Slacks	❏ T-shirt	❏ Running shoes
❏ Polo shirt	❏ Serwal	❏ Jeans	❏ Hoodie
❏ Shorts	❏ Socks	❏ Tie	❏ Sandals
❏ Business suit	❏ Dress shirt	❏ Jewelry	❏ Turban

Why did you select these items?

_____

_____

_____

Brandtrell is a lab assistant at a hospital. Check the items you think he could wear to work.

❏ Shalwar Kameez	❏ Izar	❏ Sweater	❏ Sweat pants
❏ Boots	❏ Capris	❏ Jacket	❏ Leather shoes
❏ Khakis	❏ Slacks	❏ T-shirt	❏ Running shoes
❏ Polo shirt	❏ Cargo pants	❏ Jeans	❏ Athletic shorts
❏ Shorts	❏ Socks	❏ Tie	❏ Sandals
❏ Business suit	❏ Dress shirt	❏ Jewelry	❏ Egal

Why did you select these items?

_____

_____

_____

Personal Hygiene and Grooming

In some jobs, your own health—as well as that of customers or patients—depends on your good hygienic practices. For example, the law requires health-care organizations and food-preparation facilities to enforce certain sanitary practices. Here is a list of the most commonly required hygienic practices:

Journal Activity

List the hygiene and grooming activities you practice. How often do you practice them?

- **Hairnets** Sometimes hairnets are required for jobs in food service or preparation.
- **Washing Hands** You must wash your hands with soap and water after using the restroom. This helps protect you from disease or from spreading germs and is particularly important in jobs where you prepare or serve food. Use soap and lather your hands for 10 to 15 seconds. Regulations require workers in health occupations to wash their hands each time they work with a different patient.

- **Gloves**   Wearing gloves helps control exposure to germs in the food-preparation and health occupations.
- **Aprons**   Wearing an apron might be required in food-preparation jobs to prevent germs, dirt, or other foreign particles on your clothes from getting into the food.

Additional precautions are taken in many occupations. You should become familiar with the hygiene practices required for your job. In some cases (such as with food-preparation jobs), state and local laws govern the hygiene standards.

Grooming requirements (along with dress codes) in the workplace must be reasonably accommodated according to federal regulations.[6] Note: *Accommodated* is a legal term that means the employer must adjust their rules so both the employee and the employer can arrive at an agreement that fits the needs of both parties. This means there may be occasions when an employer must allow beards and hair styles that are worn as part of a person's religious beliefs. For example, sidelocks worn by an Orthodox Jewish man must be accommodated by an employer. Imagine a typical morning preparing for work or school as you complete the Grooming Checklist.

Journal Activity

How can you improve your grooming for a job you want at a conservative workplace?

Grooming Checklist

The following is a checklist of grooming activities you should practice on a regular basis. Place a plus (+) next to those you do regularly and a minus (–) next to those you could improve.

❑ **Shower or bathe regularly.** It's not pleasant to work with someone who has body odor.

❑ **Use deodorant daily.** This helps control body odor that results from sweating.

❑ **Brush your teeth.** Brush at least twice a day and when possible after each meal. Consider gargling with mouthwash once or twice a day. Bring a grooming kit to work with floss, toothpaste, and toothbrush to use as needed during the workday.

❑ **Shave.** Some courts have ruled no facial-hair policies unconstitutional. However, many workplaces, particularly conservative-minded companies, still expect employees to remain clean-shaven (in other words, no stubble). As a general policy, groom beards and mustaches on a daily basis, keeping them neatly trimmed, and know your company's policies on facial hair. For example, food-preparation or serving jobs might require you to wear a hairnet over your beard.

❑ **Wash and style your hair.** The oiliness of your hair determines how often you need to shampoo, but hair usually needs washing every one to three days. A professional appearance includes a hairstyle that is appropriate for your specific workplace. Consider the work culture and safety reasons that may impact your employer's expectations. If you need help selecting a style you can manage every day, talk with a stylist. Understand that not all hairstyles are accepted in all workplaces. For example, in some workplaces, such as those that prepare food or in certain labs, dyed hair, dreadlocks, or extremely long hair might pose a health or safety concern and therefore are not acceptable.

Continues

❑ **Trim and clean your fingernails.** Long, dirty, and ragged fingernails are unsightly and can pose a health hazard, so trim your nails weekly and clean them at least once a day. Women who wear fingernail polish should use conservative colors for work places with a formal dress code. Avoid extremely bright or unnatural colors.

❑ **Perfume and cologne.** Many people are allergic or sensitive to perfume and cologne. Businesses do not want employees or customers to have a negative reaction to an employee's perfume or cologne. That is a reason many businesses do not allow employees to use them or other grooming products that leave a strong scent on a person's body.[7]

❑ **Use makeup sparingly.** Makeup can help you achieve a professional, confident appearance. Natural colors that complement your skin tone are appropriate. Bold colors, such as hot pinks and bright blues, may not be appropriate in your workplace. If you need help selecting an appropriate makeup routine for work, visit a salon or a makeup specialist. Initial consultations may be offered for free.

A note on piercings and body art. When it comes to tattoos, henna, and piercings, every workplace will have different policies for what is acceptable. If you accept the policies, you may need to adjust your clothing to cover body art or buy special jewelry or other temporary solutions to adhere to company policies.

Special Personal Considerations

There are three specific issues regarding appearance that justify special attention here: physical condition, weight, and skin condition. Let's examine these one at a time.

Physical Condition

This applies to everyone. You want to look and feel your best so you can perform your work confidently and fully. For more physical jobs, this may require you to exercise regularly. Exercise improves your stamina, allows you to work harder and longer, relieves stress, and alleviates job-related stress injuries. For all of these reasons, it makes good sense to maintain a healthy physical condition.

Weight

When it comes to weight, the goal is to be healthy and confident. This confidence translates directly into the first impression you make and your overall attitude at work. Maintaining a healthy weight has physical and mental benefits. If you have insecurities or health concerns related to your weight, then you may want to research healthy eating habits and exercise options. Many gym memberships include a nutrition consultation, sometimes free for new members. Do what you need to do to look and feel your best.

Journal Activity

Part of maintaining health is making time for physical fitness, even a 30-minute walk around the neighborhood. Design a one month fitness plan around an activity you enjoy.

Skin Conditions

Many people experience acne, eczema, dermatitis, warts, hives, rosacea, and other common skin irritations, disorders, and diseases. Conditions may be caused by air quality, diet, or environmental issues; other times these conditions are genetic. If your skin condition is weighing on your mind or interfering with your work performance, consult with your health insurance provider to find a skin specialist (often called a dermatologist). A dietitian or naturopath may be helpful as well.

Mannerisms and Habits

Mannerisms and habits can have as powerful an influence on people as appearance. Look at other people and determine what mannerisms they exhibit that negatively affect the way you feel about them. Examine yourself for any such behavior. Ask friends and family to tell you whether they observe undesirable traits in your conduct. (Family members will be especially willing to do this.) This list describes some common nonverbal behaviors that are generally considered to have a negative impact on how others might perceive you:

Discussion Activity

What are some common bad habits? Are there any mannerisms that are especially annoying in a workplace setting?

- **Using Tobacco Products** Most organizations have banned smoking on the job. In some cases, smoking is restricted to certain areas outside buildings or even off the premises. Chewing tobacco or using snuff also might be prohibited and may result in a negative image.
- **Wearing Earphones or Earbuds** Listening to music from streaming sources, such as computers and cell phones, may be acceptable in open work areas. But make sure your employer accepts headphone use.
- **Chewing Gum** It's hard to speak clearly when you've got a wad of gum in your mouth. Be smart—leave the gum at home.
- **Using Slang or Profanity** Slang may have a negative impact on you in workplace settings. You should use a commonly understood vocabulary. Profanity may have a negative impact on you as well. It can make co-workers uncomfortable and could even result in you losing your job.
- **Picking and Pulling** Sometimes people unconsciously develop a habit of picking at a certain part of their body—maybe their ears, nose, hair, chin, or fingers. This can be a real distraction to other people.
- **Texting and Talking on Cell Phones** Texting or talking on your cell phone may offend people in social situations and looks as though you aren't doing your job at work. Texting and talking on a cell phone while walking or driving is not only dangerous[8] but illegal in many states. You can avoid offending others and be safer if you limit your use of a cell phone at work to work-related communications.

Journal Activity

What are some habits or mannerisms that you have that might be irritating to someone else? Write a plan to overcome these habits.

Sasha started work as a secretary in a large office about four weeks ago. Today, she came into work wearing a short skirt. You can smell her perfume 20 feet away. Her nails are very long and painted purple, to match her eye shadow and her dress. Her lipstick is also purple.

1. Why might Sasha's strong perfume be a problem in the office?

_____

_____

_____

2. The office dress code is business casual—suggest an outfit that might be more appropriate for Sasha to wear.

_____

_____

_____

Dan is a maintenance worker at a hospital. He is required to wear a uniform to work. His hair is shaggy and unkempt. Some employees avoid him, saying that he smells bad. Once in a while he comes to work with a three-day growth of stubble on his face.

1. What should Dan do to properly groom himself for this job?

_____

_____

_____

2. Are there any on-the-job hygienic issues Dan should keep in mind?

_____

_____

_____

Have a Positive Attitude

During your first months of work, your superiors and coworkers will form opinions of you based on your actions and attitudes. These first impressions are important to your success on the job. They may affect the work that you are assigned and even future promotions.[9] Once they are formed, first impressions are difficult to change. Here are a few tips to create a positive impression:

- **Be a learner.** Pay attention to directions. Listen to others. Ask questions when you need help. Learn about the organization by observing the interactions of others.
- **Be a part of the work team.** Do your share of the work. Be friendly. Talk with your coworkers about their interests. Be helpful. If your boss asks for extra help for work assignments, volunteer.

Discussion Activity

How can you create a positive impression? What are ways to be a valuable team member? What are ways to retain a can-do attitude after a stressful day?

- **Be businesslike.** Speak and conduct yourself in a professional manner. Be aware that the language you would use with your friends at a weekend gathering is different from the language used in the workplace. Be organized. Know your work schedule. Be at work on time. Avoid leaving work early.
- **Be positive.** There is no doubt you will experience some stressful days. All workers do. Remember that others will judge you on how you deal with difficult situations. Develop a "can-do" attitude and use it when you experience a hard day. In other words, believe in yourself. Recognize the contribution you make to the work team. Focus on the value your supervisor has in your ability.

A Useful Skill: Good Communication

When you speak, you make an impression on others. If you speak with a clear, confident voice, others will view you as confident. However, speaking in an inaudible voice or not looking at the the person you're talking to gives the impression that you lack confidence. Always aim to use a commonly understood vocabulary and correct grammar.

To effectively communicate in the workplace, you must listen, process what you hear, and then speak. Active listening is just as important as speaking clearly.

Another type of conversation that happens in the workplace is small talk. Although small talk is not directly involved with work tasks, research has shown that it plays an important role in developing teamwork. Participating in appropriate small talk may help you become a part of the team.

Here are a few helpful hints for communicating with coworkers and supervisors:

- **Listen before you speak.** Listening will allow you to learn more about other team members. Knowing about their interests and concerns will provide information for conversations.
- **Think before you speak.** Consider what you want to convey and how you want to make the statement.
- **Avoid controversial subjects.** Don't participate in conversations that involve gossip and rumors. Controversial topics are best avoided in the workplace.
- **Be respectful of your coworkers.** Avoid asking extremely personal questions. Listen to their ideas, feelings, and beliefs. Accept their diversity.

Summing Up

Proper dress and good hygiene are crucial for two important reasons. First, they affect your appearance, and your appearance has an effect on supervisors, coworkers, and customers—either good or bad. Second, proper dress and hygiene might be important to your health and safety. Wearing clothes that protect you from injury or disease is important. Find out what the safety and health requirements are for your job, and follow them closely. Remember, how you dress and how you take care of yourself tell others a lot about you.

Your mannerisms and habits play a role in others' impressions of you. Become aware of any irritating behavior or habit you have, and try to eliminate it. When you get rid of annoying behaviors, you then have the opportunity to replace them with good behaviors.

Remember, first impressions are made only once. Make sure what you're conveying about yourself is positive. The best-dressed, sweetest-smelling grouch in the workplace is still the grouch, and everyone else will avoid that well-dressed grouch. If you are upbeat, your boss and coworkers will view you positively. Smiling, being friendly, and showing interest in your work will let others know that you want to be a part of the team.

Assessment time!

Take the Review Quiz. See your instructor or reference your student files in the ebook for additional resources.

CHAPTER 4

Being There . . . On Time!

Objectives

- Demonstrate personal accountability, reliability, and punctuality.

- Examine why being on time is important for various job scenarios.

- Summarize effective self-management (assess self accurately, set personal goals, monitor progress, and exhibit self-control).

Have you ever waited 15 minutes to get your food at a fast-food restaurant when there were no customers ahead of you? Have you waited in long lines at a discount store because not enough checkout lanes were open? Have you had extra work assigned to you at a job because another employee showed up late or didn't show up to work at all? If your answer to any or all of these questions is yes, then you've been the victim of an absent or tardy worker.

An organization can't operate without dependable workers. A supervisor must be able to rely on employees coming to work on time every day. Productivity losses from absenteeism were $225.8 billion or $1,685 per employee in 2015.[1]

You may recall that earlier in the book we mentioned some of the soft skills employers want from workers. The skill of being at work when scheduled (known as dependability) has been listed as one of the top worker skills in employer surveys for over a century. A supervisor needs to be able to count on you being at work and doing your job as expected (known as responsibility).

You may be wondering how being at work as scheduled can be a skill. A skill is a series of actions needed to perform a task. Getting to work as scheduled requires you to develop a series of actions that will lead to you being at work on time. This chapter provides you with ideas that will help you develop the skill of dependability. It includes both getting to work as scheduled and performing the job in a timely manner.

Watch the Video

Being There . . . On Time!

The Cost of Absenteeism

When you don't show up for work, you can cause problems for everyone. Here are some examples of problems resulting from absent employees:

Group Activity

Identify problems created by undependable employees. How do these problems affect the employer, supervisor, coworkers, and employee?

- **Problems for the Employer** **Employee absenteeism** can cost organizations money in three ways:

  1. **Reduced productivity means fewer products made and fewer customers served.** In some instances, the amount of goods and services remains the same but the quality suffers.

  2. **Financial loss occurs due to fees required to hire temp workers.** Some jobs require temporary workers to replace an absent employee. Common examples are home health aids and substitute teachers. When the employee is absent, there must be someone to replace the worker. This means the employer must often pay for a sick day or personal day for the full-time employee and also pay for the temp worker.

  3. **Customer dissatisfaction means potentially decreased future sales.** Customers won't be served as well as they should be. For instance, if a worker in a production job is absent, a customer's shipment might not be sent on time because there isn't enough help to complete the job.

- **Problems for the Supervisor** Worker absenteeism requires a supervisor to rearrange work schedules and plans. Another worker might have to fill in. Problems created by one absence usually continue throughout the day. Supervisors pick up the slack, which might prevent them from completing their own work during work hours. How the supervisor reacts depends largely on the reason of the absence and how frequently the employee is absent.

- **Problems for Coworkers** Everyone must work harder when one worker is absent. A person who had the day off might be called into work. Someone who just finished a shift might be asked to stay and work a double shift. This can cause tension among coworkers.

- **Problems for the Employee** Being absent or late often results in docked pay. This means that you get no pay for the time you weren't at work. The organization's policy about days off will affect how much your paycheck is reduced. Repeated incidents could result in termination.

George supervises the morning shift at a fast-food restaurant. The phone rings at 6 a.m. "George," says the caller, "this is Lee. My car won't start, so I won't be at work today." The breakfast crowd has started to arrive in the dining room. Several cars are lined up at the drive-through window.

1. What problems did Lee create by not coming to work?

   _____

   _____

2. How does Lee's absence affect his coworkers?

   _____

   _____

3. How many times do you think George will allow Lee to be absent from work before taking some kind of action?

   _____

   _____

Schedule, Attendance, and Tardiness

Work hours differ. Some companies have set hours—such as Monday to Friday from 8:00 a.m. until 5:00 p.m. In other job situations, the employees may work flexible hours and choose when they work as long as they work a certain number of hours each week. Flexible hours are more common in salaried jobs. Irregular work schedules change weekly or even monthly. Salaried workers may normally work eight hours in a day, but during the busy season of the year, they may be required to work extra hours without additional pay.

Employers can choose a variety of systems to record attendance. Manual clocking in requires a time card and mechanical clock. Automated systems record an employee's attendance, arrival, and departure during the work period using badges encoded with a special chip or cards that are swiped.[2] Employee information is stored in a computer. A salaried employee may complete an attendance sheet at the end of each pay period.

Over 50% of employers use a computer application or cell phone to record employee attendance. One advantage of using cell phones is that jobs requiring employees to be in multiple locations each day, such as office machine repairers, can use an app to record both time and location. This is done using the GPS system in cell phones to identify a **geolocation** or create geofencing around a business location.[3]

Defining **tardiness** varies from company to company. Normally a grace period, for example 10 minutes after the set hour, applies before an employee is recorded as tardy. Automated systems record the number of times a worker is tardy. Excessive tardiness can result in the employee losing the job.

What's Your Excuse?

Sometimes, being absent or late is unavoidable; more often, it's not. A CareerBuilder survey involving 2,600 managers and 3,400 employees found the most common reasons employees are late include traffic (49%), oversleeping (32%), bad weather (26%), too tired to get out of bed (25%), and procrastination (17%).[4] Read the following list of excuses. Place a check mark in the *Absent* column if that reason has caused you to be absent from work in the past year. Check *Late* if it made you late, and *Both* if it caused you to be both late and absent on different occasions. If you aren't currently employed, check the reasons you were late or absent from a former job or from school.

Journal Activity

Why have you been late to work? What excuses did you give? Did your tardiness have a negative impact?

Checklist of Excuses for Being Late or Absent

Excuse	Absent	Late	Both	Excuse	Absent	Late	Both
Overslept	☐	☐	☐	Didn't feel like going	☐	☐	☐
Missed the bus	☐	☐	☐	Family problems	☐	☐	☐
Personal illness	☐	☐	☐	Wanted to do other things	☐	☐	☐
Alarm didn't ring	☐	☐	☐	Weather was bad	☐	☐	☐
Children were sick	☐	☐	☐	Forgot the work schedule	☐	☐	☐
Car troubles	☐	☐	☐	No clean clothes	☐	☐	☐
Couldn't find a baby sitter	☐	☐	☐	Had a hangover	☐	☐	☐
Wanted to sleep in	☐	☐	☐	Took a trip instead	☐	☐	☐
Traffic was bad	☐	☐	☐	Needed a day off	☐	☐	☐

As you look over the list above, consider what you should do to reduce the number of days you are absent from or late for work. You might find it interesting to compare your answers with the following reasons for absenteeism that workers gave in a study.[5]

Discussion Activity

What are the common reasons for being late or absent? Discuss ways to avoid being late/absent.

Table 4.1 Common Reasons for Work Absenteeism

Reason for Absenteeism	Percentage of Workers Citing Reason
Illness	34%
Dealing with family issues	22%
Taking care of personal business	18%
Escaping stress	13%
Felt entitled to the time	13%

Because absences cost employers so much money, employers are always looking for ways to help employees reduce absenteeism. The next section explores common causes for absenteeism so that you can evaluate your own lifestyle and avoid being late to work or absent from work.

Your Lifestyle Affects Your Work

A lifestyle is made up of the habits and activities you develop for day-to-day living. Your lifestyle includes what you eat, when and how long you sleep, and how you spend your time.

Studies show that your lifestyle can affect the amount of stress in your daily life. Not only does lifestyle affect stress but stress affects your lifestyle. For example, stress can lead to alcohol abuse, which in turn can create even more stress.[6] Many of the reasons people miss work are directly related to their lifestyles. Here are some ways you can shape your lifestyle to increase your success at work:

- **Get a Good Night's Sleep**   Most people need six to eight hours of sleep each night. Skimping on sleep can affect your job performance.[7] Your body rests better when you sleep on a regular schedule. Many young people make the mistake of staying out late on work nights. They get less sleep and then skip work the next morning or are late.
- **Eat Well**   Eat well-balanced meals on a regular schedule and avoid eating a lot of junk food. Consume plenty of fruits and vegetables, and be sure to stay hydrated. You are less likely to be ill when you have good eating habits.
- **Exercise Regularly**   Most jobs in the United States are service and information related; they don't enable you to get much exercise. Regular exercise keeps you in top physical and mental condition and helps you release job-related stress.
- **Don't Smoke**   According to plentiful medical evidence, smoking is hazardous to both smokers and nonsmokers. A Gallup poll found that 96% of US adults want all smoking in the workplace banned or confined to a separate area.[8] Many organizations offer incentives and help for employees who want to quit smoking. Some smokers use e-cigarettes to stop smoking real cigarettes. Experts think vaping contains harmful chemicals.[9] Also, many workplaces do not allow vaping or have the same rules for vaping as they do for smoking traditional tobacco products.
- **Don't Drink Too Much Alcohol**   Abuse of alcohol can cause health problems. The more alcohol you drink, the more you can damage your body. Drinking too much alcohol will hurt your performance on the job the next day. Drinking alcohol during or before work is often considered cause for dismissal.
- **Don't Use Drugs**   Illegal drugs harm the body and mind. You should not take any drugs unless a physician prescribes them. Policies on illegal drug use vary among workplaces. Some companies periodically give their employees drug tests. If you test positive for certain drugs, some workplaces will give you a choice of entering a rehabilitation program or being fired. Other workplaces may fire you outright.

Case Study

Denzel has been stressed at his job and has a busy social life. He maintains a healthy diet, and he spends a few nights a week out late with friends to unwind. Lately he is unfocused at work and often has headaches. What are ways Denzel can improve his lifestyle?

Journal Activity

What makes you feel stressed? How can you avoid stress or ease the feelings of stress?

- **Keep Good Company**   Your relationships affect your work. For instance, if your friends don't work, they might want you to adapt to their schedule, which can leave you too tired for work the next day. If you're facing a conflict like this, you need to establish a priority for work over social activities. Avoid people who might get you into trouble with the law. Employers do not appreciate workers who miss work because they are in jail or prioritizing their social life over work.

- **Socialize Appropriately with Coworkers**   We all need time to socialize with friends and acquaintances. Our coworkers often become our best friends because we spend so much time with them. Relationships with coworkers can be positive, or they can create problems in the workplace. These guidelines can help you avoid problems in your work relationships:

  - **Approach Office Romances with Caution**   Many people think work is a good place to meet people they would like to date. However, be careful not to let a romance negatively affect your relationships with coworkers. Sometimes an office romance can create awkward and unpleasant situations while you're dating and if the romance ends.

  - **Don't Limit Friendships to Only Coworkers**   When you socialize with coworkers, you spend a lot of time talking about work. To reduce stress, you need to get away from your job sometimes by not talking or even thinking about the job.

  - **Don't Allow Office Friendships to Interfere with Performance**   Don't do someone else's work to cover for his or her inability or laziness. Avoid siding with a friend in a feud with another worker or supervisor. Try to be neutral in work relationships.

Your Lifestyle and Stress

A moderate lifestyle will serve you well throughout your life. Rate your lifestyle using the following checklist. Check each statement that is true for you. Then score your answers to see how healthy your lifestyle is.

- ❑ I do something fun on a regular basis.
- ❑ I rarely drink to excess.
- ❑ I exercise regularly.
- ❑ I have friends I can rely on.
- ❑ I have healthy coping strategies in times of stress.
- ❑ I avoid eating lots of junk food.
- ❑ I don't smoke.
- ❑ I average seven or more hours of sleep on work nights.
- ❑ I do not use illegal drugs.
- ❑ I eat at least one well-balanced meal daily.

Count the number of statements you checked. Score yourself using the following guidelines:

- **8 or more** checked items reflects a positive lifestyle that will help you be effective on the job.

- **6 to 7** checked items reflects a moderate lifestyle that will help you on the job.

- **5 or fewer** checked items reflects a vulnerable lifestyle. You might find that your lifestyle creates some problems on the job.

Plan for Success

Managing your life through good planning will help you avoid missing work. You can take the following five major steps to ensure a good work attendance record.

Step 1: Ensure That You Have Reliable Transportation

It's not your employer's fault that your car won't start. You are responsible for getting to work. Transportation problems can happen even if you own a new car. Try these strategies to ensure that you have reliable transportation:

- **Maintain Your Vehicle** If you suspect you might have car trouble, try starting your car a couple of hours before you need to be at work. This will give you time to find another method of transportation if you need to. Cold temperatures affect cars negatively in many ways. Motor oil thickens when cold, making it harder for the engine to turn over on the first start of the day, so check the car early.

- **Use Public Transportation** Most public transportation schedules are available in print and as apps for cell phones. Become familiar with the routes and how to interpret the schedule so that when you need to use public transportation you can with ease. If you know your transportation option will get you to work at 8:05 every day but you are scheduled to start at 8:00, talk to your supervisor about adjusting your start time so you won't be late.

- **Call a Coworker** Find a coworker who lives near you and has a reliable car. Make an agreement to share a ride if either of you has car trouble.

- **Carpool** Check with coworkers and friends, or advertise in the classifieds for someone who can share a ride to work with you. This arrangement will work even when you don't work together. You just need to work in the same general area.

- **Walk or Bicycle** Think about finding housing near your workplace. Even if you live two to four miles from your job, you can still walk or ride a bike to work in good weather. If you don't want to move, find a job near your home. You might actually be able to work for less money at a job that doesn't cost you high transportation expenses. Your net income (wages minus work-related expenses) might be greater if you take a job close to home.

- **For-hire Ride Share or Taxi Services** A cab, Lyft, or Uber are more expensive than public transportation but may be less costly than not getting paid for a day of work, and it's certainly less costly than losing your job. You don't want to take a taxi to work every day, but you shouldn't hesitate to do so in an emergency.

Step 2: Arrange Reliable Care for Your Dependents

Most often dependents are children. However, a dependent can be an elderly parent or a disabled spouse. If you are responsible for dependents, you need reliable care for them.

Group Activity

In groups of two, take turns being an employee and a supervisor. Practice telling your supervisor why you were late to work.

What happens if a babysitter or home health aide lets you down? What if bad weather closes a daycare center? What if your dependent is ill? What if your children can't get to school on the normal schedule?

You should plan ahead for substitute dependent care so you won't get caught off guard. Many companies offer referral services, so check with your HR representative. They may refer you to your health insurance provider, who may also offer referrals. Here are some considerations:

- **Hire Good Aides**   Choose a reliable babysitter or home health aide. You can check this person's reliability by asking for references from people who have employed the aide in their own homes and by checking websites like Angie's List.

- **Select a Good Care Center**   Learn about the center's policies for drop-off and pick-up and accepting ill attendees. There are now centers that will care for children when they are ill. You might pay more for centers with this service, but in the long run they might pay for themselves by reducing your absenteeism.

- **Investigate Healthcare Programs**   In some cases, hospitals and specialized care centers will take care of your sick dependents while you are at work. You would use many of these programs only when your child is sick. They cost more than normal child care, but they are less costly than an unpaid day off work or losing your job.

- **Have a Contact List**   Find two to three friends or relatives willing to care for your dependent for one or two days in case of an emergency. Be sure to stay in touch with them to know their most current availability, and keep your contact list up to date.

Step 3: Use a Calendar

Have a calendar and use it to keep track of your work schedule. Whether you use a simple pocket-size calendar or choose to be more technical and use a cell phone calendar, record all assigned workdays and any personal appointments that might conflict with work.

Plan to request time off in advance for doctor and dental appointments. Whenever possible, schedule personal appointments outside regular work hours. You might want to note other personal appointments and responsibilities on your calendar as well.

A calendar is one of the best tools for helping you plan your workday. You will find many free calendar apps for your cell phone. Two popular ones are Google Calendar and Outlook. You can set alarms on your phone using the calendar apps to remind you of scheduled appointments a few minutes or hours or even a day before an appointment is scheduled.

Step 4: Plan a Schedule with Your Supervisor

You can plan for many events in life, such as vacations; car maintenance; or dental, doctor, and lawyer appointments. Supervisors usually can approve and schedule a one-day absence with only a few weeks' notice. A vacation might require several months' notice. Ask your supervisor how much notice is needed to schedule days off.

Step 5: When You Can't Get to Work, Call Your Employer

Even the best planning won't cover all potential difficulties that can keep you from getting to work, so call your supervisor as soon as you know that you cannot get to work. An employer usually will understand if you miss work once in a while because you're sick or have an unexpected problem. However, being frequently absent or late may result in poor referrals down the road or even being fired from your job. By contrast, being a reliable and dependable worker can result in opportunities for a job promotion.

To better prepare for these emergencies, ask your HR representative how many days are considered reasonable to be absent from work each year and ask about the consequences for being late or having excessive absences. The discipline might range from a verbal warning for the first offense to immediate discharge. Most organizations will take disciplinary action for

- frequent or unexcused absences;
- absences that occur a day before or after a holiday;
- failure to call in and report an unexpected absence;
- absences due to nonemergency personal business.

When you notify your supervisor that you can't be at work, follow these steps:

- Identify yourself and say that you can't come to work.
- Explain the reason that you can't be at work. Don't lie.
- If you expect to be gone for more than a day, tell your supervisor how long you will be away from the job.
- Express your willingness to make up the hours you missed.

It may be appropriate to notify your supervisor that you can't be at work by emailing or texting your supervisor. You should only use one of these methods if it was previously approved by the organization and your supervisor. Many supervisors still want to be contacted by phone so they can quickly communicate about how to adjust the workflow for the day. They need to know the last task you completed or how far along you were in getting the task finished.

How Job Savvy Are You?

There are acceptable and unacceptable reasons for being absent from work. Review the following list. Check those reasons that you think justify an absence.

❑ I have a headache.

❑ My child is ill.

❑ My car isn't working.

❑ I have the flu.

❑ I have an appointment with my attorney.

❑ There's been a death in my family.

❑ My brother asked me to babysit his children.

Continues

Continued

❏ I had a fight with my spouse.

❏ I sprained my ankle and need to keep it elevated.

❏ I need to visit a sick friend in the hospital.

❏ Our house was broken into last night.

❏ I need to get a new pair of glasses.

❏ I had a car accident on the way to work.

❏ It was a long weekend, and I have a hangover.

❏ This is a religious holiday for me.

You should always tell the truth when you report to your supervisor. A lie might be discovered and cause you embarrassment. If you are caught in a lie, it will take a long time for you to regain your supervisor's trust.

Getting to Work on Time

Late workers cause the same problems for an employer as absent workers. There are reasonable causes for being late. However, some employers consider late arrivals excessive if they occur more than once a month or four to five times a year. These suggestions can help you plan ahead to be on time:

- **Use a Reliable Alarm** Many people use cell phones as a replacement for a clock or watch. Most phones come with a clock app that has an alarm that can be set for specific times of the day. Set your alarm to allow you plenty of time to get ready for work and get to work as scheduled. Don't rely on someone else to get you up. You can't afford to lose a job just because you don't get to work on time.

- **Get Up Early** Allow yourself time to get ready and get to work. Plan enough time to eat breakfast and to deal with transportation delays. You should also plan to arrive at work 8 to 10 minutes early. This cushion will help you mentally prepare for the day and reduce stress. It also shows your supervisor that you are eager to work.

- **Plan for Special Conditions** Some days you'll need more time to get to work. For example, poor weather conditions usually slow traffic. Get up and out the door earlier on such days so that you will still arrive on time.

- **Call Your Supervisor When You'll Be More than 15 Minutes Late** You should give the following information:

  - Explain why you will be late.
  - Say that you are going to get to work as soon as possible.
  - Estimate when you will arrive.
  - Assure your supervisor that you will make up the time.
  - Apologize when you get to work and make it clear that it won't happen again.

Journal Activity

What prevents you from being a dependable worker? What changes can you make to improve your dependability?

Buster was absent for two days from his job as a production worker at a shoe factory. When he returned, his supervisor, Mr. Brown, was angry. "Why didn't you call to let me know you weren't coming to work?" Mr. Brown asked.

Buster was surprised and answered, "My father-in-law died, and we had to attend the funeral."

Mr. Brown replied, "I'm sorry about your father-in-law, but I'm going to issue you a written warning. If this ever happens again, you'll be fired."

1. Why did Mr. Brown react this way?

_____

_____

2. How could Buster have avoided this problem?

_____

_____

Vanessa went out with friends Thursday night, even though she had to be at work at 7:30 the next morning. She overslept on Friday morning and got to work 45 minutes late. Two weeks earlier, she was out late with friends on Sunday and skipped work the next day. A week earlier, she was 20 minutes late because she had to pick up a friend and take her to work. Her supervisor warned her then not to be late for work. When Vanessa got to the office on Friday, the receptionist told her that her supervisor wanted to see her immediately.

1. What do you think her supervisor will say?

_____

_____

2. What should Vanessa do to keep her job and avoid this situation in the future?

_____

_____

A Useful Skill: Time Management

When employees use time effectively, production within an organization improves. Employers are looking for workers who do not just appear busy. Employers are looking for workers who get the job done. As an employee, you will also benefit from efficient **time management** because you will be less stressed at work. Your work environment will be more pleasant.

Practicing time management involves both small and big actions. Here are a few suggestions to develop time-management skills in your work life:

- **Be On Time** Whether you are clocking in for your work shift, attending a staff meeting, or taking your lunch break, be aware of the time.

Continues

Continued

- **Be Prepared to Work**   Getting enough sleep and exercise will help you work more efficiently. You want to be physically and mentally ready to work each day.
- **Focus On Assigned Tasks**   Plan and prioritize your day. Avoid distractions. Make a to-do list.
- **Do It Right the First Time**   Take the time to analyze a task to figure out how to do it most efficiently. Having to do a task a second time is a waste.
- **Evaluate How You Spend Time**   For two or three days, write a list of how you are spending your time. Identify the tasks that require the most time to complete. Look for ways to use your time more efficiently.
- **Learn How to Be More Efficient**   Breaking big tasks into small steps can help you get your work done more quickly and efficiently. For example, you can organize your emails by moving them into subject files so they can be found under labels such as a project title or a person's name. If you take a bus or train to work, consider catching up on emails during your commute so that when you arrive at work you feel caught up and ready for the day.
- **Be Focused**   Despite what people say, it is impossible to multitask effectively. When we try to do things such as talk on the phone and work on the computer at the same time, our brain simply switches back and forth between the two tasks. It actually takes longer for the brain to switch between tasks than to simply focus on one task at a time.[10]

You get 24 hours each day. You can't increase or decrease this allotted time. But by learning to manage time, you can budget your time to make both your personal and work life more productive.

Summing Up

Reliable workers are essential to an effective operation. That's why good attendance and punctuality are important to employers. Annual reviews rate an employee's punctuality, dependability, and reliability. It's important to build these key skills and then apply them at work throughout the year (not just for a few weeks or months at a time). They are often used to justify increases in salary as well as bonuses and promotions. A little planning and self-discipline will help you be a dependable, reliable, and valuable worker.

Assessment time!

Take the Review Quiz. See your instructor or reference your student files in the ebook for additional resources.

CHAPTER 5

Communicating in the Workplace

Objectives

- Organize ideas and articulate thoughts clearly and effectively in written and oral forms to people inside and outside the workplace.

- Practice active listening and understand the impact of nonverbal communication on the professional image you project at work (expanding on Chapter 4).

- Interpret and effectively respond to verbal messages and other cues.

- Write thoughts, ideas, information, and messages in letters, reports, emails, and intracompany software/apps.

A large part of being successful in the workplace depends on communicating effectively with coworkers, leaders, and customers. This means expressing ideas logically and clearly, whether verbally, nonverbally, or in writing, and making yourself understood as well as understanding others.

Part of effective communication is careful listening. And part of careful listening is hearing what someone says in context of that person's nonverbal cues.

Written communication is used when talking face to face is not possible. Communicating by writing is also used to record a permanent and accurate record of our thoughts.

Although traditional speaking and writing skills remain important for conducting daily business, technology has brought about many changes in the tools used for communication. Knowing how to communicate using technology is a necessity for people in the modern workplace. Today, effective ecommunication is important for getting along with leaders and team members. It is essential to providing good customer service. This chapter provides ideas to help you effectively communicate using both traditional and digital communication skills.

Watch the Video

Communicating in the Workplace

Good Communication Skills Open Doors

Developing good communication skills will help you find a job because employers are looking for workers who communicate well. When you check job search websites to locate job openings, you'll find numerous postings that list strong communication skills as a requirement for the position. Even professions traditionally thought to deal only with numbers (such as accounting, engineering, and coding) are hiring individuals with strong communication skills. In a recent survey of executives at 400 organizations, 85% listed oral communication as the most important practical skill for employees, and 82% identified written communication as an important skill.[1]

In a job interview, you will have more confidence if you can speak clearly. Looking the interviewer in the eye and expressing your ideas reflects your ability to do the job. Your positive manner will impress an employer.

Just as good communication skills can help you get a job, poor communication skills can result in not getting or losing a job. Employers expect to make money. Businesses lose millions of dollars each year due to poor communication by employees. An employee who causes an organization to lose money will soon be unemployed.

In the workplace, good communication skills can help avoid problems. Reading an email carefully, which is a communication skill, will keep you from making mistakes and missing meetings and appointments. Listening to your supervisor's directions will help you work efficiently when performing your assigned duties. Clear communication when leaving a phone message reduces miscommunication with customers.

Effective communication will help you keep your job. You may have some speech habits or mannerisms that you could improve on. You may need to learn a new technological communication skill. Perhaps you need to improve your listening skills. The time and effort to improve your communication skills will help you perform your job more productively.

Discussion Activity

Identify communication skills needed on the job and how they affect your relationships.

Group Activity

What jobs would you like, and what communication skills are needed for those jobs?

Practicing Effective Listening

Studies consistently point out that listening is the communication skill used most frequently in our daily lives. Listening is not a natural skill. Effective listeners have developed certain abilities. You can practice active listening to be a more effective listener using the following eight techniques:

1. **Look at the speaker.** In our culture, eye contact is important. Not looking at the speaker is an indication of not listening. Whether you are listening in a one-on-one situation or in a large group, face the speaker and maintain eye contact.
2. **Use your ears and not your mouth.** Talking while another person is speaking is rude. Talking not only interferes with your listening but prevents other listeners from hearing. When another individual is speaking, be quiet.

Discussion Activity

What is the importance of listening in the workplace?

3. **Concentrate on what is being said.** Focus on the speaker's thoughts. Taking notes is an excellent method of reinforcing what is being said. Don't multitask or try to do other things while listening. There is strong evidence that multitasking results in none of the tasks being done as well as focusing on a single task.[2]

4. **Honor the other person's opinion.** Don't let your personal biases prevent you from listening. Listening doesn't mean you accept the speaker's point of view. Listening does mean you recognize the speaker's right to have an opinion.

5. **Allow speakers to complete thoughts without interrupting.** This is not an easy task, especially if you disagree. But waiting and not interrupting lets all listeners understand what the speaker is saying and avoids confusion.

6. **Listen with your eyes as well as your ears.** Observing a speaker's body language, such as hand gestures and body posture, gives you more insight into the speaker's message.

7. **Act interested even when you may not be.** Make an effort to listen. Face the speaker. Lean forward. Concentrate on what is being said.

8. **Ask questions before you respond.** Clarify the speaker's information by asking questions. You might say, "This is what I understand you said . . . Is that correct?" Let speakers make any corrections to help you better understand their thoughts. Your response will be clearer and more intelligent if you ask questions first.

Journal Activity

Think of the best and worst listeners you have known. List the characteristics that make them good or bad listeners. Compare the two lists.

Check Your Listening Skills

Improving your listening skills begins with learning your strengths and weaknesses. Rate your listening skills using the following checklist. Check each statement that is true for you. Then score your answers to see how you measure up in terms of listening skills.

❏ I face the speaker.

❏ I maintain comfortable eye contact.

❏ I am quiet while the speaker is talking.

❏ I concentrate on the speaker's words.

❏ I avoid interrupting the speaker.

❏ I show respect for the speaker's opinion.

❏ I ask questions after the speaker has finished.

❏ I avoid multitasking.

❏ I observe body language and interpret it.

❏ I take notes.

Count the number of statements you checked. Score yourself using the following guidelines:

- **8 or more** checked items reflects positive listening skills that will help you communicate effectively on the job.

- **6 to 7** checked items reflects a need to improve your listening skills to communicate effectively on the job.

- **5 or fewer** checked items reflects less effective listening skills that might create some communication problems on the job.

Listening is essential in the workplace not just for increasing productivity, but for increasing the sense of teamwork among employees. When you're listening to directions, pay particular attention to what your supervisor says at the beginning and the end. When people give instructions, they often state the most important idea at the beginning and then repeat it at the end. Notice words that they stress, and watch for anything they write down. Ask questions to clarify the instructions, and take notes to help you review the instructions later.

Customers respond positively to workers who practice active listening. Active listening shows respect for the client. You will resolve any complaint or request with less conflict when you use active listening.

How Job Savvy Are You?

On her first day back in the office after a week's vacation, Carmen attended the monthly staff meeting. Her supervisor, Mrs. Wyatt, began the meeting by reviewing the sales records for the month. Because she had already reviewed her sales for the month, Carmen decided to text a client to schedule a lunch meeting. When Mrs. Wyatt asked her a question about the sales report, Carmen needed to have the question repeated. Mrs. Wyatt frowned, folded her arms, and repeated the question. She asked Carmen to see her following the meeting.

1. Why did Mrs. Wyatt react in this way?

   _____

   _____

2. What should Carmen do to solve this problem?

   _____

   _____

Jackson has a certificate in small engine repair and has been working at the Mower Shop for five years. Mr. Howard, the business owner, and Jackson are attending a workshop to learn to repair a new line of lawncare equipment. Mr. Howard paid the workshop fees and is quite excited about the workshop.

   The instructor's presentation is very basic. Jackson already knows much of what is being taught. In fact, the instructor doesn't really seem to be well informed. Jackson even disagrees with some information being provided. Jackson's mind is beginning to wander.

1. What listening skills can Jackson apply in this situation?

   _____

   _____

2. How could Jackson use these listening skills to impress Mr. Howard?

   _____

   _____

Verbal Communication Skills

Your voice is the primary tool used to communicate. The way you speak influences the listener's opinion of you. If you speak clearly, at an even rate, and loud enough, you appear confident and capable. If you speak too quickly or too quietly, you appear uncomfortable and incapable.

Using proper grammar and avoiding slang and cursing when communicating reflects a confident, educated individual. With an increased vocabulary, you have a greater chance of using just the right word to convey your message.

Whether you are speaking to a group or having a one-on-one conversation, the same methods apply. With practice you will become more at ease when you communicate verbally.

Check Your Verbal Communication Skills

Improving your verbal communication skills begins with learning your strengths and weaknesses. Rate your speaking skills using the following checklist. Check each statement that is true for you. Then score your answers to see how you measure up in terms of verbal communication.

❏ I speak clearly.

❏ I use correct grammar.

❏ I look at the listener.

❏ I speak loud enough for others to hear.

❏ I speak at an even rate.

❏ I vary the pitch of my voice.

❏ I avoid using slang when speaking.

❏ I avoid using offensive language.

❏ I have a varied vocabulary.

❏ I feel at ease when speaking.

Count the number of statements you checked. Score yourself using the following guidelines:

- **8 or more** checked items reflects positive speaking skills that will help you communicate effectively on the job.

- **6 to 7** checked items reflects a need to improve your speaking skills to communicate effectively on the job.

- **5 or fewer** checked items reflects less effective speaking skills that might create some communication problems on the job.

Verbal Communication in the Workplace

In the workplace, all types of conversations take place. Business talk is communication about work. Business talk may be structured, such as the agenda for a team meeting or the step-by-step instructions in a training situation. However, most conversations in the workplace are not this structured.

During a typical day, a mixture of business talk and small talk takes place. Small talk is informal conversation among workers. Although it has no relevance to the work being done, it plays the important role of forming a bond among workers that builds teamwork.

When you're communicating in the workplace, think about what you are saying before you speak. Don't spread rumors or gossip that could damage someone's reputation. Lying can cause problems in the workplace. Excessive

Discussion Activity

Identify common inappropriate conversation topics in the workplace. What ways can you make small talk with a coworker?

bragging can cause people to avoid you. Constant swearing or using vulgar language is inappropriate.

Being sensitive to the ideas, feelings, and beliefs of the people you work with will help you succeed at your job. Using offensive terms when referring to races, ethnic groups, or sexual groups is called harassment, and it is illegal.

When misunderstandings occur in the workplace, assertive communication is needed. An assertive communicator listens to all viewpoints and seeks to understand each person's thoughts. Facts and issues rather than opinions or emotions are the focus of the conversation. After all points of view have been heard, the problem is summarized for clarification. The solution is stated very specifically, with the expectation that all those involved will act on it. Assertive communication provides solutions to workplace problems instead of confusion and arguments.

Starting a Conversation

A conversation is the verbal exchange between two or more people. Initiating a conversation with a coworker or supervisor can sometimes be awkward. Here are nine techniques to use when starting a conversation:

1. **Focus on the other person.** Remember that the other individual is probably feeling as awkward as you are feeling. Forget your awkwardness by concentrating on the other person.
2. **Ask appropriate questions.** Avoid extremely personal questions. It's also best not to ask questions about controversial topics such as religion or politics.
3. **Ask open-ended questions.** An open-ended question allows the person being questioned to share an opinion or a story as opposed to a simple yes or no reply. For example, "What interested you in working with this company?"
4. **Compliment the individual.** Offer a sincere compliment, such as, "I was just admiring your ring. Is it a family heirloom?"
5. **Share something about yourself.** Sharing something personal such as a hobby, a trip, or your family background helps the listener see you as an individual.
6. **Ask about a shared interest.** If you and a coworker share interests, discussing those interests is often a good way to engage in appropriate, light conversation.
7. **Talk about books, movies, sports, or world events.** Reading newspapers or online news will help you know the current popular topics.
8. **Prepare in advance.** If you know you are going to be in a meeting or social situation with people you don't know well, plan a few things to talk about.
9. **Remember to listen.** You don't have to do all the talking. Be an active listener as well.

Communicating Remotely

A remote conversation is different from other types of verbal communication because the speaker can't see you. During a phone or conference call, your voice is the only basis for establishing communication with the listener on the other end of the line. Because listeners can't see your facial expressions and body language, they will rely on the tone of your voice to detect your mood and emotions.

The phone is designed to transmit sounds, so the caller may hear background sounds if you're not careful. Turn off the radio when speaking on the phone. Don't eat, drink, or chew gum when talking on the phone. Avoid trying to talk on the phone while talking to another person in the room.

Communicating via Phone

The first contact a customer has with a business is often on a phone call with an employee, so practicing good phone etiquette is necessary. To make a good impression on the phone, follow these steps:

1. **Greet the caller in a professional manner.** Businesses often have their employees use a special greeting when answering the phone, such as, "Thank you for calling Cathedral Painting. How may I help you?"
2. **Use a friendly, enthusiastic voice.** Smiling while you speak will make your voice sound friendly.

Case Study

Kevin doesn't like conducting business over the phone and tries to spend as little time on the phone as possible. He misses calls and then doesn't make a good connection with his customers. How can he become a better communicator using the phone?

3. **Identify yourself.** Remember that the other person can't see you and probably doesn't know you, so say your name or the company's name when you answer a call.
4. **Speak into the receiver.** Be sure the listener hears your voice. Speak clearly and loudly enough.
5. **Use voice messaging skillfully.** The caller may need to leave a voice message for an individual in your business. Learn how to transfer the caller to a person's voicemail. Inform callers that you are transferring them.
6. **Take accurate written phone messages.** The caller may ask to leave a written message for an individual in your business. Listen carefully. Print clearly. Record both the first and last name of the caller, the message, the caller's phone number, and a convenient time to return the call. Repeat the information to the caller. Date and sign the message before you deliver it to the recipient.
7. **End the call professionally.** End a call by summarizing it, thanking the caller, and saying goodbye.

When you're making a business call, remember that the receptionist may be busy with other calls. Allow the phone to ring up to six times. If the receptionist answers, ask to speak to an individual or explain the reason for your call. Your call may be transferred to the individual or to voicemail.

If you are leaving a voicemail message, include your full name, phone number, business name, and a brief message. At the end of the message, repeat your name and phone number.

Cell Phones in the Workplace

Cell phones are convenient because they allow people to be connected wherever they go. They keep us connected through texting, emailing, voice and video calling, and through other apps. Employees who make service calls, deliveries, and provide other services outside an office location may be issued business cell phones to keep connected to the main office. Sales representatives may use cell phones to arrange appointments with clients. Be aware that a cell phone issued in this manner is typically intended for business use and not for personal use.

As a courtesy, when using a cell phone to conduct business, you should inform the listener that you are calling from a cell phone. If there is interference during the call and it is impossible to reconnect, the listener will understand what has happened. In addition, cell phone calls are often made in public places; the listener may not want to talk about private subjects.

So many accidents have occurred while drivers were conducting business on cell phones that some states have made it illegal. Many businesses have issued policies concerning driving and cell phone usage. The bottom line is that using cell phones for work-related reasons while driving is unwise.

When employees make personal cell phone calls while on the job, they are not working and their productivity decreases. Others nearby may be disturbed by the call, and their productivity decreases. Ringing cell phones interrupt meetings. To prevent these disturbances, some companies ask employees to turn off their personal cell phones when entering the business facility or leave their cell phones at their desks during meetings.

Smartphones have more computing power than supercomputers had 10 years ago.[3] We can text, read and write emails, access the Internet, play games, and run specialized apps from our phones. This means there are many distractions people have in front of them while talking with another person. It is important to engage with the person or people you are talking with and not let your phone distract you. Give your full attention to those you speak to about work-related matters.

Nonverbal Communication Skills

Nonverbal communication involves facial expressions, body movements, and hand gestures. Because a speaker is usually talking as well as using nonverbal communication, a listener must use both ears and eyes to accurately interpret the speaker's message. This is one more reason to keep your attention focused on people during a conversation or meeting.

Group Activity

What cultural communication differences have you experienced?

Experts understand the importance of nonverbal communication and have discovered its complexity. A recent study identified nine major categories of nonverbal communication and how it is used in the workplace.[4] The types of nonverbal communication include body movement, eye movement, voice tone, touch, appearance, distance, time, objects, and even smell.

Developing people-watching skills and learning to understand nonverbal cues will be helpful as you communicate with others. Here are some essential elements of nonverbal communication:

- **Body Posture**   The position of a speaker's body is their body posture. Is the speaker sitting or standing (acting equal or superior to you)? Is he leaning forward or tipping backward in his chair (acting engaged or not engaged)? Are her arms folded or by her sides (acting open or closed to what is being said)?
- **Proximity**   The distance between a speaker and the listener sends a message. If a speaker "gets in your face," you'll feel uncomfortable and perhaps even threatened. Our natural tendency in this situation is to back away from the speaker.
- **Eye Contact**   In Western culture, eye contact means that the speaker and listener are interested in what is being said. Having no eye contact is considered rude. Staring, however, is eye contact that makes someone uncomfortable and can be interpreted as anger or an intimidation technique.
- **Facial Expressions**   Expressions such as frowning, smiling, or scowling indicate certain emotions. Biting one's lip might show tension or concentration. Bowing one's head might be a sign of defeat or tiredness.

An effective communicator considers the context, the nonverbal communication, and the verbal message when speaking or interpreting another speaker's meaning.

Culture and Nonverbal Communication

Communicating nonverbally can be confusing since interpretation varies from culture to culture. For example, Americans use the thumbs-up gesture as a way of accepting someone's message or actions (to indicate OK), but in many countries this gesture is an insult. In most Western countries, maintaining direct eye contact when interacting with others means you are paying attention, but in Asia and the Middle East it is considered disrespectful. While shaking hands is acceptable in most countries, using the left hand to shake hands in the Middle East is taboo. Rather than a handshake, in some parts of Europe people greet each other with a kiss in the air near both cheeks.[5]

Another nonverbal communicator is **proxemics** (the physical space between people). In many cultures people are uncomfortable when others enter their intimate or personal zones. Standing within 2 feet of a person while talking is stressful. A more socially acceptable distance is 4 feet.

Facial expressions tend to share some worldwide sameness. Happiness and sadness look alike in most cultures. Body movements and posture also express emotions. In some cultures keeping your hands in your pockets or sitting cross-legged are offensive.

Paralanguage is not the words that are spoken but rather how they are spoken (it is a type of nonverbal communication). It encompasses the tone of the voice, inflection, loudness, speed, and pitch that is used when one is speaking.[6] The meaning of a sentence changes when it is spoken loudly or softly. For example, the words "come here" spoken in a whisper have a different meaning when shouted. When whispered, it may seem sneaky or secretive, yet when shouted it may sound reprimanding or angry. The meaning of a sentence is interpreted by the paralanguage used.

Written Communication in the Workplace

Written communication is often used to clarify or formalize verbal communication. For example, after setting a meeting time while talking on the phone to Pia, Andrew emails her with the time, date, and location of their meeting. Because written communication can be saved, it is often used for reference at a later date. The written minutes of a committee meeting serve as a record of decisions made in the meeting.

Business correspondence includes letters, memos, notes, and emails. No matter what form of written communication you use, you need to follow seven rules to be effective:

1. **Use proper grammar.** Failing to use correct grammar reflects poorly on you. If you don't know the correct usage, look it up. Most popular word processing programs have grammar check that also reviews punctuation. Use this feature to check finished documents you've written, but use caution in relying solely on it because grammar check can't pick up the nuances of language (the same is true for spell-check features).

2. **Use correct punctuation.** Punctuation makes writing clearer. Incorrect punctuation can change the meaning of your writing.

3. **Capitalize correctly.** Capitalization guides the reader's interpretation of the writing. Lack of capitalized words can be very confusing.

Discussion Activity

How can you improve your writing skills?

4. **Check spelling.** When using spell check, remember that some incorrect words pass through the program without being discovered. Check the spelling yourself as backup; spell check won't know that you meant *two* instead of *to*.

5. **Use the proper format.** Your organization may have a preferred format for written correspondence. Be sure to follow it.

6. **Write concisely.** Business correspondence should deliver the message without being lengthy. Concise writing avoids repeating facts or phrases.

7. **Proofread all written correspondence.** Before you send any business correspondence, read it aloud. Make any corrections that are needed.

Communicating Electronically in the Workplace

Technology has greatly affected the way people communicate in the workplace. Electronic communication, also called **ecommunication**, occurs through emails, phones, texting, videoconferencing, social media, and workplace collaboration apps. Legal documents can be scanned and sent as a PDF file from one part of the world to another. With laptop computers and Internet connections, a virtual office can be set up in a coffee shop, a library, or anywhere. Conversations take place using instant messaging (IM) and text messaging. Checking email has become an hourly task for most people.

As the communication structure has changed, both benefits and problems have developed in the workplace. Organizations have policies concerning personal emails, text messages, and IM. Spending company time with personal electronic correspondence is no different from spending company time talking with friends and family on the phone during work hours. Most employers discourage it. Others ban it altogether.

As an employee, be aware of new electronic forms of communication. Know the regulations your company has concerning electronic communication. Learn how to effectively use new technology to do your work. Don't use it for personal communication while on the job.

> **Journal Activity**
>
> How do you use Internet communication and social media? What are the potential impacts of your online communications on your career?

Use the Internet Wisely

Each day hundreds of friends share the highlights and trials of their lives via social networks such as Facebook, LinkedIn, Twitter, and Pinterest. Keeping in touch through **social media** sites is convenient and often emotionally positive. It is also fun to share the latest news in your life with all those social connections you've acquired.

When using social networks, remember that they are not private. Many people may read your posts. If you complain about your supervisor, a coworker, a customer, or your company on a social network site, it is possible that a friend or a friend of a friend may read your post. And that friend of a friend might be your supervisor, your coworker, your customer, or even the president of your company. A good rule to follow is always think before you post.

Continues

The same is true if you're creating your own blog. A blog lets you convey your thoughts in an original manner. You choose the subject and can even include photos and videos for others to view. A blog is a creative way to communicate with others. As with social networks, postings on a blog can be viewed by anyone—your coworkers, your supervisor, or even your company's upper management. Posting critical comments about your company or work situation is unwise. Think before putting pictures (especially unprofessional ones) on your blog. Employees have lost jobs and have even been sued because of information posted on blogs or social networks.[7]

Likewise, potential employers may use the Internet to research job candidates. Don't put anything on your blog or social networks, or make any recording that might keep you from being hired in the future.

Always remember that the Internet is not secure. Whether you use email or send an IM, others have access to the information. Confidential information should be password protected or delivered via secure file transfer protocol (FTP). Highly emotional messages are best communicated in person, or in some personal manner. Remember, any communication sent electronically can be printed or otherwise redistributed.

Email in the Workplace

Because of its convenience, email is the leading communication form in the workplace, with 94% of workers saying it is the best way to contact them.[8] Understanding how to use email effectively will save work time and avoid problems on the job.

Begin by looking at the email format on your computer. Most emails have the same basic parts:

- **Header**   Includes your email address, the email address of the recipient, and the subject line. The subject line is a brief, meaningful description of the message. For many people, the message or subject line determines whether they read the email.
- **Salutation**   The greeting, such as "Dear Deanna" or "Dear Mr. Gray," will start your email. It is fine to use just the first name of someone you know well. You can also consider using a generic greeting, such as "Hi," "Hi there," or "Greetings."
- **Body**   The message being sent. Use short sentences and bullet points to keep the body concise. Keep the message to one or two paragraphs. Use complete sentences as well as correct grammar, spelling, and punctuation.
- **Signature Line**   The writer's name and sometimes his or her contact information is at the end of the email.
- **Attachment Button**   Used when a longer document is sent with the email. When you send an attachment, mention it in the message. To add an attachment to an email, click the Attachment button or the Add File button on the screen. Browse for the document or file you want to attach and then click or double click that file. You will be redirected to the email message, where you should see the "attachment."

- **Out-of-office Notification**   Creates an automatic response to emails sent to you with a message that you are out of the office. Usually the date when you'll be back to respond to emails is included.
- **Delivery Receipt**   Available on email software programs, the Request a Delivery Receipt feature allows the sender to know that the email has been placed in the recipient's inbox.
- **Read Receipt**   Available on email software programs, the Request a Read Receipt feature allows the sender to know that the email has been opened. Both acknowledgment of receipt and read receipt are part of email tracking. Tracking is not always accurate but tends to be more so within a company's computer network.

Before sending an email, check the recipient's address to confirm that it's correct. Deal with email as you do with all business correspondence: always proofread it before you click *Send*.

Getting Email

When you click the inbox, the list of your email messages appears. Because spam (junk email) as well as attachments can be the source of computer viruses, think before you open email messages. Check the sender and the subject line. If you have doubts about the origin of an email message, don't open attachments or click a link in the email because it may allow a computer virus to infect your computer. Delete the email!

Click or double click the email to open it. After reading the message, you may choose to do one of the following:

- Move the message to a different folder.
- Reply to the message.
- Forward the message to another person.
- Delete the message.
- Print the message.

In the workplace, managing email can become a problem for workers who receive large numbers of email messages. One solution is to handle email like regular snail mail. Throw away the junk mail without reading it. Look at the important mail and reply to it within a reasonable time period (typically within a week). Deal with the high-priority mail the same day.

Using work time to send and reply to personal email prevents you from giving your full attention to your job. When coworkers spend time sending jokes found on the Internet, work time is lost. Non-work-related email, especially pictures and video, can interfere with the company's network, taking up valuable space and slowing the system.

Distractions

Workers have many communication distractions that lower productivity. Email, IMs, and texts—once considered time-savers for businesses—have become time wasters in the workplace. According to a recent study by CareerBuilders, 82% of employees have a personal smartphone within eyesight when they are at work. They typically lose 1–2 hours per day by using them for nonwork-related business. Workers reported the biggest work-related distractions are phone/texting (55%), Internet (41%), and social media (37%).[9] (Note: workers could select more than one choice in some of the survey items.)

Smartphones are not the only distraction from work. There are many distractions from face-to-face communication. Workers reported that gossip (37%), coworkers dropping by (27%), and meetings (24%) are major distractions unrelated to technology.

Personal distractions are something you should avoid at work because they may cause problems. Workers reported these distractions caused problems such as compromised quality of work (48%), negative impact on their relationship with their supervisor (28%), and negative impact on customer relations (20%). In fact, 76% of employers reported they have taken actions to try to reduce distractions. You should be aware of rules and policies your employer has created for reducing workplace distractions and follow them. Managers appreciate employees who focus on their assignments.

Practice Netiquette

As email usage in the workplace has increased, some problems have evolved. Practicing email etiquette, an important part of **netiquette**, will help you avoid such problems. Here are a few tips that apply to email and the workplace:

Discussion Activity

What types of ecommunication have you sent or received today?

- Keep business email professional.
- Avoid writing words in all uppercase; it is considered "shouting."
- Follow your company's guidelines concerning email.
- Check your personal email on your own time.
- Avoid venting your anger and frustrations using email (called "flaming"). Most organizations would consider it to be abusive and are likely to fire you for such behavior.
- Don't send email messages that might offend or harass someone.
- Don't use email to avoid talking to someone in person or via the phone.
- Always remember that your email might be forwarded or posted. The message you send could be read by many people other than the person you emailed.
- Be respectful toward everyone just as though they were in the room and talking directly with you.

Read each of the following situations. In each situation, a netiquette rule is being broken. Explain how the situation could be handled in a better way.

Stan's supervisor refused to grant his request for tuition reimbursement for a class Stan recently completed. Stan emails his supervisor to vent his anger. He calls his supervisor a liar and says he intends to file a complaint with the company.

1. What is the netiquette problem?

    _____

    _____

2. What is the better way to communicate frustration?

    _____

    _____

Jana has missed two staff meetings this month. Mr. Garson, the office manager, sends the entire staff an email message written in uppercase stating STAFF MEETING TOMORROW AT 8:00 A.M. BE THERE.

1. What is the netiquette problem?

    _____

    _____

2. What is the better way to communicate the importance of being on time?

    _____

    _____

A Useful Skill: Writing

Learn to write and you will be valued in the workplace. According to a recent survey of human resource executives, entry-level workers lack basic writing skills.[10] Employers need staff members with the ability to spell correctly, use correct English grammar, and punctuate properly.

A business correspondence must state the point quickly because the recipient may read it in just a few seconds. Business writing must be both clear and concise. Using the accepted format for business letters, memos, and other correspondence provides uniformity within an organization.

Whether you are writing a memo, a business letter, or an email, knowing how to write is a useful skill in the business world. Here are five points to remember when writing in the workplace:

1. **Set the tone.** Consider why you are writing. Think about the person who will receive the writing. Remember to write in a respectful way.
2. **Be concise.** Use short sentences and brief paragraphs. Make every word count. Don't repeat words or thoughts. Make lists. Use bullets and headings.

Continues

3. **Get to the point quickly.** Begin by stating the general purpose of your correspondence and end with your request.
4. **Use appropriate language.** Write in a businesslike manner. Avoid using slang terms or jargon that is inappropriate for your type of work.
5. **Emphasize important facts.** Highlight key points using boldface type. Avoid using ALL CAPS, especially when you're emailing.

Summing Up

Businesses function as a team. When a team of workers listens and expresses their ideas clearly, productivity increases. For this reason, employers are looking for individuals with good communication skills.

You will be a valued employee if you learn to listen and communicate well. Problems occur in the workplace when team members fail to listen to directions. The ability to write a short, clear email is an excellent job skill. Observing body language and other nonverbal forms of communication will enable you to better understand what others are telling you. With practice, you will increase your ability to communicate.

The way we communicate is changing as technology changes. For this reason, it is important to recognize new technologies and learn how to use them as you continue to develop even more communication skills.

Review and Assessment

Take the Review Quiz. See your instructor or reference your student files in the ebook for additional resources.

CHAPTER 6

Learning—What It's All About

Objectives

- Discover job education opportunities.

- Evaluate the types of education and training needed in the workplace.

- Identify learning styles and skills that work for you.

Watch the Video

Learning—What It's All About

Knowing how to learn is probably the most critical skill for job success. In 2015, almost 90% of Americans spent 12 years to get a high school degree, and 33% of Americans spent another 4 years to get a college degree.[1] The 12 to 16 years spent in school gives many people the impression that learning takes place just within the four walls of a classroom. However, this idea is far from realistic. Learning begins when we are born and continues until the time we die. This is the concept called **lifelong learning** and it plays a very important role in your success on the job.

We learn in a variety of ways. It might be through watching others do a task, asking questions, watching videos, reading books, or dozens of other ways. The process of learning is continuous and a daily part of our lives. Much of our learning is incidental and occurs naturally. For example, we might ask a coworker where we can get a pen and notepad, but they instead show us a productivity app on the computer as an alternative way to jot down notes. Other times, we are intentional about our learning, as demonstrated by signing up for a seminar on time management.

Employers often provide formal learning opportunities through online learning management systems, classroom training, on-the-job training, and other methods. This chapter will help you understand the best way to use these resources and acquire new skills and knowledge. Not all employers offer formal learning resources, in which case this chapter will help you take charge of your own informal learning. In turn, you will gain the skills and knowledge employers need. Be an active lifelong learner so you will have the skills and knowledge to meet these needs and be a success at work.

Learning Is the Key to Success

Lifelong learning is the key to success in the new labor market. Management experts emphasize that a successful business is a **learning organization**. In this climate, employees learn from their experiences, both individually and collectively.

You'll have to learn many things at a new job. But learning doesn't end once you've mastered the job. In time, your job will require new skills or knowledge. For example, technology and equipment changes over time. One day you might want a promotion that requires additional skills. It is also important to keep your skills up to date in case you decide to apply for a new job with another employer.

The following reflective exercise is designed to help you understand how your past experiences can be used for planning educational goals. Planning your own learning is referred to as "self-directed learning." Teachers, trainers, career coaches, and others are good resources to help you learn, but you are in control of your educational plan and outcomes.

Group Activity

List the equipment changes that have occurred in your workplace or school over the past 10 years.

A Self-Directed Learning Project

1. Write something you learned outside of school within the past three months.

   _____

   _____

2. What was your purpose or objective? (What did you set out to learn?)

   _____

   _____

3. List the steps you went through during your learning project.

   _____

   _____

4. What resources—people, reading material, computer information, and so on—did you use in the learning project?

   _____

   _____

5. Did you learn everything you wanted to know about the subject or skill? Why or why not?

   _____

   _____

6. Are there other ways you could have learned the same thing? Explain how.

   _____

   _____

How Adults Learn

As people mature and move beyond high school, they share some common characteristics in how they learn. Adults prefer to learn using methods based on andragogy—a theory of adult learning developed by Malcolm Knowles, a pioneer in adult education. Four important characteristics of adult learners cited by Knowles are the following:[2]

1. **Adults learn better when they assume responsibility and control over learning activities.** This means that, as an adult, you will learn more if you take charge of your learning. Don't wait for someone to teach you a new skill. Instead, seek out ways that you can learn new skills.
2. **Adults learn more effectively by applying what they learn.** There are progressive steps in learning. We learn the least when someone tells us how to do a task. We learn more when someone demonstrates the task. We learn the most when we do the task ourself.
3. **As adults mature, they have a broader experience base to draw on.** This experience base can be used to help improve learning. Compare a new task that you are trying to learn to your past experiences. Determine what is the same and what is different in the situations. Linking new skills and knowledge to a past experience usually improves learning.
4. **Adults learn better when it is clear to them why gaining the knowledge is necessary.** In school you might have learned something because you were going to be tested on it and given a grade. On the job, your motivation to learn will be stronger when you understand the reasons for and benefits of learning a new skill.

Discussion Activity

How do adults learn differently than children?

Tips for Learning

All learners share certain characteristics. Following these four tips can help you become a more effective learner:

1. **The more time you spend on a learning task, the more learning takes place.** A common saying illustrates this point: Practice makes perfect. Spend time learning a new skill. In the book *Outliers*[3], Malcolm Gladwell shares multiple stories about how researchers have proven this point. People who become outstanding in performing their jobs have typically practiced the tasks they perform for more than 10,000 hours. We all can't practice tasks for 10,000 hours, but it helps us understand just how important it is to practice a task we want to do well. It also illustrates that building skills takes time.
2. **Learning patterns differ.** Don't compare yourself to someone else trying to learn the same job. Another person might excel at learning new tasks because they are a visual learner and the instructor teaches in a visual way. It might be more difficult for you to learn visually because you learn logically. Teacher-student (or in the workplace manager-employee) disconnects happen. Sometimes it can be as confusing as if the teacher were speaking in a foreign language. If you can identify such a learning communication barrier early on, you may want to let

your teacher know. Sometimes teachers can adjust their teaching style. In those times when this is not possible, you can seek the help of a classmate, coworker, mentor, or tutor, or you may research topics on your own. Also, recognize that some days are better than others. This is normal because people don't usually experience a straight line of improvement in their learning patterns. Don't let the naturally uneven pattern of learning discourage you.

3. **You can organize your learning using association.** For example, if you need to learn a list of furniture items, group them by rooms in a house. Learn codes by associating them with a special date on the calendar, telephone numbers, addresses, or such. Many people find that learning facts is easier when they associate the fact with a word and make the words rhyme.

4. **For more complex tasks, use the whole-part-whole method.** First, have your teacher go through the whole task while you watch, doing every part in one continuous sequence. Next, have your teacher break the task into small parts and concentrate on learning each part individually. Finally, have your teacher go through the entire task as a whole again. For example, learning to replace a flat tire by using the **whole-part-whole** method, you first ask someone to demonstrate the process for you. You observe the entire process of repairing a flat tire. Next, you ask the person to repeat the process, this time pausing at the end of each part so you can ask questions (Part A: raise the car using a jack. Part B: loosen and remove the lug nuts. Part C: remove the tire from the wheel. Part D: put the spare tire on the wheel. Part E: replace the lug nuts and tighten them. Part F: lower the jack and place the flat tire in the trunk). Finally, you ask the person to repeat the whole process so you can watch while anticipating each part.

You don't have to use all of the previous tips in each new learning experience. In fact, some tips will be more useful than others, depending on what you're trying to learn. Pick out the tips that you think will help you the most in learning a task, and then try them out!

Learning to Do Your Job

To be successful in a job, you must do it correctly. This seems obvious, but it's a truth that's not always easy to follow. You must know the job's essentials, which include the following:

- What tasks are assigned to the job you do?
- How do you perform each task?
- How will each task be evaluated?

Let's look at the people who can help you answer these questions and the various ways you can independently find answers to these questions.

Learning on the Job

As you read the following text, come back to this exercise and list some of the ways you can find out how to perform your job effectively. The items on your list could include things you would expect your supervisor to tell you.

1. _____
2. _____
3. _____
4. _____
5. _____
6. _____
7. _____
8. _____

Job Description

The major tasks of a job are identified in the **job description**. Ask your supervisor to explain the job description to you. Make sure you understand all your tasks and responsibilities.

Supervisors

Managers should explain what they expect, but they might forget to tell you something. That's why it's important to ask for an explanation of your job if one is not given. Although a written job description describes the tasks you are to do, it doesn't give you all the details. Supervisors help employees understand exactly how each of their tasks should be done, and, more importantly, how the tasks and the employee's performance are evaluated.

Coworkers

Watch other workers who do the same job as you and note how they complete their tasks. They might have insight into how to do the job more efficiently and how the supervisor expects the job to be done. If others were promoted from the job you have, talk with them to see how they did the job.

Friends Who Have Similar Jobs

Talk with friends and acquaintances who work at jobs similar to yours. Ask them how they do their jobs. You might get some good ideas to apply to your job. However, you should talk with your supervisor before trying out any of their suggestions.

Case Study

John is an administrative assistant for a plumbing company. What tasks and responsibilities might be in his job description?

Training

Businesses spend billions of dollars each year on classroom training to educate employees. You can expect to receive some sort of training when you begin a job. Also, employees typically will continue to receive training while on the job. Most organizations provide three basic types of training:

- **On-the-job Training**   Typically, when one-on-one instruction takes place as you do the job it is considered **on-the-job training**. Your supervisor or a coworker will explain what to do, show you how to do it, watch while you practice, and then tell you how well you did in practice.
- **Classroom Instruction**   **Classroom instruction** involves training several employees at the same time. Classroom instruction uses many methods, including lectures, digital media, discussion, role-playing, case studies, games, and learning exercises. It's important to listen carefully, ask questions when you don't understand something, and actively participate in all learning activities.
- **Multimedia Training**   Many organizations use computers to teach employees new job skills (these computer software programs are often called learning management systems). Discount stores, grocery stores, and banks use sophisticated multimedia computer programs to train cashiers. This is one of many reasons you should know how to operate a personal computer. Taking an introductory computer course in high school or community college is a good way to acquire the skills you need to learn more in the workplace.

Journal Activity

Complete this sentence: If I were training someone to do my new job, I would . . .

Schools

You might be able to take classes to learn more about your job. If, for example, you work with personal computers, there are probably software classes and certifications available in your area. Such classes are often offered through adult-education or continuing-education programs at high schools or colleges. Almost 60% of all adults participate in formal or informal adult-education programs.[4] Some employers help pay the cost of training because they know that they will benefit from their employees' improved skills. The Lifetime Learning Credit allows you to deduct a percentage of the continuing-education cost as a federal tax credit.[5]

Conferences

Professional and trade associations often have conferences where you can learn from the experts. Conferences offer opportunities to meet and talk with other people who do work like yours. In addition, there are usually expositions where vendors sell the latest equipment, programs, and services related to the field you're in. You can learn a lot from these vendors and their products. Talk with your coworkers to find out about the conferences that they have found most useful.

Workshops

Private training companies offer workshops you can attend to learn new skills. The quality of the workshops varies greatly, and you'll want your supervisor's approval before attending (especially if you intend to request reimbursement). Check with coworkers and friends to find out what they know about any workshop that you are thinking of attending. Ask the training company to supply references from people who have attended. You might want to call some of these people. Look for workshops that provide money-back guarantees.

Reading

Read about your job. The US Department of Labor has several resources that describe hundreds of occupations that can help you discover facts about your job. Two recommended resources are the Occupational Outlook Handbook (https://bls.gov/ooh) and O*NET Online (https://onetonline.org). These resources are good for workers just starting in a new occupation. Also read trade and professional magazines about your line of work. You should be able to find these and other occupational books and magazines in your local library.

The Web

Many resources are available on the web that can help you learn more about your job. Using such resources is referred to as **online learning**. You can use many sites on the web to find the type of online learning that will fit your needs. Go to a major search engine such as Google (https://Google.com) or Bing (https://Bing.com) and enter "online learning." You can also search for "online learning job skills," "distance training," or some combination of these words.

Self-directed learning allows you to explore a subject in a way that you want to learn. Resources such as YouTube offer educational videos. This is a good resource if you are a visual learner or like to see how things are done, and videos on YouTube are available free of charge. Educational sites provide a variety of learning opportunities from GED instruction to college classes. One source to explore and use is the Goodwill Community Foundation Learn Free website (https://GCFLearnFree.org). You will find computer-based training for computer software such as Microsoft Word, Internet basics, Google, email basics, reading, math, and several other subjects.

You want to be the best worker possible, so use the resources listed in this section as well as any others you can think of. Compare the resources discussed here with the steps you listed in the previous exercise.

Learning to Improve Job Performance

1. Think of the ways you can find out how to perform your job effectively, then write those ideas here. Include advice you would expect your supervisor to tell you.

    _____

    _____

    _____

2. Think of the common resources (identified in the previous pages) that you have used to get information about your job, and then write those here.

    _____

    _____

    _____

3. What resources have you used that aren't listed in this book?

    _____

    _____

    _____

The Learning Organization

In his book *The Fifth Discipline: The Art & Practice of the Learning Organization,* Peter Senge defines learning organizations as "organizations where people continually expand their capacity to create the results they truly desire, where new and expansive patterns of thinking are nurtured, where collective aspiration is set free, and where people are continually learning to see the whole together."

The basic rationale for such organizations is that in situations of rapid change, only those who are flexible, adaptive, and productive will excel. For this to happen, it is argued, organizations need to "discover how to tap people's commitment and capacity to learn at all levels."[6]

A learning organization is dynamic and growing—it changes and improves based on what it learns. As more organizations strive to become learning organizations, new principles will be identified to help them achieve this goal. You need to be an active participant in this process in any company you work for.

How Job Savvy Are You?

Marc has a computer technology degree from a technical school and is about to start his first job as a computer operator with a large accounting firm. He has never worked with the computer that the company uses. At the interview, his supervisor assured him that the company will provide on-the-job training. On his first day at work, Marc's supervisor says he is too busy to work with Marc on training. Instead, he shows Marc how to back up disk drives to the network. He then tells Marc to spend the rest of the day doing backups.

Continues

1. If you were Marc, how would you feel about this?

    _____

    _____

    _____

2. What would you do to find out more about the job that you were hired to do?

    _____

    _____

    _____

Paula began working as a receptionist last week. Her supervisor told her that she is to provide clerical support for several staff members in the real estate office. This morning, Susan asked her to file some house listings. While Paula was doing that, Karin asked her to type a letter. She had just started typing the letter when John told her to stop typing and immediately prepare a contract. As Paula was preparing the contract, she was interrupted by several phone calls. Karin came to get the letter and was upset because it wasn't finished. John came out of his office and began to argue with Karin, telling her to let Paula finish the contract.

1. If you were Paula, how would you feel?

    _____

    _____

    _____

2. What information does Paula need to help her in this situation? How can she get the information she needs?

    _____

    _____

    _____

Education for Life

You might think your education is complete when you finish school. That is far from true. You will need to continue learning throughout your life. Futurists John Naisbitt and Patricia Aburdene wrote, "There is no one education, no one skill, that lasts a lifetime now."[7]

You are responsible for your lifelong education. You can participate in company training, continuing-education classes, college classes, workshops, and conferences to improve your job skills.

You will always learn new things about your job because over time all businesses change. New machines might be installed. Policies and procedures might change. A new product might be manufactured and sold. As the business changes, so will your job. To keep up, you must understand how you learn best and practice those techniques. Whenever you begin a new job or new position in the same company, you start learning all over again. You must learn how the organization operates and how to perform your job. If you've read the entire chapter up until this point, this is probably all starting to sound familiar! That means you're learning!

Many organizations provide ongoing training. If your employer does not provide training to keep your skills current, consider getting training on your own. It will help you stay competitive in today's job market. In addition, training makes you more valuable. The following sections provide useful information that can help improve your self-directed learning.

Learning Style

You will learn more when you understand your preferred method of learning. Everyone has a **learning style**, which is determined by the unique ways each person prefers to learn something new.

My Preferred Learning Style

In the checklist below, rank from 1 (most preferred) to 8 (least preferred) the ways that you like to learn:

_____ **Reading:** You learn by reading and writing.

_____ **Listening:** You learn by listening to lectures, tapes, or records.

_____ **Observing:** You learn by watching demonstrations, videos, films, or slides.

_____ **Talking:** You learn by talking with other people or through question-and-answer sessions.

_____ **Doing:** You learn best by actually doing what you are trying to learn.

_____ **Interacting:** You learn best by interacting with computer programs, multimedia programs, or the web.

_____ **Participating:** You learn best by participating in games, role-playing, and other activities.

_____ **Smelling/tasting:** You learn best by associating what you are learning with a smell or taste.

Look at how you ranked the methods. Now list the three learning methods you like best (that allow you to learn most effectively) and use most frequently.

1. _____

2. _____

3. _____

Your three top methods show your learning style. You might like reading, observing, and interacting, or you might prefer listening and talking. You might learn by doing, participating, and smelling or tasting. Or you might use all of your senses, but typically we have one to three learning styles that we can consistently find success with.

There are other ways to determine how you learn. Assessment instruments such as the Myers-Briggs Type Indicator or the Keirsey Temperament Sorter can help you determine your learning style. You can take the latter assessment for free at https://keirsey.com.

It's important that you understand the ways in which you learn best. This understanding can help you become a better learner. When you are faced with learning a new task, try to use your preferred learning methods. If you like *doing*, you will not learn as well if you try to learn by *reading*. However, there are times when you may need to use a method that you didn't choose, such as if your employer requires group employee training by video or a written handout. When this happens, do your best to use the required method and then try to use your preferred style to review what you have learned.

Steps to Learning

You can take some specific steps to improve the way you learn.

At the beginning of this chapter, you completed an exercise in which you described recently learning something outside of school. This was called your self-directed learning project—which simply means the process of learning something new. The steps to complete a learning project are explained here. You probably listed some of them in the earlier exercise.

Journal Activity

What steps do I need to follow to reach my educational/self-directed learning goals?

1. **Motivate yourself.** Find something exciting or interesting about your learning project. If you aren't interested in the subject itself, you might be interested in something that could result from what you learn. For example, learning to fill out a new form required for your job might not excite you, but you might get excited about receiving a raise because you do such a good job completing the new form. Write down your reasons for wanting to complete education/training before you start the process.
2. **Set objectives.** The final outcomes of learning are called "objectives." You need to know your learning objectives. To identify them, ask yourself this question: "When I am done with this training, what must I be able to do?"
3. **Identify resources.** Find out what resources are available to help you reach your learning objectives. These resources can come from several areas, such as:

   * **Inhouse Learning Opportunities** Ask your supervisor whether your company offers any courses that can help you meet your learning objectives. Perhaps there is another worker who can teach you what you want to learn.
   * **Outside Education** Ask someone in your organization (a training manager, human resources manager, personnel director, or supervisor) to help you learn about courses offered at vocational schools, community colleges, universities, specialized training firms in your community, or on the web.
   * **Additional Methods** Discuss your learning needs with friends and coworkers. Find out what methods they have used to learn something similar. Ask what kinds of books, digital media, or other electronic media are available at your library. Also, check the Internet for resources and information that can help you achieve the objectives of your self-directed learning project.

Discussion Activity

What types of learning styles work best for you (visual, logical, hands-on, etc.)?

4. **Choose the best resources.** Which resources will help you the most in completing your learning project? You might decide to use more than one resource. Another factor to consider is cost. Find out whether your employer will pay for any of these resources and whether you will be allowed to take time from work to pursue your learning objective. Always keep in mind that other people are an important resource for any learning project.

5. **Schedule the learning project.** Plan the time needed for your project and decide when you want to complete it. If you need to take time from work for this, discuss it with your supervisor.

6. **Write down questions.** Decide what questions you need to answer in order to learn and then write them down. Check them off as you find the answers. Questions should ask who, what, where, when, why, and how.

7. **Implement the learning.** Completing any learning project requires self-discipline. You must follow through with the plan you create. It might be helpful to find someone who will keep you on track by checking your progress.

8. **Evaluate progress.** As you complete the learning project, evaluate your progress. Are the resources you decided to use providing you with the knowledge and skills you need? Are you following the schedule you set? Are you meeting your objectives? Have an experienced person test your new skills and knowledge. Remember, the most important step in successful learning is accomplishing your objectives.

9. **Practice.** The most effective way to become more skilled is to practice what you've learned, even after you've finished the learning project. Periodically check on how well you can apply your new knowledge.

The following exercise will help you practice the steps needed to complete a learning project.

Personal Learning Project

1. Select a skill you want to learn and write it below.

   _____

2. What is your motivation? Why do you want to learn this skill? How do you think you will feel after you learn it?

   _____

   _____

   _____

   _____

Continues

3. Choose a learning objective. What are your expected outcomes?

_____

_____

_____

_____

4. Who can help you plan your learning project?

_____

_____

_____

_____

5. What resources can you use to complete your learning project?

_____

_____

_____

_____

6. What do you think will be your best resource? Keep in mind your learning style, the cost, the availability, and so on.

_____

_____

_____

_____

7. When would you like to complete the learning project?

_____

_____

_____

_____

8. How much time will you spend daily or weekly on the project?

_____

_____

_____

_____

Continues

9. How will you (or someone else) evaluate your progress?

   _____

   _____

   _____

   _____

10. How will you practice what you learn?

    _____

    _____

    _____

    _____

The ability to learn is the most important skill you can have. Successful people know how to learn new things. Read the following case studies and develop a plan for each person to learn a new skill. Be specific about the steps for each learning project. Use more paper if necessary.

How Job Savvy Are You?

John has worked for two years at a help desk providing technical support for customers of the accounts payable software his company sells. He has an associate's degree in computer technology but would like to improve his coding skills and work as a software programmer.

What steps should John take to learn this new skill?

_____

_____

_____

_____

_____

Juan works as a bank teller. He would like to work in the accounting department, where he could earn a higher salary. If he knew more about accounting, he would have a better chance at a promotion to the accounting department.

What steps should Juan take to learn more about accounting?

_____

_____

_____

_____

_____

A Useful Skill: Active Learning

As an adult, you must take charge of your learning. Observe what skills you want or need to learn. Explore ways or places to learn the skill. Ask questions and seek answers. Build on the experience and knowledge you already have. These statements all describe the actions of an active learner.

Become an active learner. Find a method of learning that allows you to do and apply rather than just listen. Remember that adults learn best when they participate in their own learning.

As an active learner, approach your new learning by asking the following five questions:

"How can I use this new information or skill in my workplace?"
"How can I use this new information or skill to improve my life?"
"How can I use this new information or skill to solve a current problem?"
"How can I use this new information or skill to solve future problems?"
"How can I use this new information or skill to make decisions?"

Summing Up

Self-directed learning is an important skill to master. Learning in the workplace and mastering needed skills is important for retaining a job, getting promotions, and increasing earnings. Taking advantage of such training makes you more valuable to your employer.

To make learning easier, discover your preferred learning styles. Use those methods of learning as often as possible. Many times you will need to learn on your own. The more you practice learning, the better your learning skills will be.

Review and Assessment

Take the Review Quiz. See your instructor or reference your student files in the ebook for additional resources.

CHAPTER 7

Knowing Yourself

Objectives

- Discover the relationship between self-esteem and your performance at the workplace.

- Identify your different types of skills.

- Evaluate your strengths and weaknesses and assess ways to improve personal or career skills.

Studies indicate that businesses seek out employees with a positive **self-esteem** because they have a higher level of performance.[1] Self-esteem is your overall opinion of yourself—how you feel about your abilities and limitations. When you have healthy self-esteem, you feel good about yourself and see yourself as deserving the respect of others. When you have low self-esteem, you put little value on your opinions and ideas.[2] The good news is that self-esteem can be developed and improved so everyone can achieve the satisfaction and success healthy self-esteem brings.

To be a successful employee, you must believe you are a successful employee. In other words, you should have confidence in your abilities. Begin by looking at those tasks you do well. Discover your strengths and build on them by thinking about all the accomplishments you've had. Act on your strengths and achieve positive outcomes that you can celebrate. Thinking positively and acting positively will allow you to find success personally and at work.

Many of the concepts you will read about in this chapter come from **positive psychology**. It is a field of psychology that has grown rapidly in the past 20 years.[3] It focuses on helping people build on their strengths rather than identifying and fixing weaknesses. This chapter will help you identify personal strengths and skills. You will discover how to use your strengths in the workplace to achieve success. Understanding yourself and believing in yourself is the foundation for the skills you will learn in upcoming chapters. Getting along with leaders in your workplace, coworkers, and customers begins with knowing yourself. Applying your personal strengths at work creates positive relationships at work.

Watch the Video

Knowing Yourself

Work Should be Meaningful

Have you ever wondered, *Why am I here? What is the meaning of life? What is my purpose in life?* These are questions people often ask themselves. It seems finding an answer to these questions is important. Psychological studies have found people who have a purpose in life live a longer life.[4] Finding **meaning in work** has been shown to result in higher levels of satisfaction with life, work, and health. In addition, people who feel called to their work (in other words find meaning in work) enjoy work more, have lower absenteeism, and have higher levels of performance.[5]

So, we know that having a clear purpose in our work is important. How do we go about discovering this purpose? It begins by taking a look at your current lifestyle. Answer the following questions:

- **What subjects interest you the most?** These can be identified by the books you read, videos you watch, podcasts you listen to, etc.
- **What do you like to do in your spare time?** These can be identified by how you spend your time outside of the workplace. What hobbies do you enjoy? What places do you like to frequent?
- **What are your strengths?** We'll discuss this more later. For now, think about the strengths that make you feel the best about yourself. What strengths do people compliment you on?
- **What attracts you to friends and acquaintances?** To figure this out, first make a list of 5 to 7 friends. What do your friends do that attracts you to them? What do they talk about that you also like to talk about? What do you like most about times you spend with friends?
- **What do you consider an accomplishment?** Particularly, what is your most gratifying accomplishment? What ideas do these accomplishments give you about a meaningful career?

The meaning or purpose a job gives you might relate to a lifelong career purpose. For example, being a custom furniture maker might provide you with a purpose in life. It might give you satisfaction to make something beautiful from plain wood. In addition, making something with your hands might give you pleasure. You may also feel fulfilled by expressing your creativity and giving others pleasure by seeing them purchase and use the furniture you designed and built. These are just some examples of how a person can find meaning in a career. You may find a few or many reasons for finding meaning in your work. It isn't about the amount of purpose or meaning an activity provides for you, but the overall satisfaction level you gain.

While you might achieve a meaningful job in a single career move, it sometimes takes several moves. Your purpose might be accomplished through a series of jobs that lets you reach your long-term goal. A first job might involve being a cabinet installer for a home improvement store, next comes a job as a finish carpenter for a home builder, then building bookshelves in homes, and finally making custom cabinets. Your first few jobs may not satisfy your search for meaning, but you can see that they are moving you toward that goal. Be content with moving slowly toward a meaningful career

Discussion Activity

What is self-esteem? Why is it important to have a healthy self-esteem?

Journal Activity

Draw your personal circle of influence, with yourself in the middle. Include people, organizations, resources, or activities that influence how your feel about yourself.

We know from adult development experts that adults change over their lifetime. In fact, your goals, what you find satisfying, and your purpose can morph many times over the years. Be willing to change careers until you find one with a meaning and purpose that satisfies you.

Remember, your big-picture purpose in life can be expressed through multiple careers and in multiple ways. Keeping your purpose and career aligned will help you have a more fulfilling and satisfying life and a more productive career.

Now here is something you should never forget: There are many times when people do not find a purpose in their jobs but rather through something else in their lives. This purpose might include volunteer work, religious pursuits, raising a family, or improving a community. Your job then becomes a way to achieve a purpose. It provides the money you need to live a meaningful life. The key point is to understand that a purpose in life allows us to achieve the fulfillment and satisfaction from a job whether it is the job itself or a purpose outside the job. In order to fulfill your purpose in life, you need to build on your strengths, talents, skills, and abilities. The rest of this chapter is designed to help you discover these personal attributes.

Learn to Believe in Yourself

Sometimes it might seem like everyone at work knows what they are doing except you. That's not true. No one always feels confident. Anyone can experience low self-esteem, especially when circumstances change abruptly. Consider these examples:

- A teacher loses her job because there's no money to fund the gifted-student program for the coming year. She questions her ability to find a new teaching position. She wants to try a new area of work but wonders whether she's really qualified to enter a new field.
- A man is laid off after working 23 years in the same manufacturing plant. Rumors spread that the plant will close soon and move to a new location. Questions run through his mind: *Should I move my family to the new plant location? Should I start that auto-repair shop I've always dreamed about? What if I can't pay all the bills?* He has trouble deciding what to do.
- A supervisor is asked to move up in her company. Currently, 10 employees report to her. She will be responsible for 50 workers if she accepts the new position. The hours will be the same, and the pay will be better. But she'll have to take a week-long company course on leadership skills. She begins to think: *Can I handle the course? What if I don't pass? Can I supervise 50 people? Maybe I'm not ready for this promotion.*

Having positive self-esteem doesn't mean you won't ever question yourself. In fact, the people in the previous examples asked healthy questions. Questioning allows you to compare yourself with the world around you. You don't want to be put in a position where you can't perform well because you inaccurately evaluated your skills and abilities.

Group Activity

Brainstorm circumstances that might affect someone's self-esteem in a negative way. Discuss how self-esteem helps when you are facing negative circumstances.

Take Control of Your Life

Psychologists have identified a concept they call **locus of control**. This is the way people view how they control events and outcomes in their lives.[6] People either feel they control their own lives, or they feel that other people and things control them. The way you look at life greatly affects your self-esteem. The following self-assessment will help you understand how you view your control over your life.

Journal Activity

Imagine you have been granted one special wish. You may change anything about yourself that you want. What would it be?

Your Approach to Life

Answer the following questions. Put a *T* beside the statements that you think are true and an *F* beside those that you think are false. Scoring is explained on the next page.

Views of Life	Answer	Score
1. Other people control my life.	_____	_____
2. I am responsible for the success in my life.	_____	_____
3. Success in life is a matter of luck.	_____	_____
4. When things go wrong, it's usually because of things that I couldn't control.	_____	_____
5. The last time I did something successful, I knew that it was because of my own efforts.	_____	_____
6. The last time I failed at something, I knew that it was because I just wasn't good enough to get the job done.	_____	_____
7. Most successful people are born successful.	_____	_____
8. It seems that most things are beyond my control.	_____	_____
9. When I fail, it's usually someone else's fault.	_____	_____
10. When I succeed, it is usually because of someone else's efforts.	_____	_____

Total Score: _____

Continues

Continued

Scoring

- Statement 1: True = 0, False = 1
- Statement 2: True = 1, False = 0
- Statement 3: True = 0, False = 1
- Statement 4: True = 0, False = 1
- Statement 5: True = 1, False = 0

- Statement 6: True = 0, False = 1
- Statement 7: True = 0, False = 1
- Statement 8: True = 0, False = 1
- Statement 9: True = 0, False = 1
- Statement 10: True = 0, False = 1

Your Score and Your View of Life

The higher you score, the more you feel in control of your life. Compare your score to the following scale:

- 0–3 = Outside of My Control: I'm not responsible for my successes or my failures. I need to work on my self-concept.

- 4–6 = Sometimes in Control: I'm sometimes responsible for my successes and failures. My self-concept could be improved.

- 7–10 = In Control: I'm responsible for my successes and failures. I have confidence in myself and have a good self-concept.

Learn to View Life Positively

People with a positive self-concept look at their successes and believe that they are responsible for them. They also believe that although they are responsible for their failures, the outcome is also affected by events, things, and people outside of their control.

People with a negative self-concept view the world in the opposite way. They credit their successes to luck and never accept the blame for their failures. Thus, they fail to accept responsibility for their own actions. Those whose score in the self-assessment fell into the *Outside of My Control* category need to work harder to develop a positive self-concept. Those in the *In Control* category find it easier than those with lower scores to develop a positive self-concept, but they may still want to work on improving their self-esteem.

Like anything else, this approach to life can be taken to extremes. There are times when your success is due to luck or your failure is solely your own fault. But by being realistic about your personal contributions to success and failure, you'll know how to improve yourself. Most importantly, you must believe that you can improve. In fact, you can overcome problems or difficulties given enough time, effort, and, when needed, help from other people. The important thing is to have faith in yourself.

You can teach yourself to view life more positively and to gain more control over your own life. Look at the circumstances every time you succeed. Give yourself credit for your success. Remember to look at the small successes that occur every day of your life. Similarly, when you experience failure, examine the reasons for it. Look for those outside factors that contributed to the failure and understand how they affected the outcome.

Discussion Activity

How can you develop a positive attitude toward life?

Selling Yourself on You

Ryan Sauers is a dynamic entrepreneur who speaks throughout the United States. He is an author, radio show host, and sales and marketing consultant. In his book *Would You Buy from You?* he answers the question of the book title with four ideas.[7] These ideas can be remembered by the acronym PACT (passion, authenticity, creativity, trust):

- **Passion**   A person needs to be passionate about what they are doing. This means they are so excited about what they are doing that others catch the passion and want to be part of it.
- **Authenticity**   It is important to be real and genuine. Mr. Sauers says that "authenticity is about doing what is right no matter who is and who is not watching." (Sauers, *Would You Buy From You?*)
- **Creativity**   Be curious. Discover if you can learn more about how things are done or how they work and come up with a better way. Don't look back at how you have done things in the past, but think about new ways to do things in the future.
- **Trust**   When you tell someone you will do something or you can help them solve a problem, do it! Be honest with yourself just as you are with other people. Always do what you tell yourself you are going to do. If you can't count on you, then who can you count on?

Build on Character Strengths and Virtues

A ground-breaking concept that came from positive psychology is that people should build on strengths rather than try to improve weaknesses. For much of the 20th century, psychologists examined how to "fix" or manipulate people. Managers and leaders were taught ways to improve poor motivation, thinking, and emotions of employees. The emphasis is now on helping employees identify **character strengths** and build on them.

Many recent studies have been done to identify character strengths and virtues.[8] Character strengths are individual traits that have a moral or ethical factor. These studies considered ideas about character strengths going back thousands of years. Researchers reviewed history, literature, philosophy, religion, psychology, sociology, and many other fields to identify common character strengths. Additional studies used modern psychological procedures to confirm the most basic character strengths.

The following list was developed by reviewing dozens of these studies. Go through the list and check off the character strengths you possess. Then number your top character strengths from one to five. This process will give you a rough idea of your strengths.

Journal Activity

Obtain a scientific assessment of your character strengths at https://JobSavvy6 .JIST.com/Character StrengthSurvey. Reflect on these strengths. Do they seem to accurately describe you?

Character Strengths Assessment

Check off the character strengths you possess. Then number your top character strengths from one to five.

_____ **Authenticity**   seek self-knowledge and act in accordance with who you are

_____ **Collaboration**   strive to work with others in a cooperative manner to achieve a goal

_____ **Compassion**   desire to aid people who have a need

_____ **Courage**   persist even when faced with something you fear

_____ **Forgiveness**   forgive others when they mistreat you

_____ **Generosity**   give money, time, and other resources to people without expecting anything in return

_____ **Honesty**   follow moral, ethical, and legal principles as they relate to your actions

_____ **Hopefulness**   approach life in a manner that is optimistic and believe things will get better

_____ **Humanity**   care for others and seek to make friends

_____ **Humility**   realize that personal accomplishments are due to more than your own actions

_____ **Humor**   enjoy life and want others to enjoy life (you do this through smiles, laughs, and jokes)

_____ **Inquisitiveness**   desire to know more about all things

_____ **Justice**   desire to treat people fairly in all situations

_____ **Love**   care for others with a deep affection and treat them as you want to be treated

_____ **Love of Learning**   desire to acquire more knowledge and understanding

_____ **Open-mindedness**   remain willing to consider other ideas and understand what others think

_____ **Patience**   tolerate actions by others that are inconvenient to you

_____ **Perseverance**   strive to continue toward a goal despite problems, difficulties, or resistance by others

_____ **Responsibility**   take care to fulfill actions that you agreed or implied would be finished

_____ **Self-control**   restrain desires and emotional reactions

_____ **Spirituality**   seek a meaning in life and desire to make a difference in the world

_____ **Thankfulness**   deeply appreciate benefits you have in life and what others contribute to your life

_____ **Thoughtfulness**   think about other people's thoughts, concerns, and needs before your own

_____ **Truthfulness**   express the truth to others

_____ **Wisdom**   apply knowledge in a manner that uses your thoughts, emotions, and resolve

Self-Concept in the Workplace

A positive self-image helps you overcome doubt about your abilities. You will face unique challenges in the work world. Many job-related situations will be totally new to you and might make you doubt yourself. For instance, when you start a new job, you might question your ability to complete your assigned tasks. Remember that your self-confidence will increase as you gain experience. To protect your positive self-image as you begin a new job, try to remember these two simple truths:

1. **You will make mistakes.** When you make mistakes, acknowledge them. Accept any criticism or advice from your supervisor, and correct the mistake. Use a technique that business expert Chris Argyris calls double-loop learning.[9] For each mistake, examine the situation and note the contributing factors. Decide how you can avoid the same mistake in the future. This way you learn from your mistakes. You're capable of improving your self-image by learning from past mistakes— and not blaming yourself.

2. **Your employer wants you to succeed.** Employers don't hire people in order to fire them. Your employer hired you because of your skills, because they believe you have the ability to do the job successfully. Give yourself credit for your accomplishments. Learn to accept compliments gracefully. When you are complimented on your work, simply say, "thank you." If your supervisor or coworkers neglect to compliment you, compliment yourself by inwardly recognizing your own abilities.

Group Activity

Write a note complimenting each person in the group. Share your notes and then discuss the value of a compliment. Is it easier to write or receive a compliment?

Identify Your Skills

Take an honest look at yourself. You might be surprised at the variety of skills you have to offer an employer. You develop skills from all your life experiences. Occupational psychologists and other scholars have developed a classification of job-related skills. There are three broad categories: self-management (also referred to as *adaptive* skills), transferable skills, and job-related skills. There are three lists of more specific skills organized by these broad categories that follow.

Self-Management Skills

Self-management skills reflect the control you have over your life: how you plan, implement, change, and evaluate the activities in your life. Some self-management skills are necessary to please your employer. You probably have some of these skills already. Your employer expects you to use these skills most of the time. Although not all employers look for the same skills, all employers highly value the key self-management skills listed in the Self-Management Skills Checklist on the following page.

A Useful Skill: Monitoring

The ability to assess performance is a useful tool in the workplace. Whether you're assessing your personal job performance or that of a project team, you can solve problems by using monitoring skills. If you want to gain the respect of your employer and coworkers, learn to evaluate your job performance.

When evaluating yourself, acknowledge your strengths. Comparing your strongest abilities with the needs of your employer allows you to understand how you can best function in your particular job. If you are not using your strong skills, explore ways you can use them.

Seek to understand your weak areas. This will enable you to make improvements and take corrective action if needed. Find ways to overcome your weaknesses. Your supervisor and coworkers may advise you. Or you can take a course to learn more about this skill.

Self-Management Skills Checklist

Check the most appropriate column for all the following skills that apply to you. All employers value these skills highly. Employers often will not hire a person who does not have many of these skills.

Key Self-management Skills	Usually	Sometimes	Never
Ambitious	_____	_____	_____
Arrive on time	_____	_____	_____
Ask questions	_____	_____	_____
Assertive	_____	_____	_____
Businesslike	_____	_____	_____
Creative	_____	_____	_____
Demonstrate pride in my work	_____	_____	_____
Display leadership	_____	_____	_____
Enthusiastic	_____	_____	_____
Flexible	_____	_____	_____
Follow directions	_____	_____	_____
Friendly	_____	_____	_____
Get along well with coworkers	_____	_____	_____
Get things done	_____	_____	_____
Good sense of humor	_____	_____	_____
Highly motivated	_____	_____	_____
Patient	_____	_____	_____
Positive attitude	_____	_____	_____
Positive self-esteem	_____	_____	_____

Continues

Continued

Key Self-management Skills	Usually	Sometimes	Never
Produce quality work	_____	_____	_____
Responsible	_____	_____	_____
Self-directed	_____	_____	_____
Show up to work every day	_____	_____	_____
Willing to learn	_____	_____	_____
Work hard	_____	_____	_____
Work well with supervisors	_____	_____	_____
Other Self-management Skills			
Problem-solving abilities	_____	_____	_____
Results-oriented approach	_____	_____	_____
Sincere	_____	_____	_____

Review the checklist and count the number of times you checked Usually and Sometimes. Record the numbers below. Your skill points will be discussed in the section titled "A Review of Your Skills" on page 114.

Self-management Skills Record

Usually: _____

Sometimes: _____

Total Skill Points: _____

Transferable Skills

Transferable skills are skills that can be used in many different jobs. A grocery store cashier needs to understand numbers, but so do bank tellers and accounting clerks. A nurse needs good people skills, as does a receptionist or a salesperson. Employers value some transferable skills over others. The key transferable skills listed on the following page can help you get a higher-paying job, a position with more responsibilities, or both.

Case Study

Angie has been working as a shift manager at a fast-food restaurant but wants to change jobs and work as a secretary. What transferable skills has she gained from her current job?

Transferable Skills Checklist

Transferable Skills	Usually	Sometimes	Never
Accept responsibility	_____	_____	_____
Increase sales or efficiency	_____	_____	_____
Manage money, budgets	_____	_____	_____
Manage people	_____	_____	_____
Meet deadlines	_____	_____	_____
Meet the public	_____	_____	_____
Organize and manage projects	_____	_____	_____
Plan	_____	_____	_____
Solve problems	_____	_____	_____
Speak in public	_____	_____	_____
Supervise others	_____	_____	_____

Tactile Skills	Usually	Sometimes	Never
Assemble	_____	_____	_____
Build	_____	_____	_____
Construct/repair things	_____	_____	_____
Drive/operate vehicles	_____	_____	_____
Good with hands	_____	_____	_____
Make things	_____	_____	_____
Observe/inspect	_____	_____	_____
Operate tools, machines	_____	_____	_____
Repair	_____	_____	_____
Use complex equipment	_____	_____	_____

Data Skills	Usually	Sometimes	Never
Accuracy	_____	_____	_____
Analyze data	_____	_____	_____
Audit records	_____	_____	_____
Budget	_____	_____	_____
Calculate/compute	_____	_____	_____
Classify data	_____	_____	_____
Compare	_____	_____	_____
Compile	_____	_____	_____

Continues

Data Skills	Usually	Sometimes	Never
Evaluate	_____	_____	_____
Investigate	_____	_____	_____
Keep financial records	_____	_____	_____
Keep track of details	_____	_____	_____
Manage money	_____	_____	_____
Negotiate	_____	_____	_____
Observe/inspect	_____	_____	_____
Record facts	_____	_____	_____
Research/locate answers or information	_____	_____	_____
Synthesize	_____	_____	_____
Take inventory	_____	_____	_____

People Skills	Usually	Sometimes	Never
Care for others	_____	_____	_____
Confront others	_____	_____	_____
Counsel people	_____	_____	_____
Demonstrate tasks	_____	_____	_____
Diplomatic	_____	_____	_____
Help others	_____	_____	_____
Insightful	_____	_____	_____
Instruct/teach	_____	_____	_____
Interview people	_____	_____	_____
Kind	_____	_____	_____
Lead	_____	_____	_____
Listen	_____	_____	_____
Mentor	_____	_____	_____
Outgoing	_____	_____	_____
Patient	_____	_____	_____
Persuade	_____	_____	_____
Pleasant	_____	_____	_____
Sensitive	_____	_____	_____
Socialize	_____	_____	_____
Supervise	_____	_____	_____

Continues

People Skills	Usually	Sometimes	Never
Tactful	_____	_____	_____
Tolerant	_____	_____	_____
Tough	_____	_____	_____
Trust	_____	_____	_____
Understand	_____	_____	_____

Using Words and Ideas Skills	Usually	Sometimes	Never
Communicate verbally/articulate	_____	_____	_____
Conduct library and Internet research	_____	_____	_____
Correspond with others	_____	_____	_____
Create new ideas	_____	_____	_____
Demonstrate ingenuity	_____	_____	_____
Design	_____	_____	_____
Edit	_____	_____	_____
Inventive	_____	_____	_____
Logical	_____	_____	_____
Remember information	_____	_____	_____
Speak publicly	_____	_____	_____
Write clearly	_____	_____	_____

Leadership Skills	Usually	Sometimes	Never
Arrange social functions	_____	_____	_____
Compete	_____	_____	_____
Decide	_____	_____	_____
Delegate	_____	_____	_____
Direct others	_____	_____	_____
Explain concepts to others	_____	_____	_____
Get results	_____	_____	_____
Mediate problems	_____	_____	_____
Motivate people	_____	_____	_____
Negotiate agreements	_____	_____	_____
Plan	_____	_____	_____
Run meetings	_____	_____	_____

Continues

Leadership Skills	Usually	Sometimes	Never
Self-confident	_____	_____	_____
Self-motivated	_____	_____	_____
Solve problems	_____	_____	_____
Take risks	_____	_____	_____

Creative/Artistic Skills	Usually	Sometimes	Never
Artistic	_____	_____	_____
Dance, move my body	_____	_____	_____
Draw, create art	_____	_____	_____
Express	_____	_____	_____
Perform, act	_____	_____	_____
Present artistic ideas	_____	_____	_____

Office/Technical Skills	Usually	Sometimes	Never
Access and retrieve data from the Internet	_____	_____	_____
Arm/disarm a security system	_____	_____	_____
Create electronic databases	_____	_____	_____
Create electronic spreadsheets	_____	_____	_____
Create multimedia presentations	_____	_____	_____
Create PowerPoint presentations	_____	_____	_____
Create programs using a computer language	_____	_____	_____
Maintain and design websites	_____	_____	_____
Operate copy machines	_____	_____	_____
Operate DVD players	_____	_____	_____
Operate fax machines	_____	_____	_____
Operate laminators	_____	_____	_____
Operate multiline telephone systems	_____	_____	_____
Operate paper shredders	_____	_____	_____
Operate postage meters	_____	_____	_____
Operate video recorders/players	_____	_____	_____
Use collaboration software	_____	_____	_____

Continues

Office/Technical Skills	Usually	Sometimes	Never
Use database software	_____	_____	_____
Use email	_____	_____	_____
Use large-screen projectors	_____	_____	_____
Use overhead projectors	_____	_____	_____
Use presentation software	_____	_____	_____
Use spreadsheet software	_____	_____	_____
Use word-processing software	_____	_____	_____
Others: _____	_____	_____	_____
_____	_____	_____	_____
_____	_____	_____	_____
_____	_____	_____	_____
_____	_____	_____	_____
_____	_____	_____	_____

Review the checklist and count the number of times you checked Usually and Sometimes. Record the numbers below. You do not count any points for Never answers. Your skill points will be discussed in the section titled "A Review of Your Skills" on page 114.

Transferable Skills Record

Usually: _____

Sometimes: _____

Total Skill Points: _____

Job-Related Skills

You use **job-related skills** to complete the tasks required for a particular job. For example, a semi truck driver must know how to drive a large truck and abide by traffic laws. A paramedic must be able to take blood pressure and use a stethoscope. Some job-related skills are the result of years of training. Others can be learned in short time.

If you are interested in a particular job, you probably have some skills necessary to do that job. These skills come from a variety of experiences including education, other jobs, volunteer work, hobbies, extracurricular activities, and even family activities. Complete the following exercise to see what skills you have that you could use in your current job or a job you want.

Job-Related Skills Checklist

1. List the skills related to your current job that you gained through school courses or vocational training.

   _____

   _____

   _____

2. List the skills related to your job that you gained through other jobs or from volunteer work.

   _____

   _____

   _____

3. List the skills related to your job that you gained through hobbies, family activities, extra-curricular activities, and other experiences outside of school or work.

   _____

   _____

   _____

   Give yourself one point for each job-related skill that you listed. Record the total below. Your skill points will be discussed in the section titled "A Review of Your Skills" below.

Job-Related Skills Record

   Total Skill Points: _____

A Review of Your Skills

Add your total points for each skill area and write them in the appropriate spaces below. This shows you the variety of skills you have to offer an employer. You are a valuable member of your employer's team!

Journal Activity

Reflect on the results of your checklists in this chapter.

- Total Self-management Skills: _____
- Total Transferable Skills: _____
- Total Job-related Skills: _____

Identifying your skills helps to reveal your strengths and weaknesses as an employee. Now that you know your skills, you can use them to improve your position in the work world. Is there a skill you aren't using? Should you start practicing a new skill? Do you have a skill that is weak? How could you improve this skill? Include the skills you've identified in this list in résumés, performance reviews, and interviews. Whenever you are asked about your skills, you may refer back to these lists.

Skills Reflection or Skills Journal

Write a short statement describing how you feel about yourself now that you've identified specific skills that you possess.

_____

_____

_____

_____

_____

_____

_____

_____

How Job Savvy Are You?

Darren works in a formal-wear store. Last week, a wedding party of 10 came in to be measured for tuxedoes. Darren carefully measured each person and recorded the measurements on the proper form. When the groom became impatient with the long wait, Darren joked with him about the wedding. By the time the group left, the groom was smiling. Then Darren discovered that he had undercharged the group by $50.

1. What are Darren's stronger skills?

   _____

   _____

   _____

2. What are Darren's weaker skills?

   _____

   _____

   _____

3. How can Darren build upon his strengths?

   _____

   _____

   _____

Continues

Sheila works in the university research library. A professor sent a list of research articles to be reserved for his classes. Sheila went through the stacks and pulled all but one of the requested articles. Although she was unable to find the one article, she packaged the rest and sent them to the professor. Her supervisor did not okay the order. Later, the professor complained to Sheila's supervisor that his order was incomplete. The supervisor called Sheila into the office and pointed out the mistake. Sheila became angry and left the office.

1. What are Sheila's stronger skills?

   _____

   _____

   _____

2. What are Sheila's weaker skills?

   _____

   _____

   _____

3. How can Sheila build upon her strengths?

   _____

   _____

   _____

Learning from Others

A good way to learn about yourself is to ask others how they see you. Listen to the performance reviews from your supervisor at work. Work to make progress on developing your skills based on feedback from your supervisor.

Here are some simple ways to get more information from people who know you so you can build on strengths and try to improve:

1. **Send an email to about 10 friends, coworkers, and your supervisor.** The email should state the following:

   > I am working on a self-improvement plan. Please help me with this task. Please answer two questions for me. When you've seen me at my best doing a task or project, what were my greatest strengths? When you've seen me not succeed in a task or project, what suggestions would you have made to help me do better? Thank you for helping me.

2. **Make a list of all the strengths people tell you about.** Consider how you can build on these strengths to do your job better.
3. **Make a list of all the weaknesses people identified along with their suggestions for improvement.** Consider how you can begin practicing the ideas they recommend to improve your work.

4. **Go back and review these lists a month after compiling them.** Have you been able to build on your strengths? What did you do to take advantage of your strengths? Have you implemented suggestions for improvement? Which suggestions have you followed? What other suggestions could you put into practice in the upcoming weeks?
5. **Revisit your lists every few weeks, and keep on working to improve yourself.**

Summing Up

Dietitians tell us "you are what you eat" to encourage us to develop healthy bodies through good nutrition. To develop a healthier self-image, an appropriate saying might be "you are what you think." If you believe you can do the job, you can probably do it. Here are some useful tips to help you believe in yourself:

- **Think positively**   Think success, not failure. Be your own cheerleader.
- **Accept compliments**   Learn to say a simple "thank you" when you are complimented.
- **Accept responsibility**   Learn to accept responsibility for your successes as well as your failures, but recognize how other factors contribute to failure. Be proud of your successes. Strive to improve your weaker skills and correct your mistakes.
- **Identify your skills**   Use your special abilities to improve your skills and to build up your positive self-concept.
- **Reward yourself**   Treat yourself for being successful. Buy something special to remember the occasion. Celebrate!

In this chapter you hopefully discovered many things about yourself. Use this information to work more productively. The information you learned about yourself should help you appreciate others and understand reasons for differences in the ways people act and think. In the next three chapters, this information will help you understand how to get along with leaders, coworkers, and the customers you work with at your place of employment.

Review and Assessment

Take the Review Quiz. See your instructor or reference your student files in the ebook for additional resources.

CHAPTER 8

Getting Along with Your Supervisor

Objectives

- Develop good communication and collaboration skills with your supervisor.

- Identify methods to meet supervisor expectations.

- Evaluate your employee role and identify potential conflicts with your supervisor.

L eaders in organizations are responsible for planning, organizing, directing, controlling, and otherwise leading employees to accomplish the organization's purpose and goals. To accomplish these actions, leaders need help from employees. When you agree to work for an organization, you are agreeing to team up with leaders to get work done for the organization. Supervisors are usually the first-line leaders working with the employees who produce goods or provide essential services directly to customers. This chapter covers getting along with your supervisor, but the ideas apply to any leader in an organization.

Supervisors frequently make recommendations about promotions, salary increases, and employee firings, so it is important for you to get along with your supervisor. Cooperating will make your work experience more pleasant and help advance your career. It will also help you get a positive recommendation if you look for another job.

Experts on leadership tend to call employees "followers" because rather than give orders, an employee follows their leaders. A leader needs to inspire employees to follow their leadership. Leaders and followers have a relationship. A positive relationship is built on support, trust, and cooperation from both the leader and the follower. This chapter provides ideas about what followers can do to create a positive relationship.

Unfortunately, some supervisors simply don't care to have a positive relationship with employees. That is the reason this chapter ends with an explanation of the rights and protections employees have when treated unfairly.

Watch the Video

Getting Along with Your Supervisor

The Team Leader

In today's business world, the supervisor is seen as a leader, coach, cheerleader, teacher, and counselor. This person plans, schedules, orders work materials, directs the activities of employees, checks the productivity and quality of work, and coordinates all work activities with other departments in the organization. Many organizations now use the term *team leader* instead of *supervisor*. A team leader sometimes shares the responsibilities of a supervisor with other members of the team. The more traditional term *supervisor* is still used frequently, and we'll use it in this book.

Consider yourself part of a team if you participate in a work group. Each worker must do his or her job correctly for the team to be successful. The supervisor delegates work to the members of the group. Your supervisor depends on you to do your job and to do it right.

Group Activity

Define *supervision* and list the typical responsibilities of a supervisor.

Delegating

Supervisors delegate when they assign or distribute tasks to employees. When they do the work themselves instead of delegating it, their performance often slips.[1] A supervisor must delegate tasks to employees to ensure that all the work gets done. When a task is delegated to you, be sure to follow instructions carefully. Periodically, report back to your supervisor to let him or her know how the job is progressing. Let your supervisor know when you are finished with an assigned task.

Some employees think supervising is easy. It's important to realize that supervisors have responsibilities that other employees don't have. Employees are often unaware of the unseen tasks supervisors must complete. A supervisor's outlook on the workday can be affected by the stress caused by tasks that you can see as well as by unseen tasks. Hundreds of studies have been done about a concept called leader-member exchange, also known as LMX.[2] This idea focuses on the two-way relationship between leaders and followers. Leaders create **in-groups** of followers who are willing to go above and beyond the job requirements. In addition, members of this group work well with their leaders. Followers who insist on doing only the work required by their job descriptions become members of the **out-group**. Members of the in-group typically receive preferred treatment, more access to the leader, and richer feedback. A lesson employees can learn from the LMX concept is that they are more likely to experience success at work by learning to become better followers.

An excellent resource for helping followers become part of the in-group comes from US Air Force Colonel Phillip Meilinger. He wrote the following Ten Rules of Good Followership:[3]

1. Don't blame the boss.
2. Don't fight the boss.
3. Use initiative.
4. Accept responsibility.

Discussion Activity

Think back to jobs you've had. What support did you need from your supervisor that coworkers could not provide?

5. Tell the truth, and don't quibble.
6. Do your homework.
7. Be willing to implement suggestions you make.
8. Keep the boss informed.
9. Fix problems as they occur.
10. Put in an honest day's work.

Leaders appreciate workers who follow these 10 principles and often show their appreciation in many ways, such as by offering flexible schedules, better assignments, or more learning opportunities. Some people think that being a good follower is "kissing up to the boss." However, being a good follower is just a good strategy for creating a pleasant work environment and being a success at work.

Communicate with Your Supervisor

When employees and supervisors communicate effectively, businesses benefit. A recent study shows that supervisors' communication abilities had a significant effect on the job satisfaction and productivity of their team members.[4] Effective communication creates a domino effect, leading to positive interactions with customers, investors, and the community. Both the company and the workers benefit.

Good communication with your supervisor is important to both of you. It fosters a mutual understanding that creates a good working relationship. Let's explore four important ideas you should remember when communicating with your supervisor:

1. You must be able to follow instructions.
2. You need to know how to ask questions.
3. You should report any problems and the results of your work.
4. You need to discuss your job performance.

Follow Instructions

It's important to follow instructions at all times, especially during training. Your supervisor will be watching to see how well you do this. Use all of your senses to follow instructions correctly. Here are some tips to help you do this:

- **Concentrate**   Focus your attention on the supervisor. Don't be distracted by noise and movement.
- **Listen**   Pay attention to the words being spoken. If you hear unfamiliar words or terms, ask for clarification. Listening also means interpreting body language, voice inflections, and gestures. If this nonverbal communication is confusing, ask the supervisor to clarify what you don't understand.
- **Watch**   If you don't completely understand the task your supervisor is demonstrating, ask him or her to repeat the process until you understand it completely. Sometimes a task can be too complex or too time-consuming to demonstrate. In such cases, you probably will receive general instructions. If there are details you don't understand, ask for guidance.

Group Activity

List nonverbal communication types. Take turns demonstrating to your group.

- **Ask**   After you have listened and observed, ask questions. A good supervisor will encourage you to ask questions. It's better to ask a question than to make a mistake because you didn't understand something.
- **Write**   Record notes on paper or an electronic device to document the important points to remember. Try not to write while your supervisor is talking or demonstrating something. Do it during a break in the instructions (you may have to request a break occasionally to jot down your notes).
- **Practice**   With your supervisor's permission, perform the task. Make sure you have fully completed the job. This can include putting away tools or cleaning up your work area. Don't leave your work partially completed.

Jargon/Acronyms

Every organization develops its own terminology called **jargon**. Jargon might be the most difficult thing for a new employee to learn. It can be in the form of words or acronyms. For example, your supervisor might tell you that you will be "pulling" today. This could mean you'll be taking packages off a conveyor belt to be loaded onto a truck.

An acronym is an abbreviation. Your supervisor might say you can't get a computer until you submit an RFP, which might refer to a "request for purchase." When you hear a term that is unclear, ask for an explanation. Some organizations give new employees a booklet that defines unique terms to that business.

The following exercise will help you understand how easily instructions can be misunderstood. It illustrates why the tips suggested for communicating with your supervisor are good ideas.

How Job Savvy Are You?

1. Get a sheet of 8½" × 11" paper.

2. Fold the paper in half.

3. Now fold the paper in half again.

4. Fold the paper in half one more time.

Following these directions can result in at least four possible outcomes. For example, your folded paper could have any of these measurements:

- 2¾" × 4¼"

- $2^1/_8$" × 5½"

- $1^3/_8$" × 8½"

- $1^1/_{16}$" × 11"

Continues

Job Savvy: How to Be a Success at Work

Continued

The results differ because the instructions are not entirely clear, just as some instructions you receive from a supervisor might not be completely clear.

1. What questions could you have asked to better understand the instructions?

_____

_____

_____

2. How would you rewrite the instructions so that only one outcome is possible?

_____

_____

_____

Ask Questions

If you don't understand something, ask questions. Your supervisor can't read your mind. It's better to ask a question than to make a major mistake.

Many people are reluctant to ask questions for fear of appearing unqualified. If this applies to you, concentrate on overcoming your reluctance. Not asking questions can result in broken equipment, angry customers, and other mistakes that will negatively affect your performance rating. It might even cost you the job.

Here are some simple guidelines for asking questions:

- **Ask Immediately**   You should ask a question as soon as it arises. The longer you wait, the more irrelevant your question will seem, and then you won't ask it at all.
- **Summarize the Response**   When the supervisor answers your question, repeat the answer in your own words. This lets you make sure that you clearly understand the answer.
- **Memorize or Record the Answer**   It's irritating to answer the same question repeatedly. Your supervisor might grow impatient with you if this happens. Record answers in a notebook or smartphone if you have trouble memorizing information during training.

Report on Results

Your supervisor needs to be kept informed of your work. Sometimes the supervisor will be close enough to observe your work at all times, but this is not always the case. It is *your* responsibility to keep the supervisor informed about your progress on a task. Contact your supervisor in the following situations:

- **When You Complete a Task**   The supervisor needs to know whether a job has been completed. If you don't report back, he or she will have to find you to ask whether the job is done. A busy supervisor doesn't have time to track down all employees to see whether they have com-

Case Study

A new mother has developed a serious infection. The head nurse, Aisha, needs José to move the mother to another area of the hospital. What questions should José ask Aisha?

Case Study

A supervisor has asked Jack to make 15 copies of a memo for all employees. There are 25 employees in the office. What questions should Jack ask?

pleted their assigned tasks. A supervisor will appreciate knowing when you've finished a task.

- **When You Aren't Sure How to Proceed**   At times, you won't know how to complete a task. Whenever this happens, ask your supervisor for guidance. Remember to document the answer so that you'll know how to handle a similar situation in the future.
- **When You Have a Problem**   Problems can develop when you are trying to complete a task. The less experience you have, the more difficult it will be to solve the problem. Equipment might not work properly. Customers might have questions you can't answer. Someone else might have completed a job incorrectly, preventing you from finishing your assignment. When you aren't sure how to solve a problem, contact your supervisor immediately. Doing so can keep the problem from getting worse.

Some tasks might take several hours, days, weeks, or months to complete. Keep your supervisor informed about ongoing assignments. This tells your supervisor that you are assuming responsibility and that you can be trusted to complete assignments.

Request Coaching on Your Job Performance

Your supervisor should communicate with you frequently about your job performance. If this is not happening, you should request it. This communication is called **coaching**, and the goal is to help workers do the best job possible.[5] Just as a sports coach can help improve an athlete's performance, a good supervisor can help you improve your work performance.

Coaching techniques should include periodic encouragement and feedback about your work. Sometimes you might have negative feelings when a supervisor suggests ways to improve your work. Keep in mind that coaching is designed to be a win-win situation. It helps the organization because your performance is improved, but it also helps you become a more skilled worker. Coaching helps you do a better job for your organization.

Follow these simple guidelines to communicate effectively with your supervisor about your job performance:

- **Respond Positively to Feedback**   Feedback from your supervisor is important. No one enjoys criticism, but it is sometimes necessary. If you get angry because your supervisor gives you negative feedback, get control of yourself before responding. Count to 10 if there is no other way to cool off, or simply know that you don't have to respond at all. You can sleep on it, and then respond in a calm manner the next day. Avoid getting into a shouting match with your supervisor.
- **Know What You've Done Wrong**   Your supervisor might be so upset with something you've done that you aren't sure what the problem is. Apologize if you made a mistake, and ask for an explanation of exactly what you did wrong. Don't repeat the mistake. Make the correction in the future and move on.

- **Thank Your Supervisor** You must learn to accept praise as well as criticism. Acknowledge compliments with a simple "thank you."
- **Ask for Feedback** Some supervisors are not good about giving feedback. If you aren't sure what your supervisor thinks about the work you are doing, ask! Let him or her know that you want to succeed on the job and that you need to know how you're doing.

Performance Appraisal

A **performance appraisal** is a formal report about your job performance based on your supervisor's evaluation of your work. You are rated on various aspects of your job for a quarterly, semiannual, or annual period, depending on your organization's policy. Performance appraisals are similar to report cards in school.

You usually review the appraisal form with your supervisor and have an opportunity to respond to the evaluation. Coworkers might even be asked to rate your performance. Some organizations give you a chance to rate yourself. If so, you are usually expected to explain the ratings and back them up with examples. Be honest, but don't give yourself a rating lower than you deserve. New employees usually receive performance appraisals at the end of their probation periods.

How Job Savvy Are You?

Bryan has worked for Armstrong Dry Cleaners for two months. He works behind the counter, taking customer orders. His supervisor tells him the business is going to expand and will begin cleaning leather garments. Bryan will need to fill out a special order form for leather clothing, and he is not sure that he understands all of the instructions.

    What should Bryan do at this point?

_____

_____

_____

_____

Yvette has just finished loading the heating and air conditioning service van when her supervisor comes up to her and starts yelling. He tells Yvette that she took too long when inspecting a furnace yesterday and is costing the company too much money. He says that Yvette had better get her act together if she expects to keep her job.

    How should Yvette respond?

_____

_____

_____

_____

Meet Your Supervisor's Expectations

This section reviews some of the little things you need to know to get along with your supervisor. These are important because *little things* to you can become *big things* to your supervisor when they are multiplied by all the employees he or she is supervising.

Practice the following six actions in order to satisfy your supervisor's expectations. These actions can help you become part of your leader's in-group. Following these actions increases the likelihood that courtesies you extend to your supervisor will be reciprocated.

Discussion Activity

Supervisors manage many workers. How do problems multiply when workers start breaking "little" rules?

Be Truthful

Your supervisor expects you to tell the truth at all times. If you make mistakes, don't try to cover them up by lying. Lies usually are discovered and can be grounds for disciplinary action. Supervisors need employees they can count on to tell the truth. Without honesty between a supervisor and workers, it's impossible for either to do a good job.

Don't Extend Your Breaks

Your supervisor expects you to work during your scheduled hours. Normally, a full-time worker is allowed a 15-minute break midmorning and midafternoon in addition to a 30- to 60-minute lunch break. When you don't return from a break on time, it can cause problems. A customer might have to wait, another worker might not be able to take his or her break, and others might not be able to finish a task until your work is completed.

If you can't get back from break on time, explain the reason to your supervisor. Make sure you aren't extending your breaks unless there is an exceptionally good reason, and always request the extension in advance.

Get Your Work Done

You should complete all assigned tasks as quickly as possible while doing the best job possible. It's difficult for a supervisor to check your work all the time. You are expected to continue working productively without a supervisor present.

If circumstances prevent you from completing a job, notify your supervisor immediately. Balance your work between completing a task as quickly as possible and producing the highest quality of work you can. Ask your supervisor for feedback about how well you are meeting these priorities.

Be Cooperative

Cooperate when your supervisor asks for your help. When someone can't work at a scheduled time, be willing to change your schedule if possible. Help with a task that's not normally your responsibility. In special situations, your supervisor might need more help from everybody. Of course, if you think the supervisor is taking advantage of you, don't be hesitant to let him or her know you can't help out.

Cooperation can be mutual, and most supervisors will remember your help the next time you need a day off for a special reason. Thus, cooperation benefits you and creates a more pleasant work atmosphere.

Be Adaptive

Be willing to adapt to new situations. The organization you work for needs to change as the world around it changes. Employees sometimes resist change because of poor self-esteem, threats to personal security, fear of the unknown, a lack of trust, or an inability to see the larger picture. When you understand the reason for resistance, you can work to reduce it. Adjustments are difficult, but your life will be more pleasant if you adjust instead of resist.

Supervisors probably don't want to make changes any more than you do, but sometimes it is their responsibility to do so, and they need your cooperation. It might help to think about the positive things that result from the changes. For example, if your work schedule changes, think about the new opportunities it might provide at work or in your personal life, such as providing an opportunity to meet new people, spend more time with family, or learn new skills.

Take Initiative

Find ways to help your supervisor. After your own work is completed, take **initiative** to look around the workplace for other tasks to do. But remember, it doesn't help anyone if your work suffers because you were trying to help with something else.

Meeting a Supervisor's Expectations

1. Why might a worker lie to a supervisor?

   _____

   _____

2. What problems could these lies cause for the supervisor?

   _____

   _____

3. What are some acceptable reasons for extended breaks?

   _____

   _____

4. What obstacles might make it difficult or impossible for you to do your job?

   _____

   _____

Continues

5. How can you benefit from cooperating with your supervisor?

_____

_____

6. What are some typical reasons for change within an organization?

_____

_____

7. How can you take the initiative to help your supervisor?

_____

_____

How Job Savvy Are You?

Tonight, Lei has a date. Sara, her supervisor at the Bureau of Motor Vehicles, is going directly from lunch to a supervisor's meeting. Lei knows Sara won't be back in the office until 2:30 p.m. On her lunch break, Lei passes her favorite hair salon and considers stopping in for a hair cut.

1. What should Lei do?

_____

_____

_____

2. What could happen if she stops to get her hair cut?

_____

_____

_____

Ryan has three days off work this week. On his second day off, his supervisor calls. Ryan isn't home, but his sister takes a message and gives it to Ryan later that afternoon. One of the other employees is sick, and the supervisor needs Ryan to work the next day. Ryan has already made plans for the day.

1. What should Ryan do?

_____

_____

_____

Continues

2. What will be the result if he goes into work? What will happen if he doesn't?

_____

_____

_____

Brandon works second shift as a lab technician at Mercy Hospital. Brandon has just finished the last lab report for the shift and is preparing to leave when the phone rings. His supervisor has just stepped out of the lab. Brandon is alone in the lab. Typically his supervisor answers the phone.

1. What should Brandon do?

_____

_____

_____

2. Whose responsibility is it to answer the phone?

_____

_____

_____

Performance Reviews

Many organizations use a performance review, or appraisal, to periodically evaluate employee performance. This formal process is conducted by a supervisor and includes completing a written report about your performance. Management often uses performance appraisals to determine pay increases, promotions, and training needs.

Organizations differ in how frequently they conduct performance appraisals. Some organizations do an appraisal at the end of an employee's probationary period. Most companies conduct reviews once or twice a year, and a few have quarterly appraisals. Regardless of how often your workplace conducts reviews, you should be prepared for them.[6] Here are some tips:

Journal Activity

Draft your own mock performance evaluation.

*   **Keep a Record of Accomplishments**   Once a month, write down your accomplishments. Examples include a special project you completed, customer feedback that was very positive, the number of sales you had, or the quality of goods that you produced. You might want to compile these accomplishments and give a written report to your supervisor before the performance appraisal is conducted. It will help your supervisor remember your accomplishments.
*   **Communicate Regularly with Your Supervisor**   Information given in a performance appraisal shouldn't be a surprise. Talk frequently with your supervisor about your performance. Ask what you can do to improve your job performance. Try to have any performance issues resolved before your review takes place.

- **Know What Coworkers Think**   Some organizations use a review process called "360-degree feedback." This includes reviews from yourself, coworkers, and your supervisor. Supervisors in organizations that don't use 360-degree feedback appraisals often rely on the impressions coworkers have about an employee when conducting an appraisal.
- **Listen with an Open Mind**   Assess the feedback from your supervisor honestly. We all have strengths and weaknesses. Encourage the supervisor to consider your strengths. Accept constructive criticism about your weaknesses. Ask for specific examples of unsatisfactory behavior or performance.
- **Develop a Plan for Improvement**   Ask your supervisor to give you specific recommendations about how to improve your performance. The plan might include a change in behavior, training, job restructuring, and other strategies. Work with the supervisor to develop objectives that are possible to achieve. Make sure there is a timetable established for achieving the objectives.
- **Implement the Plan and Get Feedback**   Determine how you will implement the plan and how specifically you will improve your performance. Periodically review your performance with the supervisor and verify that your performance is improving in a satisfactory manner.
- **Be Realistic**   Consider the performance review and determine whether it is fair. It is possible to receive a poor performance review even though your work has been good or satisfactory. A supervisor might give you a poor evaluation because that person is unrealistic, unfair, or constrained by company policy to give only a certain number of excellent, good, and fair ratings. A poor performance review that you objectively consider unfair should motivate you to think about your future with the organization. If you regularly receive unfair reviews, you might want to consider looking for another job. Of course, be sure you have a new job lined up before you resign.

Courageous Followership

Much of this chapter has presented ideas about how to get along with your supervisor and other leaders. However, there may be times when it is not appropriate to go along with what your supervisor tells you to do. For example, a supervisor instructs you to bypass a step in food preparation because there is a backup in customer orders. Another example might be if your supervisor tells you to leave a door propped open even though it is against company security policies. A further example is being told by your supervisor to dispose of cooking oil in a city drain outside a restaurant. Each of these examples describes a situation where each action will result in serious consequences for you. Skimping on food preparation just means a lower quality product for customers. Leaving a door open might result in a person—possibly a friend of the supervisor—entering the restaurant to steal something. The last example may be a violation of city or state law. What should a follower do in each of these situations?

Most of us subconsciously realize when we are asked to do something wrong. When this happens, you need to stop and think. If you believe you have been asked to do something that contradicts company policy or law, you need to refuse. A more serious example of being asked to do something wrong was faced by Pfizer sales reps in 2002. Pfizer leaders asked sales reps to convince doctors to use a new pain-killing drug in a dangerous manner. They told physicians they could use it for medical conditions and in amounts that the Federal Drug Administration (FDA) didn't allow. Leaders and sales reps knew the drug could potentially cause patients to have heart attacks. Because six employees refused to follow this order and contacted the FDA, Pfizer was fined $2.3 billion and some leaders were sent to prison. Ira Chaleff writes about **courageous followership**[7] and the need to question an order when it doesn't seem right. Refusing to carry out a supervisor's order is a last resort, but the following principles can help you make the decision when needed.

- Have the courage to assume responsibility for carrying out the order. You can't blame others for your action.
- Have the courage to follow your leader's orders when they are reasonable, ethical, and moral. Do this even when it isn't something you like to do.
- Have the courage to challenge the leader. If you think the order is inappropriate or wrong, share your concerns and reasons with the leader.
- Have the courage to support leaders when they try to do the right thing. Other followers may still want to resist even though the reasons to do so no longer exist.
- Have the courage to resist when there is a reason to do so.

In addition to abiding by company policy and laws, there are several scenarios when an employee should resist following a leader's order. One situation is when it violates moral principles. You might be asked to do something that violates your religious or moral beliefs.

Whether corporate policy, legal, moral, or religious offense has occurred, evaluate whether you feel safe addressing your leader directly. If you feel safe, you may want to tell the supervisor why you are refusing an order. It is even more important to report the supervisor to HR or the supervisor's direct report/leader. Fortunately, most organizations have set up procedures to help employees when a supervisor has put them in a compromising situation. The rest of this chapter is written to help you understand some of the principles that organizations typically establish to protect employees along with procedures required by the state and federal governments to protect workers' rights.

A Useful Skill: Emotional Intelligence

The skill of **emotional intelligence** (EI) is useful when you're dealing with others and is an important skill for the 21st century.[8] When you develop this skill, you have a clearer concept of how others will react to your actions. Practicing EI involves two basic steps:

1. **Being aware of the reactions of others.** Some individuals are oblivious of others' emotions and opinions, and they act with total disregard for anyone else. EI requires listening and learning to recognize nonverbal clues when communicating with others, as well as remembering to observe what an individual does.
2. **Understanding why others react as they do.** An emotionally intelligent person is conscious of factors that may play a role in the responses of individuals. Knowing the cause of reactions gives insight into how to approach individuals. For example, scheduling a meeting to discuss your recent performance review on the day your supervisor just returned from vacation and has meetings scheduled from 9:00 a.m. until 4:30 p.m. might result in a negative reaction. A meeting on a less hectic day would be to your advantage.

Resolving Problems with Your Supervisor

Each person looks at a situation from his or her own point of view. You might not always agree with your supervisor, and sometimes your supervisor will make mistakes. You might not do a good job at certain times. A number of problems can arise when conflicts occur. Such disagreements can be resolved by conflict resolution, through a grievance procedure, or through disciplinary actions.

Conflict Resolution

Conflicts are a part of life. You should face them head-on when they arise. Talk with your supervisor about any disagreements. The act of addressing conflicts and finding solutions is called **conflict resolution**. These simple suggestions can help you keep conflicts to a minimum:

- **Own Up to Your Mistakes**   Everyone makes mistakes. When you make a mistake, you should do what you can to correct it. It's typically not a good idea to accuse your supervisor (or anyone else, for that matter) of making a mistake.
- **State Your Feelings**   Don't say "you" when explaining your perception of a situation. It will sound like you're accusing someone. Instead, focus on using "I" statements. Say "I feel" or "I think" or "I am" to describe your view. The supervisor will not know how you feel unless you voice your feelings.
- **Ask for Feedback**   Ask your supervisor whether you understand the situation correctly and have acted appropriately. It is possible that you misunderstood what happened. You might find that you feel differently about the situation once it is clarified.

- **State What You Want**   Know what you want done about a situation before you confront your supervisor. State your wishes clearly and respectfully.
- **Get a Commitment**   After you state your feelings and what you want, ask what your supervisor can do about the situation. Maybe no action is necessary. If no immediate action can be taken, your supervisor should commit to a date and time to let you know what will be done.
- **Compromise When Appropriate**   Not all problems can be resolved the way you want. You might have failed to consider your supervisor's needs or the needs of the organization. How can your needs as well as your supervisor's be met? The ideal result of any conflict is that both parties are satisfied.

Most problems with a supervisor can be solved with these techniques. However, some problems can't be resolved in this manner. When such a situation occurs, you might be able to file a grievance.

Grievance Procedures

If your supervisor cannot resolve a conflict, you might resolve the problem by going through a **grievance procedure**. Some organizations have standard procedures, and you should learn about them. Be aware that filing a grievance almost always creates tension between the employee and the supervisor.

Organizations with unions usually have a procedure that has been negotiated between management and the union. If you are employed by such an organization, you will probably have a union representative with you at all steps in the grievance process. An arbitrator makes the final decision.

Studies show that many nonunion companies also have formal grievance procedures. Many government or government-funded organizations are required by law to have them. Some smaller organizations, though, have no such process.

You need to know your organization's procedure before filing a grievance. In nonunion organizations, you typically have no assistance filing a grievance, and the organization's personnel director or chief executive officer probably makes the final decision. Complaints of discrimination or sexual harassment often receive special attention. Such cases might require a different procedure.

You should make every attempt to resolve a conflict with your supervisor before filing a grievance. Don't tell your supervisor that you are considering such action until you have tried every other means possible to solve the problem.

Disciplinary Action

Sometimes your work performance or behavior might be unacceptable. It is your supervisor's responsibility to address the problem and to advise you on appropriate performance. If you don't correct the problem, you could face **disciplinary action**. Make sure you understand your employer's disciplinary process. Such procedures usually apply only to employees past their probation period. Those still on probation might be dismissed without warning.

Disciplinary procedures, like grievance procedures, vary from one employer to another. The action taken will depend on the seriousness of the violation. The disciplinary responses explained here are common to many organizations:

- **Oral Warning**   Your supervisor warns you that your performance is not acceptable. This applies to less serious problems. Serious problems such as drinking or drug use probably will result in immediate suspension or dismissal. The oral warning goes into your personnel record but is removed later if no further problems arise.
- **Written Warning**   Repeated performance problems result in a written warning. This step takes place after an oral warning is issued. A written warning might become a permanent part of your personnel record.
- **Suspension**   Suspension means you aren't allowed to work for a short period of time, sometimes three to five days. This is unpaid time. The disciplinary action becomes a permanent part of the personnel record.
- **Dismissal**   The final step of any disciplinary process is dismissal. This means the organization won't tolerate your job performance any longer. Dismissal becomes a permanent part of the personnel record. It also means that any future employer who contacts your former employer might be told that you were dismissed from your job.
- **Immediate Response**   Some organizations immediately escort a terminated employee out of the building. They will stop at your desk, workstation, or locker to allow you to remove personal articles. This action is designed to protect employees, equipment, computer systems, or other assets from disgruntled employees. It is often a required security procedure, so don't take it personally.

Most organizations don't want you to fail. If you are being disciplined, follow your supervisor's instructions and you should not encounter further problems. Smaller businesses might not follow the procedure described previously. You might simply get an oral warning before suspension or dismissal. If you think you are going to be dismissed from a job, you might want to look for another job. You might also consider looking for another job when you can't resolve a problem with your supervisor.

Resolving Employee Rights Issues

It's important to know your rights as an employee. Your rights are based on these factors:

- **Federal and State Employment Laws**   The federal and state governments place certain restrictions and requirements on all employers. The US Department of Labor contains an "Employment Law Guide" that can be found at www.dol.gov/elaws/elg. In addition to federal employment laws, there are local laws. Local employment laws vary from one location to another and are impossible to summarize here. The US Department of Labor has created a link to help you discover the employment laws in each state at https://www.dol.gov/whd/state/state.htm.

- **Personnel Policies**   Some organizations have personnel policies that describe the behavior expected from an employee, as well as employee rights. Courts consider personnel policies to be a formal contract between an employer and employees.
- **Union Contract**   An employer might sign a contract with a labor union. The contract might describe some personnel policies. Employees are expected to follow all of these policies; the employer must do likewise.

Understand that an organization or supervisor might not follow all laws and policies. Employees might be unhappy with these circumstances. Remember, a disagreement with an employer caused by a violation of a law or policy is called a "grievance."

You might want to file a grievance with a supervisor. However, decide how important a problem is before you discuss it with your supervisor. Employees who question possible violations of laws, policies, and procedures might be viewed as troublemakers. If the problem is serious and you do decide to pursue the matter, follow these three guidelines:

1. **Discuss the problem with your supervisor.** Approach the conversation in a calm and respectful manner. Keep in mind that you might not correctly understand the situation. Give your supervisor an opportunity to explain why the problem might not be as serious as you think, and then request a solution.

2. **Contact the personnel office or the organization's owner.** This action is recommended if the supervisor doesn't correct the problem or if you feel the explanation is inadequate. Personnel handbooks usually describe the process you should follow when appealing a supervisor's actions. Discuss your concerns and how they can be satisfied. Always do this in a polite and nonthreatening manner. Be aware that your relationship with your supervisor might be negatively affected by this action.

3. **Contact a law-enforcing government agency.** If the company doesn't correct the problem, the government agency responsible for enforcing the related laws may be able to help. Sometimes specific laws protect employees from being fired. When you approach a government agency to file a complaint, you'll find that the follow-through—such as finding the right person to talk to, meeting with government officials to explain the problem, documenting your claims—requires a great deal of time. You might be required to testify at formal hearings.

It's important to weigh the time requirements and pressures that are a part of such formal complaints against the benefits of having an employer change its illegal practices. Also, consider that if you apply for another job and that employer discovers you have reported another employer to a government agency, the organization might be reluctant to hire you. A job coach, career counelor, or legal advisor may be helpful in these situations.

Summing Up

Supervisors are people, too. Whether they are excellent or poor leaders, all supervisors appreciate good employees. Supervisors can't do their jobs without them. If you practice the guidelines in this chapter, you will increase the chances of establishing a positive relationship with your supervisor. If a problem does develop between you and your supervisor, try to resolve it. If a formal procedure is necessary or your supervisor takes disciplinary action against you, make sure that you understand how your organization handles such situations. Always try to abide by your employer's rules and guidelines.

Review and Assessment

Take the Review Quiz. See your instructor or reference your student files in the ebook for additional resources.

CHAPTER 9

Getting along with Coworkers

Objectives

- Evaluate personality traits and personal values and how they work together in the workplace.

- Assess the ways diversity makes a team stronger.

- Identify ways to resolve conflicts with coworkers.

Teamwork is important in any business operation. Most managers and supervisors use **teams** to get work done. A survey of over 7,000 executives found that 90% of them thought improving organization design was critical and that teams were an important part of that activity. The use of teams is common in modern organizations and is a growing trend worldwide.[1]

Sometimes organizations use terms like *quality circles, self-managing groups, self-directed groups,* or *project pods* to refer to their teams. Even if your organization does not use the word *team* to refer to a work group—also known as department, office, center, division, unit, branch, or store—leaders expect you to work with other employees as part of a team. Team members maximize productivity if they can learn to work together and adapt to each other's working styles. In this way, teams are truly a way for everyone to win—you, the leader, the group, and the organization.

As you read this chapter, some ideas may sound similar to those in previous chapters. This chapter also looks at positive human relationships. Learning to have good relationships with everyone you work with will make a job more interesting and enjoyable. Specifically, collaboration is a key to success and promotion to a leadership role.[2]

Collaboration means working well with others to accomplish work. The ideas in this chapter will help you better understand how to collaborate with employees.

Watch the Video

Getting along with Coworkers

Get to Know Your Coworkers

It is difficult to be part of the team if you don't know how to get along with the other members. Getting to know your **coworkers** and being accepted by them will help you succeed in your job.

Gaining Coworker Acceptance Checklist

Here are several situations describing how you might interact with coworkers. If you think the situation will help you gain acceptance from coworkers, write a *Y* in the space provided. If not, write an *N*.

_____ Greet your coworkers when you arrive at work.

_____ Join the office intramural sports league.

_____ Ask a coworker to join you for lunch.

_____ Invite your coworkers to a party at your home.

_____ Tell the group how much another worker spent on a new car.

_____ Bring Aunt Sally's handmade rugs to sell to your coworkers.

_____ Tell the latest ethnic joke during a coffee break.

_____ Loan a book you enjoyed to a fellow worker.

_____ Offer to take on additional duties when a coworker has to leave suddenly to tend to a sick child.

_____ Repeat the latest rumor about the boss's relationship with a coworker.

_____ Tell the boss when one of your coworkers leaves early.

_____ Tell the group how to do the job better.

_____ Tell the group how well the boss thinks you are doing.

_____ Offer to give a coworker a ride to the auto-repair shop.

Fitting into a team is an important skill to learn. It requires patience to become part of a team. It takes some time before you know how to work well with the other employees in your work group. Everyone likes to be respected for skills, knowledge, or other contributions to the group productivity, but that respect doesn't come right away. If you do your job well, your coworkers' respect for you will increase over time. Meanwhile, these tips can help you earn that respect:

- **Know Your Position**   Find out what other workers expect from you. Keep in mind that these ideas should be balanced with your supervisor's expectations. Other workers might have a specific method they use to do a job. If you do it differently, you might upset their system. Other workers also might expect a newcomer to take over certain tasks, for instance cleaning up after a project at the end of the day. Go along with reasonable tasks the group expects you to do as the newest employee. Eventually, another new worker will be hired and will take over these tasks.

Discussion Activity

How does each of the tips that help you earn respect from team members relate to your answers in the Gaining Coworker Acceptance Checklist?

- **Accept Good-natured Teasing**   Workers sometimes play jokes and tease new employees to test what kind of person they are. If this happens, don't get angry. Let others know you appreciate a good joke. If this behavior doesn't cease and makes it difficult for you to do your work, you might want to talk to coworkers about it. If this doesn't reduce the teasing, you might consider discussing it with the supervisor. However, if you think the jokes or teasing constitute bullying or racial/sexual harassment, immediately inform your supervisor.

- **Do Your Fair Share**   All team members are expected to do their best. If you don't do your fair share of the work, your coworkers have to do more. After a while, they might complain to the supervisor. The flip side is that other workers also might complain if you do too much work because that can make them look bad. Supervisors reward good workers with salary increases and promotions, but you should try to balance the expectations of your supervisor and your coworkers. When in doubt, do what the supervisor expects.

- **Don't Do Other People's Work**   As a team member, you should cooperate and help others when asked. However, some people try to take advantage of this cooperative spirit and push their work off on others. Remember, your supervisor will evaluate you based on how well you do *your* job. If your job suffers because you are doing someone else's work, you are likely to receive a lower evaluation.

- **Know How Your Team Functions**   How does your team relate to other teams in the organization? What are each team's responsibilities? Remember that all teams work to accomplish the employer's goals. However, conflicts sometimes occur. Discuss these problems with all people involved. Avoid letting conflicts affect your working relationships with members of other teams. Contact your supervisor when you can't resolve conflicts with other teams. You should all be working for the best interests of the organization.

Synergy

Synergy describes the extra energy and capability that results in combined group efforts to accomplish an objective. Because of synergy, a team can accomplish more than the same number of individuals working independently can. With synergy, $1 + 1 = 3$. That's why teamwork is so important to an organization. You should cooperate in every effort to develop synergy with your coworkers.

In the month that Rick has worked in the warehouse, he has gotten to know a couple of the other workers pretty well. In fact, he went to a baseball game with Don last weekend. When he unwrapped his sandwich at lunch today, there was no meat in it. Rick turned to the other workers and yelled that he was sick and tired of their jokes and then stomped out of the lunchroom, slamming the door behind him.

1. How do you think the other workers will react to Rick's outburst?

   _____

   _____

   _____

2. What should Rick have done in this situation to create a more positive relationship with other workers?

   _____

   _____

   _____

Lynette has worked at Hoover's Pharmacy for four days. Yesterday, a customer broke a bottle of perfume. Mika, who has worked at Hoover's slightly longer than Lynette, told Lynette to clean up the mess. Lynette cleaned up the mess. Today, a small child knocked over a display of cough medicine. Tim, who has worked at Hoover's for five years, told Lynette to restack the boxes. Lynette got upset and told Tim to do it himself.

1. How do you think this will make the other workers feel about Lynette?

   _____

   _____

   _____

2. What do you think Lynette should have done in this situation?

   _____

   _____

   _____

The Value of Diversity

You will work with many people who are different from you. The growing **diversity** of the US workforce described in Chapter 1 affects most organizations. Diversity in an organization can be good. Diverse teams work well when they share information, cooperate, trust each other, and have a leader who makes everyone feel included. However, organization experts have not found a definite answer as to whether diverse teams perform better than teams where all members are similar.[3] Let's explore three common ways people differ: preferences, temperaments, and individual characteristics (such as gender, ethnicity, and age).

Group Activity

Write five of your positive characteristics. Gather the lists and shuffle them. Try to guess which list belongs to each person.

Preferences

Preferences are the values we give to ideas, things, or people. Parents, friends, teachers, religious and political leaders, significant events in our lives, the media, and our community all influence the development of our preferences.

Sometimes these preferences are referred to as "values." These values are not the same as moral or ethical values. Rather, they are situations, behaviors, structures, personal interactions, or other things on which we place value. Although our values can be quite different, organizational behavior expert Stephen Robbins suggests that based on their values, people fall into one of three categories:[4]

1. **Traditionalists:** People in this category value (prefer)
   - hard work;
   - loyalty to the organization;
   - doing things the way they've always been done;
   - the authority of leaders.

2. **Humanists:** People in this category value (prefer)
   - quality of life;
   - loyalty to self;
   - autonomy (self-direction);
   - leaders who are attentive to workers' needs.

3. **Pragmatists:** People in this category value (prefer)
   - success;
   - loyalty to career;
   - achievement;
   - leaders who reward people for hard work.

Which category do you fit into? Look over the values in each of the three categories. Circle those items that you value most. Note which category has the most items circled. Then in the space below, write the category that best describes you. Explain your reasons.

_____

_____

_____

_____

_____

_____

_____

_____

_____

_____

Discussion Activity

How might people with different preferences strengthen a work team?

An effective work team includes people who have values in each preference category (traditionalist, pragmatist, and humanist). At times, the team needs the traditionalist to make sure that the team does what is best for the organization. At other times, the team needs the humanist, who stresses the need to balance life and work. There also are times when the team needs the pragmatist, who will strive to advance the team because this also advances personal achievement. Each person's values contribute to the team.

Few people fit neatly into one category. However, we can better understand and appreciate our differences when we think about which category we and other people might fall into. We can't think in terms of right or wrong, or good or bad, when we talk about these value differences. Each set of values is sometimes positive and sometimes negative. Learn to appreciate the differences and be tolerant of people who hold a different set of values from your own.

Temperaments

Your **temperament** is the distinctive way you think, feel, and react to the world. Everyone has a unique temperament. However, it's easier to understand differences in temperaments by sorting people into categories. Management specialists assess temperaments through tests. One of the most famous tests is the Myers-Briggs Type Indicator. David Keirsey has adapted the Myers-Briggs to identify the following four categories of temperament:[5]

Discussion Activity

Consider four occupations (like judge, teacher, scientist and soldier). What types of temperaments are associated with each profession?

1. **Optimists:** People with this temperament
   - must be free and not tied down;
   - like to try new things;
   - are impulsive;
   - can survive major setbacks;
   - enjoy the immediate;
   - are generous;
   - enjoy action for action's sake;
   - are cheerful;
   - like working with things.

2. **Realists:** People with this temperament
   - like to belong to groups;
   - feel obligations strongly;
   - have a strong work ethic;
   - need order;
   - are realistic;
   - find tradition important;
   - are willing to do a job when asked;
   - are serious;
   - are committed to society's standards.

3. **Futurists:** People with this temperament
   - like to control things;
   - want to be highly competent;

- are the most self-critical of all temperaments;
- strive for excellence;
- judge people on their merits;
- cause people to feel they don't measure up;
- live for their work;
- are highly creative;
- tend to focus on the future.

4. **Idealists:** People with this temperament
   - are constantly in search of their "self;"
   - want to know the meanings of things;
   - value integrity;
   - write fluently;
   - are romantics;
   - have difficulty placing limits on work;
   - are highly personable;
   - appreciate people;
   - get along well with all temperaments.

What kind of temperament do you have? Go through the preceding descriptions and circle the items in each style that apply to you. The category in which you circle the most items is probably your temperament style.

1. What is your temperament style?

   _____

2. What is your secondary temperament style (the one with the second highest number of answers)?

   _____

No temperament style is better than another. In fact, a strong team includes people of varied temperaments. That said, people with different temperament styles often find one another difficult to deal with because of their distinct approaches to life. When differences arise between you and a person with a different temperament, follow these steps to resolve conflict:

1. Look for positive contributions the person makes to the team.
2. Identify characteristics of your temperament that conflict with the other person's temperament.
3. Talk with the person and explain what characteristics seem to cause conflict between you.
4. Ask the other person to describe which of your characteristics is most difficult to deal with.
5. Discuss a plan of action that you both can pursue to reduce conflict. Often just acknowledging the differences and being willing to discuss them will reduce the conflict.

Individual Characteristics

In Chapter 1, you saw that the US workforce has become more diverse over the past 20 years. This trend will continue throughout the coming decade. While the workforce of tomorrow is projected to grow at a slow rate of just 0.6%, the assorted groups within it will continue to differ in the following ways:[6]

- **Gender**   The percent of women participating in the workforce is expected to decline somewhat over the next 10 years. But women are still projected to make up 47.4% of the labor force in 2026.[7]
- **Ethnicity**   Increasing racial and ethnic diversity in the workplace will continue to be the trend. Blacks and Hispanics are expected to be nearly 33.3% of the workforce by 2026. Asians and members of other ethnic groups will make up another 11.1%. This means ethnic minorities will make up more than one-third of the workforce.
- **Age**   The number of workers ages 55 and over is expected to increase from 22.5% in 2016 to 24.8% in 2026. To put this in perspective, the number of workers in the 55-plus age group will grow three times faster than those of any other age group in the labor force. Employees in this age group will be the healthiest and most vital group of older workers in history.

Studies of team composition have found demographic differences to be less important to team success than differences based on preferences and temperaments.[8] However, having diversity based on demographic composition provides positive impressions about the appreciation leaders have for inclusivity. We know that leaders who create an inclusive environment have more productive teams.

No matter how different they are, each person can contribute to the team. It's important for all members of a team to share their thoughts and ideas. Understanding one another's viewpoints will help overcome many differences.

A Useful Skill: Persuasion

Persuasion is the ability to convince others to change their minds or behavior. Because workers are expected to make decisions as a team, being able to convince your coworkers to reach a point of agreement is a very useful skill. Gaining a promotion or making changes in your workplace may depend on your ability to use this skill.

Studies have shown that some people may be more gifted at convincing others; however, persuading others is not a natural talent. Learning how to persuade others is a soft skill that is being taught in business schools.

When developing this skill, you need to observe people. Study how your coworkers and superiors think when making decisions. Some people ask questions when processing information. Others make statements. Some people approach decisions in a calm manner, whereas others become very emotional. Recognizing these differences in individuals will make a difference in the methods of persuasion you use.

Basic Human Relations

Psychology and organizational behavior studies have helped us gain a better understanding of **human relations** in the workplace. To get along with workers on your team, consider some practical steps derived from these studies:

1. **Get to know other workers.** Take lunch breaks with your coworkers. Join employee recreational and social activities. Listen to the things your coworkers share about their personal lives and interests.

2. **Avoid trying to change everything.** You're "the new kid on the block" the first few months on a job. Know and understand the organization before you think about changing something. Listen to others. Talk to coworkers about your ideas and get some feedback before you suggest changes.

3. **Be honest.** One of the most important things you own is a good reputation. Honesty with your coworkers will build up your reputation. It's one of the best ways to gain and keep respect.

4. **Be direct.** Let people know when they do something that bothers you. Most people want to know when there is a problem. However, don't be a constant complainer or a whiner. Make sure that your problem is important before you discuss it with others.

5. **Avoid gossip.** Don't listen to other people gossiping about coworkers. More important, never gossip about others. When you gossip, people wonder what you say about them and often avoid you.

6. **Be positive and supportive.** Listen to the ideas of other people. When someone makes a mistake, don't criticize. It's irritating to have someone else point out a mistake. When you realize you've made a mistake, admit it and try to do better next time.

7. **Show appreciation.** Be sure you thank a coworker who does something to make your job easier. Let coworkers know you appreciate their contributions to the team. People like to be recognized and praised.

8. **Share credit when it's deserved.** Take credit for the work you do. When other coworkers assist you, make sure you credit them. People often feel they have been taken advantage of if someone else takes credit for their work.

9. **Return favors.** A coworker might help you out by exchanging a day off with you. Return that favor. A sure way to make people dislike you is to only take and never give.

10. **Live in the present.** Avoid talking about the way things used to be. People are often irritated to hear about how great your old job was or how great former coworkers were.

11. **Ask for help and advice when you need it.** People like to feel needed. Your coworkers can be a great resource. When you aren't sure what to do, coworkers can give you advice and assistance.

12. **Avoid battles.** Let coworkers in conflict work out their own differences. Don't take sides in their arguments. This is likely to cause problems with coworkers. When you take sides, other people usually resent the interference. Often both sides will become unhappy with you.

13. **Follow group standards.** Every group has standards—sociologists call these "mores." For example, your coworkers might take a coffee break at 9:15 a.m. Stop work and go on break with them if you are able. These group standards help build teamwork. Most standards are not major and require little effort to follow.

14. **Take an interest in your coworkers' jobs.** People like positive attention. Taking an interest in another worker's job gives that person positive attention. It also helps you better understand how your team works together.

How Job Savvy Are You?

Rosa's family has seven children and enjoys doing most things together. Her grandmother is celebrating her 85th birthday next Thursday, and the family has planned a surprise party for her. On Monday, when the work schedule is posted, Rosa sees she is scheduled to work Thursday evening. She is quite upset, although she knows she should have asked for the evening off before the schedule was made.

1. As a coworker, what could be your positive reaction to Rosa's problem?

   _____

   _____

   _____

2. What could be your negative reaction?

   _____

   _____

   _____

Tyler belongs to an animal rights group. He brings literature about animal rights to work and leaves it in the break room. He refuses to eat meat because he believes killing animals for food is wrong. Tyler has invited you to join him at the next animal rights meeting.

1. How could you react positively to Tyler's invitation?

   _____

   _____

   _____

2. How could you react negatively?

   _____

   _____

   _____

Continues

Gwen is a very hard worker. She comes to work early and stays late. She has to be reminded to take breaks. Her main interest is her job. Sometimes, she seems to be trying to outdo her coworkers.

1.　How could you react positively to Gwen's work habits?

_____

_____

_____

2.　How could you react negatively?

_____

_____

_____

Chang doesn't work on Saturdays because it's a holy day in his church and he attends services. Last Saturday, all personnel were required to work on a special project. Chang was excused from working. The entire work group is upset with him.

1.　How could you react positively to Chang's situation?

_____

_____

_____

2.　How could you react negatively?

_____

_____

_____

Good Electronic Manners

Most organizations today use voicemail, fax machines, email, texting, and collaborative software such as Slack and Google Hangouts. Experts say that fax machines are less popular than they were 10 years ago but are still used in law, healthcare, and government offices, and other offices where original signatures and security are important. Frequent use of technology has resulted in a new electronic etiquette. The following are guidelines for using communications technology:

Journal Activity

Look back at your answers to the previous How Job Savvy Are You? exercise. Reflect on your positive and negative reactions.

1.　**Leave voicemail messages that are short and concise.** It's frustrating to listen to long, rambling messages. Let the person know why you called, how urgent it is, and when you need a response.

2.　**Make sure that voicemail messages contain essential information.** Most important are your name, phone number, and when you can be reached.

3.　**When you place a voicemail greeting on your phone, keep it short.** Callers don't want to waste time hearing a poem or cute message, and they don't need your schedule for the week. Just let them know whether you are going to be able to return their call shortly or whether it will be a while.

4. **Avoid leaving messages that convey anger or frustration.** Otherwise, your message might not be returned. If it is returned, the person might be defensive or angry. Usually, it's better to have a face-to-face discussion about a serious problem.

5. **Avoid reading faxes sent to another person.** Reading someone else's fax is an invasion of privacy, similar to opening someone's mail.[9]

6. **Call, text, or email someone before sending a fax so the person knows it's on the way.** Include a cover page so that others at the receiving end know who should receive the fax.

Discussion Activity

Why are good manners important in email, fax, and voicemail communications?

7. **Follow company email policies.** For example, some organizations consider all email to be company property, and management may read any message. Employees have lost their jobs due to violating email policies.

8. **Avoid sending email messages on important matters if your message could result in a negative emotional reaction.** For example, sending a critical email might anger the recipient much more than a direct conversation would. A personal conversation lets you observe the person's reactions. It also lets you make clear anything that could be misinterpreted.

9. **Carefully consider whether to send copies of messages.** A general rule is that messages containing information can be copied to other people. A message that contains opinion, criticism, or private information should be kept private.

10. **Avoid "flaming."** This is a situation with electronic messaging that involves an exchange of a series of messages that become increasingly negative. For example, someone might make a suggestion and your response might be negative. The person returns a negative email to you. You send another email that is even more negative, and the process continues until someone has the good sense to stop. When it appears that flaming is happening, talk with the person directly to avoid more conflict.

11. **Don't use someone else's computer without asking.** Computers can contain confidential information. Using a computer without asking might be considered a violation of privacy, similar to going through someone's desk.

12. **Computer files should also be considered personal and confidential.** Files stored on a computer hard drive or any other media are private. You shouldn't take or look at any electronically filed information that doesn't belong to you.

13. **Be careful when you use social media.** Posting complaints about your coworkers, supervisor, managers, or company on Twitter, Facebook, Google+, or other social media is unwise. In some cases such statements might be viewed as bullying. Unless you want someone to report you for negative information you've written online, it is best not to post it. Employees have been terminated after they vented online. So think before you tweet.

Cubicle Etiquette

Many companies set up offices with worker cubicles because of the economic benefits and the flexibility of space. Working in a cubicle gives people easy access to coworkers; however, it limits their individual privacy. Because workers are so close together, problems can develop if they don't practice good cubicle **etiquette.**

Existing in the cubicle world can be challenging. Here are nine tips for working in a cube:

Discussion Activity

What are some privacy problems created in a cubicle environment? What tips might you use to overcome these problems?

1. **Use a reasonable voice volume.** Cubicles are not soundproof. Others can hear what you say. Use a quiet voice when conducting business.
2. **Use personal devices as per company policy.** Mute electronic devices. You might want to use headphones or ear buds not just to keep noise down in your area, but also to keep from being distracted. Take your personal cell phone with you when you leave your cube.
3. **Treat your coworkers' cubicles as offices.** Knock before entering. Wait until the person responds to you before walking in. If a coworker is on the phone or busy with someone else, leave and go back later.
4. **Hold conversations in the cube.** Sitting in your cube and talking to the person in the next cubicle disturbs everyone around you. Leaning over the wall for a conversation is just as distracting. When you need to speak to anyone, enter their cube for the conversation.
5. **Avoid overcrowding in the cubicle.** Unless you are meeting with only one other person, a cubicle is not large enough to hold a meeting. A conference room is a more appropriate place to have a meeting.
6. **Be considerate of others.** A cubicle office is shared space. Coworkers who hum, chew gum loudly, or clip their fingernails annoy others.
7. **Express your concern.** If you are unable to do your work because of a coworker's actions, politely discuss the problem with the individual. A direct approach is much kinder and more effective than gossiping about the individual or avoiding the problem.
8. **Avoid strong odors.** It is best to avoid using strong-smelling soaps, colognes, or perfume; setting items on your desk that are fragrant; or eating strong-smelling foods in your cubicle. Strong odors are not only offensive to some people, but they can also stimulate headaches, coughing, or sneezing reactions among your fellow employees.[10]

Special Problems with Coworkers

Some problems require special attention. These include **harassment**, dating conflicts, and violence. This section reviews what you should know about each topic.

Sexual Harassment

Sexual harassment is unwelcome verbal or physical conduct of a sexual nature. The following list provides examples of sexual harassment but is by no means a complete list:

- Staring at another person
- Touching another person without their permission
- Telling sexual jokes
- Making sexual comments
- Commenting on a person's sexual characteristics or appearance
- Displaying nude pictures or obscene cartoons

Employers are required by law to protect employees from sexual harassment. You could be severely disciplined or fired for harassing a coworker sexually. The safest course is to reference the company policies and act professionally at all times. Even if a person doesn't object to your behavior at the time, this does not make the behavior acceptable. Just because someone doesn't confront you directly doesn't mean the issue hasn't been brought to the attention of a supervisor or HR.

Discussion Activity

What should you do if you are the victim of harassment?

Racial Harassment

Racial harassment is unwelcome verbal or physical actions directed at people because of their race. Racial harassment might include these behaviors:

- Telling racial jokes
- Using racial slurs
- Commenting on a person's racial characteristics
- Distributing racist materials
- Excluding someone from company activities because of race

This form of harassment may result from ignorance. It may be difficult to stand up for yourself or others in the face of harassment, but don't participate in any of these behaviors. Also, you may want to point out the harm that can result from harassment, if you feel comfortable doing so. You can also report the harassment privately to HR if you are concerned for your own safety or the safety of others.

Dating Conflicts

You can get to know someone well by working together, and office relationships sometimes develop into romantic relationships. Many people find that the workplace is a natural place to meet people to date. But dating a coworker can be risky. For one thing, romantic advances might be considered sexual harassment. In fact, repeatedly asking someone for a date after being turned down *is* considered sexual harassment.

Dating a coworker can have a negative effect on your relationships with other workers. They might think that you take advantage of your romantic relationship, that you are not doing your own work but sharing work with your romantic interest, or that you support that person's ideas or actions simply because you are dating him or her.

Another problem that can result from dating a coworker is that your attention would no longer be on your job. You might be thinking about the other person instead of concentrating on your work. You might engage in romantic small talk rather than work, or find yourself supporting your sweetheart's actions and ideas even when you have doubts about them.

Breaking up is another concern to think about. What effect will your breakup have on your job performance and working relationship with the person? When you must work with that person every day, you might experience a great deal of discomfort and stress.

Some organizations have a policy prohibiting coworkers from dating or limiting who can date whom (for example, they might not allow a supervisor to date a person who reports to him or her). Be sure to find out whether your employer has such a policy. If you develop a romantic interest in a coworker, follow the company policies first. As a general rule of thumb, be discreet. Don't talk about your relationship specifics in the office. Don't spend any more time with that person than is normally required as part of your job when you are on the clock. Try to separate how you behave toward the person at work from how you behave on a date.

Conflict Resolution

As we learned in Chapter 8, conflict resolution seeks to solve a disagreement between individuals or groups within an organization. The purpose of conflict resolution is to avoid emotion, stress, and violence while dealing with the facts. Companies usually have a process in place for employees to use.

First, attempt to resolve the problem between you and the other person. Go to the other person and calmly discuss the problem. If this attempt fails, go to your supervisor. Calmly and concisely explain the problem. Given time, your supervisor may be able to deal with the problem. If your supervisor is unable to resolve the problem, go to human resources for help. If your firm doesn't have a human resources department, go to your supervisor's manager.

Remember that if another person violates the law and no one in the organization takes action, you should report it to legal authorities. Realize that you may lose your job, but your safety is more important.

Violence in the Workplace

In 2016, there were 16,890 workers who suffered injuries form workplace violence. There were 500 homicides.[11] People who are critically injured at work make headlines, but fistfights are far more common in the workplace. So what can you do to avoid violence? Thomas Capozzoli and Steve McVey are two experts on the workplace who provide the following advice.[12]

Discussion Activity

How can you avoid violence in the workplace?

- People sometimes get angry. When you get angry in return, it creates the potential for violence. When you feel angry, tell the person that you want to solve the problem at a later date when you are not feeling angry. Walk away from the person, if necessary.

- If a coworker threatens you with violence, notify your supervisor. Co-workers who threaten violence can be fired.
- Violence sometimes occurs because a worker has mental or emotional health conditions—disorders that affect mood, thinking, and behavior. Examples of mental illness include depression, anxiety disorders, schizophrenia, eating disorders, and addictive behaviors.[13] Other workers might appear to always be angry; they might verbally or physically strike out at everyone. Talk with your supervisor when you observe behaviors that are impacting a coworker's communication or professional performance. If a coworker has done self-harm or is considering doing so, take the person to the hospital or call for emergency help.
- Violence often occurs due to marital disputes that spill over into the workplace. Don't hesitate to call the police when a spouse who should not be there enters the workplace.
- Follow all security procedures to protect yourself and coworkers. Keep doors locked, don't allow strangers into the building, and report suspicious behavior.
- Working in places open to the public—such as convenience stores—requires special security guidelines. Every retail chain has security guidelines. Take time to learn the guidelines and follow them for your own safety and that of your coworkers.

Not all violence can be prevented, but following some simple guidelines can reduce it. Carefully observe your surroundings and people in the workplace. Report unusual situations to your supervisor or security guards.

Summing Up

Becoming part of the work team is important to your success on the job. Your relationship with other workers will affect your performance. Your contribution to the team will influence how your supervisor appraises your job performance.

Getting along with your coworkers is not difficult. It takes an understanding of yourself and an appreciation of differences among people. Finally, it takes a commonsense approach to human relations. When all else fails, treat your coworkers as you would like to be treated.

Review and Assessment

Take the Review Quiz. See your instructor or reference your student files in the ebook for additional resources.

Meeting the Customer's Expectations

Customers are very important. They buy products or services that then allow an organization to function and make a profit. Without customers, an organization will fail. This is why organizations conduct studies to learn what their **customers** want. Government and nonprofit agencies also need to serve customers well because customer satisfaction affects public support and funding.

A recent study indicates that after experiencing poor service one time, 33% of customers will not go back to the business. If a customer experiences two to three cases of bad service, 60% of them will not return. Good **customer service** results in increased customer spending and referrals. Employees who provide good customer service are highly valued. In fact, 69% of customers report they will spend more at a business with good customer service, and 90% of customers tell other people about their good experience. By providing good service experiences, businesses build customer loyalty.[1]

In this chapter, you will learn about good customer service and related skills. You have already learned many of the skills you need to provide good customer service, specifically in building relationships with leaders and colleagues at work. One key difference is that your contact with customers occurs less frequently and usually for brief time periods. That is why you must work harder to make the time you spend with them positive. This chapter will help you learn how to be successful at serving customers.

Watch the Video

Meeting the Customer's Expectations

The Customer Is Always Right

Providing good customer service is a key ingredient of any organization's success. Businesses spend billions of dollars advertising and promoting products or services in an effort to get new customers. A customer's decision to buy now and in the future is affected by how an organization can satisfy his or her needs in three areas: price, quality, and customer service. This means manufacturing workers should strive to make high-quality products. Knowledge workers should create valid, reliable, and dependable information. Service workers should provide a pleasant and productive experience for customers. Every employee should work efficiently to keep prices low.

According to one study, businesses lose customers primarily for the reasons listed in Table 10.1.[2]

Table 10.1 Reasons Customers Don't Return

Reason for Not Returning	Percentage of Respondents
Natural reasons (death, moved, etc.)	4%
Influenced by friends	5%
Price	9%
Dissatisfied with product	14%
Turned away by indifference on the part of an employee	68%

This study illustrates how critical customer service is. The service you provide to customers makes a major difference in their decision to patronize your organization or spend their money elsewhere.

Most of us experience customer service daily when we go to the grocery store, buy gas for the car, eat at a restaurant, call a business, or buy clothes. Our most common activities often make us customers. Use the following exercise to think about your experiences as a customer and what good customer service means.

Discussion Activity

What does good customer service mean?

Customer Service Checklist

In the following checklist, mark the items that demonstrate good customer service.

- ❑ Smiling at customers
- ❑ Greeting customers
- ❑ Opening doors for customers
- ❑ Answering phone calls in a cheerful manner

- ❑ Forwarding a customer's call without first asking what their needs are
- ❑ Talking with friends while customers wait
- ❑ Telling customers that you want to address their concerns

Continues

- ❑ Asking customers if they need help
- ❑ Letting customers wander around the store looking for something
- ❑ Listening politely to what customers are saying
- ❑ Calling back customers who leave phone messages
- ❑ Doing exactly what customers request
- ❑ Putting customers on hold for a long time
- ❑ Expressing anger at customers who yell at you
- ❑ Telling customers about all the bad customer service you've had at other businesses

As a customer, what has made you feel good about a business?

_____

_____

_____

_____

What has made you upset with a business?

_____

_____

_____

_____

One simple definition of good customer service is treating customers the way that you would like to be treated—perhaps the way that you would want your grandmother treated. The exercise you just completed gave you some guidelines for how to do this. In the next section, we look at some specific ways to provide good customer service.

Providing Good Customer Service

Customer service begins the moment customers contact your business. Contact can be a face-to-face meeting, a phone call, a letter, a fax, an email, or even a visit to the organization's website. Your treatment of customers results in several possible reactions. First, it affects how customers treat you. Second, it determines whether customers buy the product or service your business is selling. Third, it affects how customers think about your organization and whether they will return.

It's helpful to understand some base customer service statistics relevant to our world today. When customers have simple inquiries, 63% of them want to use electronic resources (website, mobile app, online chat, or voice response system). When there are complex issues, such as disputes or complaints, 23% of customers want face-to-face contact with an employee and 40% want to talk with an employee on the phone.[3] The desire for personal contact means when customers get in touch with an employee they are expecting a high level of service. The following suggestions for customer service will help customers feel good about the service they receive.

Have a Good Attitude

Customer service begins with you and your attitude. It's easy to get caught up in the busywork that makes up every job and to think that it's the most important thing you do. But think again. Serving customers is actually the most important thing you do. When a customer asks for assistance, don't think of responding promptly as an interruption of your work. Instead, consider it your primary job.

Too often, employees see customers as a nuisance. Frequently, these employees might keep talking on the phone, doing paperwork, or working on other things while the customer waits. A customer senses this attitude, and the encounter starts off on the wrong foot. The next time you think of a customer as a disruption, remember this: The customer is the person who actually pays your salary. Without customers, there are no jobs.

Make the Customer Feel Good

You should go out of your way to help customers who seek service from your organization. Be polite and **courteous**, and always think about the customer's needs. Courtesy makes a business competitive. A nice smile helps make people feel happy. When you encounter customers, politely ask how you may help them. Say please and thank you. Thanking customers, holding doors open, and carrying packages are all courteous actions that help customers feel good about your service.

Greet Customers

An organization's customers should feel welcome when they enter or contact the business. Many large discount and grocery stores now employ greeters to specifically welcome shoppers. Think about times when you've gone into a business only to have an employee ignore you. You probably don't feel like going back to the business again.

Whenever customers enter a business, immediately acknowledge their presence. A greeting should be polite and make the customer feel that you're interested and ready to help. For example, say "Hello, may I help you?" Some employees make the following three mistakes at this point—mistakes that you should avoid:

1. **Don't talk too long with customers.** Balancing the needs of several customers at once can be difficult, but it's important, otherwise a customer might feel unwelcome. When a second customer comes into your work area, politely excuse yourself from the first customer. Go to the new customer, and tell the person you'll help as soon as you're done with the first customer.

2. **Don't focus on other tasks.** Remember, giving customer service is your first and most important task. Have you ever gone into a business and had to wait for an employee to finish a task? How did it make you feel? Finishing up a task instead of acknowledging a customer could result in the customer feeling less important. Put aside your task, even if it means repeating steps when you go back to it.

3. **Don't try to talk on the phone or text.** Customers who visit your workplace in person took the time to travel there. You should show an appreciation for this by immediately paying attention to their needs. This is particularly true if the visit is to specifically talk to you. Even when you are talking to another employee, it should be understood that the customer comes first. If you are talking with a customer on the phone and another customer walks in to visit you, you might want to tell the person on the phone that you have to put him or her on hold for just a few seconds. While the first customer is on hold, explain the situation to the new customer and let the person know you'll be available shortly.

Case Study

Jackson is showing a customer a video camera. The phone rings. How should he handle this situation?

Listen to the Customer

Practice good listening skills when talking with customers. The customer has all the information you need to provide top-notch service.[4] However, customers can't always express their needs clearly. Your role is to make sure that the customer's needs are unmistakable and understood by both parties. The following tips can help:

Group Activity

Work together to create two lists with examples of body language that communicates "I'm listening" and "I'm not listening."

- **Be Attentive**   Assure customers that you are listening. A greeting can verbally express this fact. Look a customer in the eye and display body language that shows your interest. Smiling, nodding, and similar body language indicate that you are paying attention.

- **Listen Without Interrupting**   Let customers explain what they want without interrupting. Getting your point across and remembering your train of thought are more difficult when someone interrupts. You might have questions as customers speak, but wait until they have finished talking to ask those questions. In fact, when you take time to listen to everything that customers have to say, many of your questions get answered.

- **Control Your Reaction**   There are times when customers may be angry. It is important to control your emotional reactions. You don't need to fully understand what has caused a customer to use harsh words, yell, or even use abusive language. Here are some ways to handle difficult customers: explain that you are there to help them, that you understand they are upset, and that you will try to solve their problem. Be honest about what you can do to resolve their problem. It may be necessary to ask a manager or more experienced employee to talk with the customer if you are unable to offer a satisfactory solution. Should a customer threaten you or continue to use abusive language, warn them you will end the call if you are talking by phone. When face to face with a customer, warn the person you will call security or the police if the threatening behavior continues. This action is a last resort but leads to a safer workplace for everyone.[5]

- **Ask Questions**   Once customers have expressed a need or placed an order, ask open-ended questions (that can't be answered yes or no) to make sure you fully understand everything they need from you. When customers use a word or term that isn't familiar to you, ask for an explanation. When customers ramble on and you aren't sure what they need, ask specific questions to identify the exact needs. For example, you might ask, "Exactly what would you like to do?" or "What do you want to happen?"

- **Repeat the Need**   When you think that you understand what a customer wants, repeat it. This ensures that you both are clear about what is expected. If the customer confirms that you are correct, then you can provide the requested service. If there is still some misunderstanding, ask more questions and then repeat what you believe the customer wants. Continue this process until everyone is in agreement about what the customer wants.

- **Negotiate the Final Result**   It's not always possible to give the customer exactly what he or she wants. When this happens, you must negotiate.[6] Your goal is to create a win-win outcome, in which the customer and you each get something positive out of the situation. You might be able to do this by offering an alternative to what the customer wants.

    For example, suppose that a person comes into a government employment program office and asks for assistance with preparing a résumé. However, the program does not provide this service. It does offer a workshop on job-seeking techniques, which would serve the person better than a single résumé would. The workshop teaches how to prepare a résumé, but, more importantly, it teaches job seekers everything they need to know about finding a job. This is really what the customer needs. The customer wins because the person has a real need met, and you win because the office can serve one more person.

Take Action

As soon as you know what the customer wants, you can take action to provide the service or product. This is where you can make a positive impression. Give customers the product and service they want . . . and more. Meeting a customer's expectations results in a satisfied customer, but going beyond what is expected creates a satisfied and loyal customer. How do you go beyond what customers expect? Do exactly what they request. Then do something special. For example, let's say a customer orders a diet cola. Get the cola as quickly as possible, because this action is expected. Then tell the customer that refills are free (if this is restaurant policy). Even when a free-refill drink policy is assumed—regardless if you might know it, and regular customers might know it—telling the customers there are free refills makes them feel good and appreciate the service.

Discussion Activity

What can you do to exceed a customer's expectations? Why is it important to do so?

How Job Savvy Are You?

Omar works as a certified nursing assistant in a hospital. A patient in his assigned area just had back surgery, making it difficult for him to get out of bed without assistance. In the past hour, the patient has turned on the service light three times. Omar has always been busy doing something else when he called for help.

1. If you were Omar, what would you do to create a positive relationship with the customer?

   _____

   _____

2. What could Omar do to show exceptional customer service to the patient?

   _____

   _____

Janet works as an auto mechanic in an independent repair shop. One afternoon, she is at the shop by herself working on an alignment job when a customer comes in. Janet is at a point where it is difficult to stop what she is doing without having to repeat some of the work.

1. What should Janet do?

   _____

   _____

2. What can she do to make the customer feel welcomed?

   _____

   _____

Iliana works for an insurance agent. A policyholder comes into the office and wants to get an insurance rider for her new computer. The customer didn't bring the serial number for the computer with her. Iliana can't complete the necessary forms for the coverage without the serial number.

1. How do you think this situation makes the customer feel?

   _____

   _____

2. What can Iliana do to help satisfy the customer's needs?

   _____

   _____

Basic Customer Needs

Every customer has specific needs. However, all customers come to an organization with some basic needs. Marketing and branding consultants Karen Leland and Keith Bailey identify six basic customer needs:

1. Friendliness
2. Understanding and empathy
3. Fairness
4. Control
5. Options and alternatives
6. Information[7]

As you serve customers, keep these basic needs in mind and try to meet them. If you do, the customer usually will be satisfied, even when you can't meet a specific need.

For example, let's say you go into a sporting goods store looking for a particular brand of running shoes. The clerk smiles and greets you in a friendly way, tells you the style you want is very popular, and comments on your wise choice in running gear. Next, he checks the stockroom and tells you that your size is not in stock. When he checks the computer record, he tells you that a new shipment of shoes will be delivered next week. The clerk gives you the option of reserving the shoes in your size, making it clear that you don't have to buy the shoes if you don't want them. He also tells you that the running store in the mall might have the shoes you want.

When you leave the store, you don't have the shoes, but chances are you feel good about the service you received because the clerk met your basic needs.

Providing Good Customer Service on the Phone

Most businesses serve customers via phone. Some enterprises, such as carry-out restaurants, catalog dealers, and computer-support hotlines, do business primarily by telephone. Consequently, knowing how to give good customer service by phone is important.

Answer the Phone Promptly

People calling a business expect to get an answer quickly. If the phone rings too many times, the caller often hangs up. Many businesses direct employees to answer a call in no more than three rings.

You should make an attempt to answer the phone as quickly as possible. Stop whatever you're doing and come back to the task after answering the phone. If you're talking with someone else, consider politely putting the caller on hold and going back to fulfill the first customer's needs, then going back to the caller.

Greet the Caller Properly

You should give callers several points of information when you answer the phone. First, identify your business by name so that customers know right

> **Journal Activity**
>
> Call or visit three different businesses in your area and record your positive and negative feedback to their customer service.

away that they have reached the right number. Second, identify yourself by your first name. Giving your last name isn't necessary at this point because the caller probably won't remember both. Third, ask how you can help the caller.

Your greeting should change slightly if a receptionist or automatic answering service has greeted customers previously. In that case, customers already know that they have reached the proper business. You need only give your name and ask how you might help.

Listen to the Customer

To find out a customer's needs over the phone, follow the previously discussed guidelines for listening to a customer who comes to your business. Listening carefully to what the person is saying in a phone conversation is even more important than it is in a face-to-face encounter because by phone you aren't able to observe body language. Ask questions that help you understand what the customer needs. When you are certain that you know what the customer wants, repeat the information.

Take Action

Once you have heard what the customer wants, explain exactly what you are going to do. This reassures the caller because he or she can't see what you are doing. Once the customer understands what you plan to do, you can complete the action.

Phone Etiquette

Putting a Customer on Hold

While trying to satisfy a request, you might have to put a caller on hold. Being put on hold can be frustrating. To make this a more pleasant experience for the caller, follow these steps:

1. Briefly explain what you need to do and why it is necessary to put the person on hold.
2. Estimate the time it will take to complete the action. For example, you might say, "It's going to be approximately a minute before I can get back to you."
3. Ask whether you may put the caller on hold.
4. Offer to call the customer back if your actions will take more than two or three minutes.
5. It might take longer than you had anticipated to complete the task, and your caller might become anxious. Time waiting on the phone often seems longer than it actually is. You can reduce a customer's frustration by picking up the phone and explaining the situation.
6. Inform the customer of the action you have taken, and thank him or her for waiting.

Putting a customer on hold can cause a negative reaction. The person might get tired of waiting and hang up, get irritated, call back and ask for a manager, or decide not to wait and never patronize the business again. Unless it is absolutely necessary, you should avoid putting a customer on hold.

Continues

Transferring a Call

At times, a customer needs help that only one of your coworkers can provide. In this case, you need to transfer the phone call to the other employee. Like being put on hold, being transferred can irritate customers. From their point of view, you are passing the buck or don't know your job. Keep in mind that their perception might not be reality. Following these steps will help keep the customer happy:

1. Explain why you can't satisfy the request.
2. Tell the caller the name of the person who can fulfill the request.
3. Ask the caller whether he or she understands or has any questions before being transferred.
4. Make sure that the employee to whom you are transferring the call takes it.
5. If the employee is not available, explain that you will take a message and have that person return the call.

Taking a Message

If a customer needs to talk to another employee but that person is unavailable, you should take a message. Assure the customer that the call will be returned. As you take a message, follow these steps:

1. In a positive way, explain that the employee isn't available. For example, say the employee is in a meeting, currently out of the office, or whatever other task the employee might be doing.
2. Tell the caller when you expect the employee to be available. Use a general time frame such as today, tomorrow, at the end of the week, or next week. If you expect the employee to return a call the same day, you might say the person is expected to be available before lunch, after lunch, or by the end of the workday.
3. Ask the caller whether he or she would like to leave a message.
4. Ask the caller for a name, a phone number, and the reason for the call. If you aren't sure how to spell a name, ask.
5. Repeat the information to make sure it's correct.
6. Assure the caller that the message will be passed on and that a return call will be made.
7. After the caller hangs up, be sure to send the message by text or email to the employee. If you write a message on paper, write clearly and place the message where the employee will see the message.

Good customer service requires that messages be received and calls be returned. Make sure that you do your part by getting the message to someone else. When you receive a message that a customer called you, return the call as quickly as possible.

Providing Good Online Customer Service

Customer service is not limited to face-to-face encounters and phone conversations. With the use of online shopping, banking, and bill paying, dealing with customers online is an important part of the business world. Customers may be unhappy with merchandise or services. They might ask billing questions. Customers might not understand how to use the business's website and need help.

Good customer service online requires understanding what the consumer wants. The ability to write a clear, concise response is very important. Many businesses have standard responses that can fulfill these principles for clarity.

Chatting, another form of online communication, allows customers to communicate with customer service representatives as if they were face-to-face. When you are dealing with customers online, it is important to reply in a helpful and courteous manner as if the customer were actually standing in front of you.

How Job Savvy Are You?

Burton works at Marconi's Pizza Shop. The shop has a dining room and a delivery service. Burton answers the phone between making pizzas. His hectic job allows little time for breaks.

1. What problems might Burton have with giving good customer service?

   _____

   _____

   _____

2. If you were Burton, how would you answer the phone?

   _____

   _____

   _____

Allison is a sales clerk in a dress shop. While waiting on a customer, she hears the phone ring. She is the only employee in the shop.

1. How should Allison handle the situation?

   _____

   _____

   _____

2. What should she tell the customer before she answers the phone?

   _____

   _____

   _____

Continues

Continued

Stephen, a reference librarian at a university library, is looking up information for a patron when the phone rings. The caller needs to verify some statistics for a term paper.

1. What should Stephen do with the customer he is serving?

   _____

   _____

   _____

2. How should Stephen handle the customer on the phone?

   _____

   _____

   _____

Dealing with Difficult Customers

Occasionally you will have to deal with difficult customers. The difficulty can result from the customer's complaint, anger, or rudeness. You can take some simple steps to help yourself and the customer in each of these situations.

Customers with Complaints

Every business receives customer complaints. Customers might complain because of a problem your organization created. For example, a customer might have bought a faulty product or received an order late. A customer might feel that the product doesn't do what it should or that he or she received poor service.

At other times, a "problem" with your product or service might be the customer's fault. For example, a customer who broke the product, gave the wrong address for the product to be shipped to, or didn't read a description carefully before ordering a product might still want the company to fix the problem or share the blame. Regardless of the reason for the complaint, keep in mind that resolving a customer complaint will probably result in a happy and loyal customer. Try these eight steps for resolving customer complaints:

1. Listen carefully as the customer explains the problem.
2. If the customer is angry, let them vent their anger as long as it is kept in control and doesn't offend you or other customers.
3. Ask questions until you are sure you understand the complaint, and then repeat what you understand the complaint to be.
4. Find out what will satisfy the customer. Often, the complaint can be satisfied with a direct action. For example, a faulty product can be replaced. Other times, a complaint can't be resolved immediately. For example, late delivery of a product can't be undone. However, efforts can be made to be on time with the next delivery.

Discussion Activity

What types of complaints might customers have? What might cause customers to be angry or rude?

Group Activity

Identify ways to handle difficult customers who are disturbing other customers.

5. Compare what the customer wants with the actions you can take. You may not be authorized to do everything the customer requests. If this happens, tell the customer that you must discuss the matter with your supervisor. You should also contact the supervisor when the customer requests to speak to someone with more authority.

6. Tell the customer exactly what you plan to do to resolve the problem. Be sure that you can follow through on everything you promise, or you'll end up with a bigger complaint later.

7. Take the action you promised, and let the customer know what is going to happen. Sometimes this is clear when you simply hand over a new product. Other resolutions are more involved—such as reprimanding an employee for rudeness.

8. Contact the customer after the action is taken, and make sure the person is now satisfied.

Angry Customers

Customers sometimes become angry, and there can be many reasons for their anger. Usually, the anger is in reaction to poor service or bad products. Now and then, customers carry over their anger from another event and unload it on your business. For example, a customer who has been arguing with a spouse over a purchase might come into your store angry. Use these guidelines to respond positively to an angry customer:

- Tell the customer that you want to help correct the situation that made the person angry.
- Explain to the customer that being angry makes it difficult to understand the problem.
- Ask the customer to explain the reason for the anger, and use the same process for clarifying a need that was described previously.
- Explain what you can do to resolve the problem, and ask the customer whether the solution is satisfactory. Most of the time, a solution will satisfy the customer.
- When a customer does not respond to your attempts to resolve the problem, tell the person you'll get the manager to address the situation.

Journal Activity

Write down some ways you control your reactions when listening to an angry customer.

Rude Customers

Rudeness can be as mild as a simple lack of courtesy or as extreme as sexual or racial harassment. Most people are rude because of ignorance. Often, when someone points out that their behavior is rude, they stop. Some rude people get satisfaction from putting down others. You will not change their behavior by returning their rudeness or getting angry.

Discussion Activity

Discuss effective ways to handle rudeness.

Giving good customer service doesn't require you to tolerate customer rudeness, however. You can deal professionally with a rude customer in a number of ways:

- Express to the customer that rude behavior makes you uneasy.
- Tell the customer that you can give better service when you are treated with respect.
- Ask how you can help and provide the best service possible.
- Provide service without mentioning the rude behavior again, if it doesn't continue.
- If the rude behavior continues, contact your supervisor and ask for assistance.

How Job Savvy Are You?

A man with a pile of shirts comes into the dry cleaning business where Abby works. He says the shirts weren't properly starched and packaged. Abby looks at the shirts and doesn't see any problem.

1. How should Abby deal with this complaint?

   _____
   _____
   _____

2. What should she do to keep this customer coming back?

   _____
   _____
   _____

Roscoe works in the produce department of a grocery store. A customer comes up to him and complains that she can't find the apples featured in the sales ad. When Roscoe looks for the apples, he can't find them, either.

1. How do you think the customer will feel when Roscoe says he can't find the apples?

   _____
   _____
   _____

2. What should Roscoe do to satisfy the customer?

   _____
   _____
   _____

Continues

Marlene works in a child care center. A mother comes into the room early one morning and begins yelling that her son's teddy bear wasn't sent home with him the day before. The children in the room are becoming upset.

1. What can Marlene do to immediately help calm the situation?

    _____

    _____

    _____

2. What can Marlene do to help resolve the mother's complaint?

    _____

    _____

    _____

Pete works as a teller in a large bank. This morning a customer came into the bank to close a joint savings account. When Pete told the customer that the account could not be closed without the signature of the other account holder, the customer began swearing loudly. Other customers seemed anxious to complete their business and leave the bank.

1. What can Pete do to make the other customers more comfortable?

    _____

    _____

    _____

2. What can Pete do to help resolve the customer's complaint?

    _____

    _____

    _____

A Useful Skill: Service Orientation

Business leaders are looking for workers who are service oriented. **Service orientation** is the skill of actively looking for ways to help people. Workers with this skill listen to customers to learn their wants and needs. Because workers often have more direct contact with customers, business owners use this customer knowledge to provide the materials or services customers need.

When workers are service oriented, their customers develop a loyalty to that particular company. This is profitable for the business. When a business can depend on returning customers, it becomes stabilized. Service orientation is a skill that you can use in any job that causes you to interact with others.

Summing Up

Knowing that the customer is the most important person in the organization and should receive good service is the key to business success. Employees must make customer service their number one job. You can discover and meet customer needs by following some simple but critical steps.

Many suggestions and principles for providing good customer service were presented in this chapter. Apply these ideas in your work to be successful on the job. Keep in mind this fact: Customers don't interrupt your work—they *are* your work.

Review and Assessment

Take the Review Quiz. See your instructor or reference your student files in the ebook for additional resources.

CHAPTER 11

Problem-Solving Skills

Objectives

- Analyze a situation and produce creative solutions.

- Interpret data to solve problems.

Managing an organization today is complicated. Competition from other countries is increasing, technology continues to become more complex, and government regulations are sometimes difficult to understand and follow. Faced with these complexities, employers are looking for workers who are problem solvers.

The challenges organizations encounter in the world today are often referred to by the acronym **VUCA**.[1] The acronym stands for volatility, uncertainty, complexity, and ambiguity. Volatility is not only unexpected change that occurs in an organization, but the fact that changes are almost endless. Uncertainty is being unable to predict present and future events from past ones because they are so different. Complexity means there are many causes for factors affecting the organization. Ambiguity is a situation where the meaning of an event is unclear.

Problem solving is a highly marketable skill. It is made even more valuable because of the existence of a VUCA world. Employers need people who can think on their feet, adapt to new situations, and apply new problem-solving techniques. Knowing how to solve difficult problems is important to your success on the job. In this chapter, you'll practice seven steps to improving your problem-solving skills.

Creativity works hand in hand with problem solving. VUCA makes it clear that we are often unable to consider how things have worked in the past to solve new problems. It is then necessary to consider creative ideas and solutions. It appears that the temperament and learning styles of some individuals makes creative thinking easier. But there are skills everyone can practice that will help them be more creative. The last part of this chapter explains how to develop these skills.

Watch the Video

Problem-Solving Skills

Management through Teamwork

Managers in today's business world rely on employees and work teams to help solve many problems. This leadership approach is called **employee involvement**. Studies about employee involvement show that when employees are trained, recognized, and rewarded for their work, the quality of their problem solving improves.[2] Sometimes organizations develop problem-solving procedures through systems such as quality management systems or other processes. There are several reasons for the growth of employee involvement in problem solving, including the following:

Discussion Activity

Why are the employees of today's workplaces more involved in problem solving than in years past?

- **Reduction of Management**   In the last several years, businesses have made drastic cuts in the number of managers and supervisors they employ, thus saving a great deal of money. Consequently, employees must assume some leadership responsibilities that managers previously performed.
- **Complexity**   Worldwide competition, technology growth, government regulations, and a diverse workforce all make businesses more complex than they were in the past. An organization needs help from every employee to solve problems in these complex areas.
- **Motivation**   Employees are motivated to do a better job when they are involved in solving problems related to their work.
- **Proximity**   Employees work closer to most problems than managers and supervisors do. Employees often see solutions that escape managers.
- **Change**   Modern organizations go through a great deal of change due to business acquisitions and mergers, changes in production means, expansion of products and services offered, and entry into world markets. If employers want their employees to be willing to change, they must involve them in problem-solving and decision-making processes.

Employees who develop good problem-solving skills become valuable members of the team.[3] They are seen as good workers who should be rewarded with promotions and raises. The following section examines skills you need to develop to become a good problem solver.

Problem Solving

Problem solving is essentially a social process. It involves managing your thoughts and those of the group in an orderly and systematic way. Several models provide a system for problem solving. This section combines the best ideas from many of these models.

Would-be problem solvers begin by adopting these three basic assumptions that provide a foundation for good problem solving:

1. **Problems can be solved.** The belief that a problem can be solved has motivated some of the greatest problem solvers of history. Thomas Edison, inventor of the light bulb; Henry Ford, creator of modern manufacturing processes; and Jonas Salk, discoverer of the polio vaccine, all persisted despite many failures. Edison failed nearly 1,000 times before he produced a light bulb that worked.

Discussion Activity

Why is it important to believe that a problem can be solved?

2. **Everything happens for a reason.** Problems have causes. Before you can solve a problem, you must look for the causes. Often, you can find only probable causes.

3. **Problem solving must be a continuous process.** In other words, after finishing the last step in the process, you must return to the first step and begin the process again. This gives you the opportunity to evaluate whether the solution is working and whether it can be improved.

The problem-solving process can develop in a number of ways, but the steps and order that you follow are important. Leaving out any of the steps or doing them in a different order will limit your problem-solving abilities. Following are seven steps to effective problem solving.

Step 1: Identify the Problem

The biggest mistake you can make in solving a problem is to work on the wrong problem. Take time to discover what the real problem is.

Here is an example of the importance of this step. A tea shop manager notices that the store is frequently out of certain flavored teas. She tries to solve the problem by asking, "How do we get employees to reorder these teas when they see that we have run out of a flavor?" She then begins to work on getting employees to reorder teas.

However, the real problem could be something else. Perhaps the store orders a standard number of teas for each flavor when it should order larger quantities for more popular flavors. In this case, the question should be, "How can we improve inventory control?"

Journal Activity

Identify a problem you have at work. Write it in your journal. Follow the seven steps to effective problem solving, starting on this page, to resolve the problem. Write your responses for each step in your journal.

Step 2: Gather and Organize Data about the Problem

You should gather as much data on the problem as possible. The best way to collect data is to observe what happens. Other good methods include talking with people affected by the problem and reading reports.

Organize the data in a way that will help you arrive at a solution. Organizing data, a process called "data analysis," requires some mathematical skills. You can **analyze** data with three simple methods: frequency tables, percentages, and graphs.

Step 3: Develop Solutions

After collecting data about the problem, you can use the following five and many other ways to develop as many solutions as possible:

1. **Talk to a coworker.** Talk about the problem with coworkers who have experienced it. Find out how they have solved it in the past. One of the best ways to learn about something is to ask questions. Ask friends from other organizations whether they have had a similar problem and how they solved it. (When talking to people outside your organization, do not reveal information about your business that would be considered confidential.)

2. **Hold a group discussion.** The two most popular types of group discussion are:

- **Brainstorming** In **brainstorming** sessions, a group of workers tries to come up with as many ideas as possible. There are some important rules to follow when brainstorming. First, don't criticize any ideas. You want those involved to suggest as many ideas as possible without being concerned about their quality. Second, stretch for ideas. When the group thinks it has exhausted all ideas, try again. Third, write all the ideas on a flip chart or board so that the entire group can see what's been suggested.
- **Nominal Group Technique** This is a method of discussing a problem that is more controlled than brainstorming.[4] First, each person thinks of as many ideas as possible and writes them on a piece of paper. Second, people in the group share these ideas, taking one idea from one person at a time in a round-robin manner. Third, people in the group discuss the ideas. Fourth, everyone in the group ranks or rates the ideas from best to worst.

3. **Change places with other employees.** Spend four to eight hours in another department. See how other employees handle problems similar to the ones in your department. A change in roles often provides a new viewpoint that can help you solve a problem. This method also allows employees in another department to ask for your ideas about their problems. This interaction can generate many creative solutions.
4. **Visit other organizations with similar problems.** You can learn a lot by discovering how other organizations solve their problems. Many businesses will let you visit if you don't work for a direct competitor. Look at their solutions and evaluate how they solved similar problems. Ask how well they think the solutions work. Decide whether the solutions could be used in your organization.
5. **Read about the problem.** Trade journals provide valuable information about how organizations like yours have solved problems. Trade journals exist for computer dealers, retailers, publishers, fast-food restaurateurs—the list goes on and on. Because trade journals deal with businesses just like yours, they publish articles that give helpful ideas for resolving problems. Other business magazines, books, or related websites can also give you some good ideas.

Step 4: Evaluate Possible Solutions

You should ask a number of questions when evaluating possible solutions:

1. **Is the idea logical?** Look for a direct relationship between the problem and the solution. For example, giving dissatisfied customers a discount doesn't solve a customer-service problem.
2. **How much will it cost?** You might have a great idea, but if it isn't affordable, it doesn't do the organization any good. Some problems are not complicated, so the solutions are not costly. However, costs for solutions to more complex problems can vary greatly. For example,

Job Savvy: How to Be a Success at Work

grocery delivery time might improve if a store bought a new truck customized for grocery delivery, but it might not be able to afford one.

3. **Does the organization have workers who know how to implement the solution?** Some solutions require specialized knowledge. Without employees who have that knowledge, the solution won't work.

4. **Is the solution timely?** Some problems need immediate solutions. Some ideas are good but take too long to implement. Sometimes, you must choose two solutions: one that works immediately and another that will be a better solution in the future. For example, a new copier will improve the quality of the company's printed documents, but it can't be delivered for three months. The immediate solution might be to keep the current copier and arrange a short-term contract to outsource more complex or large copy work.

Even after applying these rules, it's often difficult to select the right solution from a large number of ideas. Two ways to help sort ideas are rating and ranking:

- **Rating**   A process in which each idea is evaluated separately. You apply all four of the preceding questions to each idea. Then you rate the idea on a scale of 1 to 5, 1 being a great idea and 5 being a terrible idea. One drawback to this method is that you might end up with several ideas that are rated equal or almost equal.
- **Ranking**   A process that involves looking at all ideas, choosing the best, and ranking it number one. Then you compare the remaining ideas and select number two. Continue this process until all the ideas have been ranked. A weakness of this method is that ranking more than 10 ideas at a time can be difficult.

Probably the best way to select the number one idea is to use both rating and ranking. First, rate all ideas. Then rank the top 10. This uses the strengths of both methods and omits their weaknesses.

Step 5: Select the Best Solution

By the time you complete the analysis, you should be able to decide the best solution. The best solution might not always be the top idea, but it will usually be among the top three to five ideas. Keep the following three principles in mind when choosing a solution:

1. **The best idea should be practical.** This means that you should select an idea that will solve the problem, can be done in a timely manner, and can be done without being too costly. If the top two or three ideas are basically equal, select the one that is most practical.

2. **Problem solving always involves risk.** No solution will be foolproof. Fears of risk often keep people from making a decision. You can try to reduce the risk, but you can't eliminate it.

3. **Don't worry about being wrong.** Mistakes can't be totally eliminated. Think about what to do if the solution fails. Planning ahead for errors enables you to correct them more quickly.

Step 6: Implement the Solution

A good idea can be ruined if you fail to implement it correctly. Try these tips for putting solutions to work:

1. **Believe in the idea.** Never implement an idea that you don't think will solve the problem. If people believe an idea will be successful, it's usually easier to overcome difficulties that would otherwise jeopardize the solution.
2. **Convince others to support the idea.** When a group solves the problem, you already have this step covered. Getting your supervisor's support for any idea is critical. Reaching a group solution helps convince your supervisor to support the idea. However, if you develop a solution by yourself, you need to "sell" it to other people and convince them that it's the right idea.
3. **Don't let fear hold you back.** It's normal to be afraid of failure. You need to keep in check worries about losing your job or reputation if an idea fails. People sometimes wait too long before implementing a solution. Remember, inaction can kill a good idea.
4. **Follow through.** A solution shouldn't be immediately rejected because it doesn't work. It often takes time for ideas to work. Continue trying the solution until you know why it isn't working before taking a new approach.

Step 7: Evaluate the Solution

Within a reasonable period of time, evaluate the effectiveness of the solution and decide whether it's working. One good way to evaluate effectiveness is to repeat the analysis step (Step 2). For example, go back and do another frequency table to find out whether customers are happier or whether production or quality has improved.

Creative Thinking

Many organizations realize that they must be innovative to compete with other businesses, so employers want workers who think creatively. **Creativity** is the ability to think of new ideas. This might mean applying old ideas to new problems or coming up with entirely new ideas. The following suggestions can help you think creatively.

> **Group Activity**
>
> Discuss different ways to approach a problem.

Don't Let the Problem Limit Your Thinking

Our thinking process sometimes limits the way we look at a problem. The following exercise illustrates a common block to creative thinking.

Thinking Outside the Box

Connect all nine dots with four straight lines without lifting your pencil off the paper.

Look at the Problem from Different Viewpoints

Here's a simple way to do this. List ridiculous solutions to the problem. Then turn those ideas around and ask how they might make sense. The following example illustrates this process.

Your supervisor has asked you and the other employees how to increase the number of customers who visit the shoe store where you work. Here are some "ridiculous" ideas:

- Give shoes away.
- Yell at people to come into the store.
- Carry every style of shoe made.
- Pay customers to take shoes.

Making these ideas workable would give you the following:

- Discount shoes as much as possible.
- Get people's attention through advertising.
- Have a wide variety of styles.
- Include a free pair of socks with each purchase.

Case Study

Since the new pizza place opened nearby, the Burger Castle where Jason works has had less business. The manager has asked all employees for ideas to increase business. What ideas might Jason share?

Use Hazy Thinking

Other words for hazy are *unclear* or *vague*. Sometimes we're very specific and take things too literally in the problem-solving process. Maybe our thinking should be hazy and unclear. The next exercise illustrates how literal thinking can block creativity.

A Different Perspective

Look at the letters below. Eliminate five letters to find one familiar word in the English language. After you've tried solving the problem, look at the answer at the end of this chapter. This exercise shows that thinking in such specific ways blinds you to alternative ideas.

FHIEVLEILCEOTPTTEERRS

Joke about the Problem

Humor is a good way to find alternative solutions to a problem. Humor often relies on expectations. You are led to think one way and then are surprised after seeing another way. This old riddle is an example:

Question: What is black and white and read all over?

Answer: A newspaper.

When this joke is spoken, *read* is usually interpreted as *red* because *black and white* lead a person to think about colors. Humor might allow you to view the problem in an entirely different—and unexpected—way.

Give Yourself Time to Think

Take time to think about the problem and solutions. Relax and look at the ideas you've come up with. Don't allow anything to distract you. Get away from phones, customers, coworkers, radios, televisions, and computers. Write down your thoughts during this time. Better yet, make an audio recording so that you're not distracted by writing.

Then get away from the problem. Work on something else that is not related to the problem, or have a social break with coworkers. Often this relaxation frees your subconscious to come up with more possible solutions.

There are other methods for being creative, such as brainstorming and researching a problem. There are many excellent books on creative thinking. Find one, and learn more about this valuable skill.

Discussion Activity

Why is it important to develop problem-solving skills? Why is practice needed?

Yvonne works as a sales manager for a computer training company called Endevlo. Large companies send their employees to Endevlo for training during the day to learn about project management and a variety of problem-solving techniques. The computer classrooms are seldom used at night. Yvonne's manager has asked her to assemble a team and develop a plan to use the classrooms during the evening hours.

1. Whom should Yvonne recruit for this problem-solving team? (Think in terms of job positions for members of the team.)

   _____

   _____

   _____

2. Describe the characteristics you think team members should possess.

   _____

   _____

   _____

   _____

   _____

3. What are some ideas that you would suggest to solve this problem? Why are these ideas good solutions?

   _____

   _____

   _____

Cyrus works as an assistant manager at the Clean-Up Car Wash. A customer complained to the manager that the car wash damaged her rear window wiper. The manager, Jia, asked Cyrus to determine whether this is a serious problem. If so, Jia expects Cyrus to come up with a solution.

1. What are some reasons that Jia would not automatically assume that damage to rear window wipers is a problem for the business?

   _____

   _____

   _____

2. What techniques would you suggest Cyrus use to determine whether this is a serious problem?

   _____

   _____

   _____

Continues

3. Assume Cyrus discovers that several customers have experienced wiper damage at the car wash. How can he find a way to solve the problem?

_____

_____

_____

4. What ideas for solving the problem would you suggest to Cyrus?

_____

_____

_____

Lymon works as a sales clerk for a large retail store. The company wants more customers to sign up for a credit card. Lymon is assigned to a team that is expected to propose a solution to help increase the number of credit card applications. Reporting to the store manager, the group has suggested the following:

- Offer a bonus to the employee who signs up the most customers for credit every week.

- Offer customers a gift for signing up for the card.

- Give a gift certificate to employees every time they get a certain number of customers to apply for a credit card.

- Tell customers that every time they use a company credit card, a store employee will carry their bags to their cars.

- Give all employees a free lunch if the number of cards applied for in one month is higher than the count for the previous month.

- Offer a 10% discount to customers the first time they use a credit card.

1. How can Lymon's team determine which solution would be the best?

_____

_____

_____

2. Are there common characteristics in these ideas that can be used to classify them into two or more groups? How can this help the team decide on the best solution?

_____

_____

_____

_____

Continues

3. Identify the idea that you think would be the best solution, and explain the reason for your answer.

_____

_____

_____

_____

A Useful Skill: Complex Problem Solving

You will encounter problems on the job. Solving those problems requires individuals with complex problem-solving skills. As an employee, you will be valued if you develop these skills. As with other skills, your expertise will improve with practice.

The first step in complex problem solving is identifying the problem. Perhaps the problem seems obvious. However, it is unwise to assume that you recognize the problem without carefully reviewing the facts and observations.

One technique used to identify the basic problem is called "the five whys." In this technique, the obvious problem is stated followed by the question, "Why?" Each answer is followed by asking "why?" Typically, after five whys, the real problem will be discovered.[5]

Once the problem is defined, examine different solutions. Consider each solution and its merits. After this evaluation, choose the best answer. Establish a plan to implement the solution.

Summing Up

Because they have a direct connection to the problem, employees involved with production and services at the basic level of a business are a valuable source of information to their employers. When communicating with clients, employees learn about customers' needs or dissatisfaction. In day-to-day work, employees may observe ways to increase efficiency in the workplace. Their knowledge is useful in correcting problems.

Problem solving is an important skill for employees in modern business. Many organizations expect every worker to contribute solutions to problems. You should practice your problem-solving skills whenever you get the chance. These skills will improve as you apply the techniques in this chapter.

Daniel Kahneman is a psychologist and Nobel Prize winner in economics. His best-selling book explains how people think fast and slow.[6] Thinking slow is the analytical problem-solving process described in this chapter. Thinking fast is something we do continuously, and it drives our intuitive thought process. Dr. Kahneman discusses the relationship between thinking fast and creativity. The last part of this chapter focused on ways to tap into your creativity. Everyone needs both the fast and the slow processes of thinking to be successful on the job.

Review and Assessment

Take the Review Quiz. See your instructor or reference your student files in the ebook for additional resources.

CHAPTER 12

Doing the Right Thing

Objectives

- Identify common ethical dilemmas within a work setting.

- Evaluate and choose the most ethical course of action.

- Demonstrate integrity and ethical behavior.

- Act responsibly with the interests of the larger workplace community in mind.

E thics are principles or standards that people in our society believe should govern everyone's behavior. Society usually sets many ethical principles. Communities, organizations, religions, and families establish additional ethical principles that guide people in their daily actions. For example, fairness, honesty, truthfulness, respect, and kindness are just some of the ethical practices people expect others to follow.

There are three levels of ethical behavior. First, there is the expectation that employees will follow all federal, state, and local laws and regulations that apply to the organization. For example, stealing copper pipes from a business is theft under the law, regardless if you are an employee. Second, employees are expected to follow company policies. Human Resources typically helps write, organize, and distribute these policies. Violating them will not result in criminal charges but may result in civil charges (meaning you can be sued in court). Disobeying a minor policy usually results in a warning or maybe a suspension. However, major policy violations might result in a firing. The third type of ethical behavior is moral or virtuous in nature. Defying a moral principle usually will not result in any discipline, but it damages your reputation. An example of this type of unethical behavior would be taking credit for someone else's work.

This chapter examines ethical principles and behavior in the workplace. Ethical ideas govern the ways people behave toward employers, supervisors, coworkers, and customers. You'll discover basic principles to help guide you in making ethical decisions. To begin, let's look at how you view ethical behavior.

Watch the Video

Doing the Right Thing

Your Ethical Behavior

1. Why is ethical behavior important?

_____

_____

_____

2. What common ethical principles or ideals are commonly observed by most people?

_____

_____

_____

3. What are some job situations in which you would need to apply ethical principles?

_____

_____

_____

Ethical Problems for Business

There are many reasons businesses are concerned about the ethical behavior of employees. A few reports that illustrate why businesses are disturbed about unethical behavior are contained in the following points:

Discussion Activity

How are ethical principles formed? Why are they important in a job?

- A recent study of employers discovered employee theft costs US businesses $50 billion each year. It also revealed 75% of employees said they have stolen from their employer and 37.5% have stolen at least twice. An even more disturbing finding was that 33% of all business bankruptcies were caused by employee theft.[1]
- When employees copy software illegally, their employer could be sued. It is estimated that software companies lost $46.7 billion globally last year because of illegal use of software. Approximately 15% of software used by businesses in the United States was illegally installed on their computers.[2] Many times, the software was illegally downloaded by employees.
- Cyber theft is another major ethical problem for businesses. Employees are responsible for 66% of successful cyber attacks. These occurred because of employee negligence and deliberate acts to harm the company.[3] Business leaders are becoming aware that installing pirated software increases the risk that companies will have computer systems affected by malware (harmful software). An employee making illegal copies of software can be costly to an organization because it can face large fines, and leadership could even face imprisonment.
- It may seem surprising, but 70% of drug abusers are employed. The use of drugs and alcohol on the job results in 47% of accidents that

cause serious injuries and 40% that result in death. Higher accident rates cost an employer more money in workers' compensation insurance payments and loss of productivity.[4]

Unethical employee behavior costs businesses money and causes morale problems. Employees who commit serious illegal or unethical actions are often fired. In addition, bad conduct hurts those employees' reputations. Most people feel guilty about unethical behavior—even if they are not punished for it.

Common Ethical Dilemmas

At first glance, ethical behavior seems easy. All you have to do is "do the right thing." Knowing what the right thing is for every situation is the hard part. Also, what you consider "right" or "ethical" might differ from others' ideas about what is right or ethical. Most people learn ethical behavior while growing up and use the same principles as adults.

Sometimes it's hard to know what is the right behavior. Most people face the same basic dilemmas when trying to decide what is the right thing to do. We call this uncertainty an **ethical dilemma**. The following sections identify these common ethical dilemmas.

Uncertainty about What Is Expected

At times, you may face a situation and not know what your organization considers to be the right or wrong response. For example, suppose that you deliver a package and the customer offers you a tip. As a new employee, you don't know whether the company allows you to accept tips. You also don't know whether you're supposed to report any tips. What would you do in this situation?

_____

_____

_____

_____

_____

_____

_____

_____

_____

Conflicts in Ethical Standards

A major problem can result when your ethical standards conflict with those of others. This kind of conflict can occur between you and your coworkers, you and your supervisor, or you and the organization itself. For example, you believe in the need to practice environmental stewardship. Everyone, from other workers to the company owners, discards used oil from large lawn mowers by pouring it down sewer drains. Let's explore some of these ethical conflicts individually.

Conflicts between You and Your Coworkers

Suppose that you and two other workers are out on a repair job for a cable company. The other workers decide to report that the job took three hours when, in fact, it took only two hours to complete. They plan to spend the extra hour drinking in a bar. What would you do in this situation?

_____

_____

_____

_____

_____

_____

_____

_____

_____

Conflicts with Your Supervisor

You might have ethical conflicts with your supervisor. Imagine that you work for a painting contractor. At the end of a day's work, your supervisor tells you to take some partially empty paint, varnish, and turpentine cans to the county landfill. You know that it's illegal to dispose of these materials in a landfill. What would you do?

_____

_____

_____

_____

_____

_____

_____

_____

Conflicts with the Organization

Your **ethics** might conflict with those of the organization. This can happen when a company supports policies that you believe are wrong. For example, say that you work for a restaurant that regularly substitutes a lower grade of meat than is advertised on the menu. What would you do in this situation?

_____

_____

_____

_____

_____

_____

_____

_____

Dilemmas about a Situation

Not every ethical decision is strictly right or wrong. In ambiguous situations, it can be very difficult to decide how to behave. For instance, imagine that you are a bank teller. A coworker confides that he is working on a GED. You know that a high school diploma or GED is one of the bank's hiring requirements. The coworker apparently lied on his application. In the entire time you have known him, he has always done an excellent job as a teller. You know that he has a wife and two children who depend on his income from this job. Should you tell your supervisor?

_____

_____

_____

_____

_____

_____

_____

_____

Another example might include an overheard conversation. In the break room at an auto-parts factory, you overhear a coworker say that he would sure like to get Joe—a supervisor—alone in the parking lot one night. You know that the coworker has never done anything violent but can get very angry at times. Should you report the person to a supervisor or some other authority?

_____

_____

_____

_____

_____

_____

_____

_____

Guidelines for Making Ethical Decisions

The problems illustrated in the preceding section show the difficulty in making ethical decisions. Did you have trouble trying to decide how you would act in the sample situations? Most people would have some difficulty. You can ask yourself some questions to help make ethical decisions and guide your behavior. You might need to answer several or all of the questions before you can make the right decision. Just because you can answer one of the following nine questions positively doesn't mean that the act you are considering is ethical.

Journal Activity

What are some ethical values you have? What influenced you in forming these values?

1. **Is it legal?** Will your decision and subsequent action violate local, state, or federal laws? Laws express the ethical behavior expected of everyone in a society. You should consider whether you could be arrested, convicted, or punished for your behavior. In the example of disposing of paint cans in a landfill, it's clear that doing what the supervisor wants is illegal. When you do something illegal, your behavior will not be excused simply because you were ordered to do it.

2. **How will it make you feel about yourself?** Positive self-esteem is one key to doing the right thing. The book *The Power of Ethical Management* by Norman Vincent Peale and Ken Blanchard states, "People who have a healthy amount of self-esteem tend to have the strength to do what they know is right—even when there are strong pressures to do otherwise."[5] What you're really asking is, "Am I at my best?" Most of us want to do our very best. We want to look at ourselves in the mirror without feeling guilt and say, "It feels like the right thing to do."

3. **How do others feel about it?** You should discuss ethical problems with others. Sharing the problem with your supervisor might be uncomfortable or might put your job at risk. In that case, talk with a coworker you trust. Some organizations have appointed ethics officials (called "ombudsmen") or have a person in the HR office fill that role. You can seek advice from those officials when facing an ethical problem. You can talk to friends, relatives, religious leaders, or anyone whose opinion and confidentiality you respect. Don't just talk to people you think will agree with you. Listen to advice from others but don't assume that the majority is always right.

4. **How would you feel if the whole world knew about it?** What if someone made a video recording of what you did and posted it to YouTube? If you wouldn't want coworkers, supervisors, friends, relatives, the community, or everyone in the world to know what you are going to do, *don't do it.*

5. **Does the behavior make sense?** Is it obvious that your proposed action could harm someone—including yourself—physically, mentally, or financially? Is it obvious that you will get caught? This last question shouldn't be the only thing you consider, but you should keep it in mind.

6. **Is the behavior fair to everyone involved?** Ethical behavior should protect everyone's best interests. Look at how everyone can benefit but realize that everyone will not benefit equally by the decision that you make. No one should receive a great gain at the expense of someone else.

7. **Will leaders at your organization approve?** How does your supervisor feel about the behavior? What would the manager of your department say? Would the organization's lawyer approve of it? Find out what those in authority think about the situation. This doesn't guarantee the right decision. Sometimes people in authority support unethical behavior. You aren't necessarily relieved of responsibility because a supervisor approves a certain act.[6] However, receiving approval indicates what behavior is thought to be right by people in authority at your organization.

8. **How would you feel if someone did the same thing to you?** This is the Golden Rule: Do to others what you would want them to do to you. When applying this principle, you should look at the situation from another person's point of view. Another way to view this issue was voiced by philosopher Immanuel Kant, who suggested that what individuals believe is right for themselves, they should believe is right for all others.[7] Avoid doing things you think would be unfair to you because they're probably unfair to someone else as well.

9. **Will something bad happen if you don't make a decision?** You might decide to do nothing, and it won't affect anyone. You might have good reasons for not wanting to get involved. However, you might be aware of a situation that could result in someone being hurt by your inaction. Not taking action when you think you should can result in a major problem.

Discussion Activity

What are the important issues to stress when considering ethical issues?

Roger works at a branch office of the DMV. Recently he saw one of the driving examiners take a bribe from an elderly woman. Roger knows the woman. She lives alone and needs to drive her car to run errands and visit friends. He has never seen the examiner take a bribe before.

1. What do you think Roger should do?

    _____

    _____

    _____

    _____

2. Explain your answer.

    _____

    _____

    _____

    _____

Adilah works for a screw and bolt manufacturer that has a contract with the Air Force. She knows that the bolts being made for the Air Force do not meet the required standards. She talked with her supervisor, and he said not to worry about it. He said it was up to management to correct the problem.

1. If you were Adilah, what would you do?

    _____

    _____

    _____

    _____

2. Explain your answer.

    _____

    _____

    _____

    _____

Jayreene works in a jewelry store. A customer left two rings for cleaning, but Jayreene accidentally gave her a receipt for just one ring. The customer didn't notice the mistake and left the store before Jayreene realized what she had done. One of the rings is quite beautiful. Jayreene thought about how nice it would look on her. She began to think about keeping the ring for herself and telling the manager the customer left only one ring. After all, the customer is very wealthy and can afford the loss.

1. What do you think Jayreene should do?

    _____

    _____

Continues

_____

2. Explain your answer.

_____

_____

_____

_____

Now go back to the situations presented earlier in the chapter. Apply the ethical questions to them. What, if anything, would you do differently? Explain your reasons for each of the following situations.

1. Take a tip from a customer.

_____

_____

_____

_____

2. Take an extra hour with the repair crew.

_____

_____

_____

_____

3. Dump paint cans in the landfill.

_____

_____

_____

_____

4. Substitute lower-grade meat.

_____

_____

_____

_____

5. Report a worker who lied on his application.

_____

_____

_____

_____

Common Ethical Problems

Workers often face common ethical problems on the job. This section covers seven situations in which knowing how to behave can keep you out of trouble.

Discussion Activity

Have you encountered any of these common ethical problems? What other issues come to mind?

Favoring Friends or Relatives

Favoritism poses a particular problem in any business that deals directly with the public. Some businesses allow employee discounts for immediate family members (father, mother, spouse, children, brothers, and sisters), but friends might expect special deals and service, too. As a result, paying customers do not get proper service because of attention shown to friends. Know what your employer permits and expects in these situations.

List some ways that workers might show favored treatment to friends and relatives.

_____

_____

_____

_____

_____

_____

_____

_____

Cheating Employers out of Time

An employer pays employees for time spent at work. Some workers cheat the employer out of this time in a number of ways, including these:

- taking a break for longer periods than is allowed
- talking excessively with friends and relatives while at work
- coming to work late or leaving early
- hiding someplace to avoid working
- conducting personal business using office equipment
- texting or sending personal email messages
- **cyber loafing** by playing games

This kind of behavior is irritating to supervisors. Less work gets done, and customer needs might not be satisfied. When employees behave this way, managers might take disciplinary action.

List some other ways workers can cheat employers out of time.

_____

_____

_____

_____

_____

_____

_____

Stealing from the Company

Taking money from the cash register and taking merchandise from a store are obviously stealing. Here are some other items workers steal:

- **Supplies**   People often take pens, pencils, paper, paper clips, and other supplies from their employer. It doesn't seem like a big thing because the organization has so many supplies. However, multiplied by all the employees, this loss can cost an organization a great deal of money.

- **Photocopies**   Many employees use the copy machine for personal use without thinking of it as theft. However, it usually costs a business 2 to 5 cents per copy. Making 20 copies can cost $1.00. If every employee in an organization with 1,000 employees did this once a week, it would cost the employer almost $52,000 a year. Small thefts by workers can add up to major expenses for an organization.

- **Data theft**   One study[8] on data theft found that 85% of employees took documents and information they helped produce. Computer code and patent filings were stolen by 25% of employees. Customer database information (identify theft) was taken by 35% of employees. And 20% of employees said they would be more likely to steal data if they were fired from their jobs. This may be one reason that many organizations have a policy of escorting fired or laid-off employees out the door without letting them touch a computer. Computers make it easy to copy software programs an organization owns. This is known as "piracy." Global spending from malware attacks, usually due to counterfeit personal computer software, in 2017 was $359 billion.[9] Some organizations fire employees caught pirating software.

What are other ways employees steal from their employers?

_____

_____

_____

_____

_____

_____

_____

_____

Software Piracy, Freeware, and Shareware

Copying software illegally is called **software piracy**. Just like books, music, and videos, software is protected by copyright laws. Commercial software is purchased, and the right to make copies is restricted.

Typically, you should follow three rules to avoid pirating commercial software:

1. Install the program on only one computer.
2. Make only one copy. This copy must be stored and used only if the original is damaged.
3. Never make copies for anyone else. A much more serious violation is to make a pirated copy and sell it.

Sometimes software is made available as freeware or shareware. *Freeware* means that the program developer allows anyone to freely make copies. *Shareware* means you can use the software and make copies for others. However, you are expected to pay the program developer if you continue to use the program.

Abusing Drugs and Alcohol

Drinking alcoholic beverages or using drugs on the job is wrong. Taking recreational drugs or prescription drugs (such as pain killers) without a doctor's prescription is against the law. Using them on the job can result in immediate termination. Substance abuse can generate three major job problems:

1. **Lower productivity.** Employees under the influence of alcohol or illegal drugs produce fewer goods or services.
2. **Lower quality.** It's impossible to perform at your best when you are under the influence. Your quality of work will be lower than your employer is paying you to provide.
3. **Safety hazards.** Substance abuse can cause many safety problems. Reactions are slowed, judgment is impaired, and workers are more likely to suffer serious or fatal injuries.

List other problems that can be caused by substance abuse on the job.

_____

_____

_____

_____

_____

_____

_____

Violating Confidentiality

Some employees have access to a great deal of information. If you are in a position to handle such information, don't talk to anyone about it. This includes other workers. Sharing confidential information about a company can cause great harm. Competitors can use trade secrets to duplicate proprietary products or services. With knowledge of another company's financial data, competitors can identify that business's weaknesses and strengths. Customer lists can be used to lure customers away. Following is a list of information you should keep confidential.

- **Customer Confidentiality** Customers' private information, such as salary, credit history, or employment history should be kept confidential. Stealing customer data, such as credit card information, can result in criminal prosecution and imprisonment. Accessing less critical information such as the amount of money spent with your organization or a customer's mailing address, email address, or telephone number could still cause harm to someone.

- **Employee Confidentiality** Employees' salary, personnel records, performance appraisals, and attendance records should be kept confidential. Talking about any of this with others could harm the employee's reputation or cause other problems.

- **Healthcare Confidentiality** Employees who work for any organization that serves the medical needs of patients (hospitals, physician offices, dental offices, pharmacies, insurance companies, etc.) are guided by the Health Insurance Portability and Accountability Act (HIPAA).[10] Information that is unknowingly released by an employee can result in civil fines that can amount to thousands of dollars. Knowingly releasing patient information can result in fines and years in jail. It is important to be very careful about keeping patient information confidential.

- **Education Confidentiality** Employees who work for educational organizations that serve students (public and private grade schools, middle schools, colleges, etc.) are governed by the Family Educational Rights and Privacy Act (FERPA).[11] This law requires all employees of educational organizations to keep most information about students confidential. A school may lose federal funding for violating student confidentiality. As a result, most schools take harsh disciplinary action when an employee violates a student's confidentiality.

Many companies have policies about **confidentiality**. You should know your employer's policies. However, it's in everyone's best interest for you to keep all information confidential.

List other work information that should be treated as confidential.

_____

_____

_____

_____

_____

_____

_____

Knowing about the Unethical Behaviors of Others

One of the most difficult situations to face is knowing that another employee has done something wrong. You may discover that an employee has behaved unethically in one of the following ways:

1. The other employee tells you personally.
2. You see the employee do something wrong.

Gossip is a less reliable way of finding out about another employee's misdeeds. You should not feel obligated to report to a supervisor any gossip you hear. In fact, when you don't have firsthand information about a situation, it's usually best not to repeat to anyone what you've heard.

List some things that you might discover about other workers, that you might need to report to your supervisor.

_____

_____

_____

_____

_____

_____

_____

Violating an Organization's Policies

Many organizations have a set of personnel policies to govern employee behavior. Policies are communicated through a policy manual, memos, or email. As an employee, you are expected to follow these policies. You can be disciplined for violating them. It's important to know what the policies are and to follow them. Even if other workers get away with breaking the policies, you should not accept this as a good reason for breaking them yourself.

List some common personnel policies that an organization might establish.

_____

_____

_____

_____

_____

_____

_____

How you deal with ethical problems determines how successful you will be at your job. The wrong behavior could cause your supervisor to be dissatisfied with your performance and could, in fact, cause you to be fired from your job.

How Job Savvy Are You?

Shane works in the payroll department. He has several friends in the computer department. One of these friends, Fran, told him that she just got a raise. Her supervisor told her that she is now the most highly paid programmer in the company. Shane knows that several other programmers have higher salaries than Fran has been promised. The supervisor has obviously lied to Fran.

1. Should Shane tell Fran what he knows?

    _____

2. Explain your answer.

    _____

    _____

    _____

    _____

Justine works in a doughnut shop. Some of her friends stop by late at night. She spends a lot of time talking with them, but there aren't any customers in the shop. A customer comes in, and Justine immediately asks whether she can help him. She then returns to her friends' table and starts talking with them.

1. Do you think Justine is doing the right thing by spending so much time talking with her friends?

    _____

2. Explain your answer.

    _____

    _____

    _____

    _____

Lance works at a fast-food restaurant. His family is very poor. The restaurant has a policy of throwing out hot sandwiches that aren't sold within 15 minutes. The policy also states that employees may not take any of the sandwiches for themselves. Lance's supervisor tells him to throw away 10 cheeseburgers. He thinks about how much his family could use the sandwiches. Instead of throwing them in the dumpster, he hides them in the back of the store and takes them home when he leaves work.

Continues

1. Should Lance have done this?

   _____

2. Explain your answer.

   _____

   _____

   _____

   _____

Demos is preparing to resign from a state small business administration agency. He plans to begin a consulting firm and knows it would help his new business to have a list of all businesses the agency has helped along with owners' names, addresses, and phone numbers. Demos decides to download the information to a flash drive and takes it home.

1. Is Demos doing the right thing?

   _____

2. Explain the reasons for your answer.

   _____

   _____

   _____

   _____

A Useful Skill: Critical Thinking

Decisions made using critical thinking are based on logic and reason rather than emotions. A critical thinker identifies the strengths and weaknesses of alternative solutions to situations. Critical thinking requires a person's time and effort. After an evaluation, the individual reaches a conclusion and takes action.

Critical thinking is needed in a variety of work situations. A worker may use critical thinking when making ethical decisions or when solving a technical work-related problem. Workers who can assess problems and initiate solutions are valued in the workplace.

Summing Up

Supervisors evaluate workers based on their behavior. If they see workers doing something that they consider unethical, those workers will be disciplined. To maintain a good self-concept, you need to behave in a way that you feel is ethical. It's not always easy to know what is ethical. But if you apply the questions in this chapter, you will make the best decision when you face ethical problems and be a success at work.

Review and Assessment

Take the Review Quiz. See your instructor or reference your student files in the ebook for additional resources.

CHAPTER 13

Getting Ahead on the Job

Objectives

- Create a career plan.

- Evaluate job opportunities.

- Assemble facts to know your worth as an employee.

- Prepare a request for a raise.

- Tell an employer why you need to leave a job and submit a professional resignation.

According to a study done by Automatic Data Processing (ADP) Research Institute on 12,000 companies and 12.5 million employees, 5% of employees leave their jobs every month. This same study found the main reasons employees voluntarily leave their jobs are pay and promotional opportunities.[1] Pay relates to supplying basic physical needs for food, clothing, and housing. But money earned from a job also allows people to buy things that make life easier and more enjoyable. Receiving a promotion meets our basic psychological needs of achievement and recognition.

People want more from a job than just money and status. In fact, a study by the Society for Human Resource Management found there were other important reasons people stayed at their jobs.[2] Having flexibility to balance family and work is a key factor as is job security. An opportunity for meaningful work is a main reason to work for many people because people need a purpose other than making money. Another reason for staying with an employer is the location—people don't want to move.

You will be faced with many difficult decisions as your career advances in an organization. It can be challenging to find a perfect balance when deciding whether to accept a promotion or take a job offer from another company. It is never easy to decide whether to stay or leave an organization, even when a new job seems like a great opportunity. This chapter will help make these decisions easier for you.

Watch the Video

Getting Ahead on the Job

197

You, Incorporated

A basic way to thrive in the workplace today is to think of yourself as a business. In Chapter 1, we looked at how you must be prepared to work as a core employee, temporary employee, or independent contractor. It is a gig economy, and you must sell yourself to employers. Even core employees are not guaranteed full-time employment and must keep selling their value and importance to leaders. You are your own business and there is no one else who will be as concerned about your success in the workplace as you are. The following six principles will help you better understand how to sell yourself.

Discussion Activity

Would you be satisfied in the same position in a company at a constant rate of pay for your entire career?

1. **Understand that skills are the product you sell to an employer.** The strategy for selling yourself should focus on your skills. That is why you should know what your strongest skills are. Refer to the exercises in Chapter 7 to help identify your skills. For example, an employer pays cashiers at a store for their ability to scan items, operate a cash register, and maintain good customer relations.

2. **Market your skills.** Discuss your skills with the employer during your job interview. When the opportunity comes up to use your skills within the organization, remind your supervisor about them. Apply your skills whenever you have the chance. Let coworkers know the skills that you can use to assist the team in accomplishing projects and tasks. Keep records of accomplishments that illustrate your skills. An oil-change mechanic who demonstrates an ability to use a computer may get promoted to a customer service representative position when the opportunity arises.

3. **Continually improve your skills.** Businesses today emphasize ongoing quality improvement. This means always trying to provide customers with more quality for their money. You can improve skills through experience and education by doing jobs and tasks that give you this experience—even when you are frightened by the possibility of failure. You can also improve your skills by taking advantage of educational opportunities that employers provide. An administrative assistant who attends a course to learn how to use advanced PowerPoint features or some other software program has one more valuable asset than an assistant without this skill.

4. **Learn new skills through experience.** Many skills are learned through experience. Volunteer for new tasks and projects. Working with project teams may give you a chance to network with employees outside your department or work team. You can learn from these employees by watching how they work and asking them questions. It is also possible to learn new skills by volunteering for nonprofit community groups—particularly ones sponsored by your company.

5. **Monitor trends.** Keep track of changes in your occupation and the industry in which you work. Know how these trends will affect future activities and the skills you will need to keep pace with the change. For example, elevator operators were plentiful in the first half of the last

century. These days, the job is so rare the US Bureau of Labor Statistics doesn't recognize it. If elevator operators in the 1940s and '50s had tracked the growing trend in automated elevators, they could have trained as elevator inspectors, retail salespeople, or some related occupation.

6. **Improve your performance through job crafting.** After several months of experience on the job, you will discover ways to improve your performance. This improvement can happen through **job crafting**.[3] Job crafting is the process of making changes in your job on your own so the job fits your abilities and preferences better. Examples include doing tasks so they fit your physical and thinking skills, clarifying tasks, and taking on new tasks related to your job. Crafting your job so it better fits you makes your work more meaningful. It also sets apart the quality of your work from that done by other employees.

Lifelong Learning

Lifelong learning is the concept that a person's education never ends. Even after a person reaches educational goals such as high school graduation or completing a degree, the learning continues. Lifelong learning takes many different forms. Formal classroom education, online courses, seminars, and on-the-job training are examples.

Companies may offer their own courses for employees through the human resources department. Some businesses have tuition-reimbursement programs, which help pay for college courses for workers returning to college. On-the-job mentoring programs use experienced employees to teach skills to other workers. Industry-related conferences and seminars give employees a chance to learn about relevant topics from leaders in their field.

Getting a Raise

Organizations give pay raises for many reasons. Good pay helps businesses attract and keep good people. Raises are one way to reward good performance. The thought of earning more money can motivate employees to do a better job, but it's important to know when you can expect a raise. Unreasonable expectations can create misunderstandings between you and your employer. This could cause you to lose interest in your job and your employer to lose some respect for you.

An organization's policy on pay increases is usually discussed at the job interview. If it hasn't already been explained to you, ask your supervisor how pay raises are determined. The following list describes some common instances that result in pay increases:

- **Completion of Probation**   **Probation** is considered a training period, and it usually lasts from one to six months. Organizations often give raises after an employee completes the probation period. After a worker completes probation, he or she has demonstrated the ability to do the work the organization expects.

- **Incentive Increases**   Organizations using this method give raises according to the quality of work during a certain time period. Typically, supervisors evaluate the work every six months or once a year. Pay increases are based on evaluations and job performance. Organizations that stress teamwork might give pay increases based on a team's evaluation.
- **Cost-of-living Increases**   Companies sometimes give these raises to help employees offset inflation. Inflation is the increase in prices of things such as rent, groceries, and entertainment that lowers the value of the dollar. For example, if the cost of living rises 3% a year, at the end of that year it costs $1.03 to buy what cost only $1.00 the year before. In this situation, an employer might give employees a 3% cost-of-living increase so that the buying power of their pay doesn't decrease.
- **To Keep Employees**   Organizations may give highly valued workers pay increases to keep them from taking other jobs. If you receive a higher-paying job offer, it's appropriate to ask your employer for a raise. Don't use this approach unless you really have a better offer that you would realistically consider accepting. In addition to damaging your credibility, your employer may not be able to afford a raise and might tell you to take the other job.
- **Reward for Special Efforts**   Sometimes employees take on added job responsibilities. Employers may reward this behavior by giving raises. Some organizations reward employees for learning new skills. The more skills you learn, the more money you earn.
- **New Assignments**   Companies normally give raises to workers who accept new positions in the same organization, especially if it means a promotion to a more responsible position. Some businesses give pay increases based on the number of jobs a worker learns to do. The more jobs you are trained to do, the higher your pay.

Discussion Activity

What are some added job responsibilities or new skills that could result in a pay raise? Why might an employer offer a raise in an attempt to keep an employee?

When you start a new job, make sure you understand your employer's policy on pay increases. You are less likely to be disappointed by the size of your pay raises if you know what to expect. Knowing how your employer determines raises gives you an advantage and the motivation to work hard to receive a raise.

Wage and Salary

A **wage** is a specific amount of money earned for each hour worked. A **salary** is a flat payment per week or month regardless of hours worked. Employers are required by federal law to pay hourly workers an overtime rate for hours they work in excess of 40 hours per week. Salaried workers usually are more highly paid because they don't receive overtime pay. If the hourly workers are working a lot of overtime, it's possible for salaried employees to make less money than hourly employees in the same organization.

How Job Savvy Are You?

Enoch is a grill cook at Humpty Dumpty Hamburgers. He was told he would receive a raise after working for three months and that he could be considered for another raise after six months. Enoch has worked at the store for six months and still hasn't received a raise. Enoch's supervisor has never talked to him about his job performance.

1. Do you think Enoch deserves a raise? Why?

    _____

    _____

    _____

2. What approach should Enoch take when asking for a raise?

    _____

    _____

    _____

Abeer has worked as a clerk for Golden Auto Parts for more than three years. Each year she receives a 3% raise. During the past year, inflation was 5%. Abeer does a good job, and her supervisor frequently praises her for her work. She is concerned that if she receives the same pay increase this year as she has in past years, it will not be enough for her to live on.

1. What percentage of pay increase should Abeer ask for?

    _____

    _____

    _____

2. How did you decide on the percentage?

    _____

    _____

    _____

3. What approach should Abeer take when discussing her raise?

    _____

    _____

    _____

Barb has been a secretary at Newton Manufacturing Corporation for two years. Her performance appraisals have always been good, and she has received a good pay raise each year she's been with the company. Recently, Barb saw an ad in the newspaper for a secretary. The advertised pay was $1,000 more per year than she is currently making. Barb believes she has the qualifications needed for the advertised job, and she is upset that she isn't being paid more by Newton. She plans to go into the office on Monday and tell her supervisor she could have a job that would pay her $1,000 more than she is making.

Continues

1. Do you think Barb's plan is a good one? Why?

   _____

   _____

   _____

2. What plan would you suggest?

   _____

   _____

   _____

Wayne is a bookkeeper for Hall's Home Oil Company. A few months ago, his supervisor asked him to set up all the ledgers on a new computer system the company purchased. The new system has many advantages, and the managers now receive financial reports that help save the company thousands of dollars each month. Wayne works hard to keep the computer system operating. He has begun to wonder why he has been given this new responsibility but no pay raise.

1. Do you think Wayne deserves a raise? Why?

   _____

   _____

   _____

2. What plan would you devise for Wayne to get a raise?

   _____

   _____

   _____

Getting Promoted

Many people want a more responsible position at their company, but organizations limit the number of supervisory and management jobs available. This means that **promotions** are difficult to get. Promotions are often worth working hard for, however, because they have several advantages, including these:

- **Increased Pay**   Normally, pay raises accompany promotions. However, sometimes a promotion to a salaried position is not much more money than an hourly worker earns with overtime pay.
- **More Respect**   A promotion often increases your status within the organization and in society.
- **Better Assignments**   A promotion usually provides more challenging work. Lower-level positions usually require less ability, and sometimes workers become bored in these jobs. A promotion offers a release from boring duties.
- **Improved Self-esteem**   Your own self-esteem will improve when other people recognize you and your work. You'll feel better about yourself because of your success.

Discussion Activity

What are the two major criteria for promotions? Discuss how a promotion can change a person's status and self-esteem.

- **Future Promotions**   The typical path for promotions is to advance one level at a time. For example, you typically will be a supervisor and then a manager before becoming a director rather than moving directly from supervisor to director. Therefore, if you aspire to a higher-level position at your company, you need to begin with a promotion to the first level of management.

Preparing for a Promotion

Promotions typically are based on two major criteria: seniority and merit. *Seniority* refers to the amount of time on the job. Workers with more seniority often understand the organization and job better. *Merit* refers to the quality of job performance. Merit factors that most often result in promotions include leadership, communication, and technical skills. Both merit and seniority are considered when deciding which employee to promote. If specific skills or knowledge are required for the job, they are factored into the decision as well. If you want to be promoted, follow these tips:

Group Activity

Write a list of items that could influence a supervisor to promote an employee.

- **Keep Track of Job Openings**   When a job opening occurs in your company, apply for the job. Talk to other workers. They usually know when someone is going to retire, be promoted, or leave for another job. Companies post job openings by placing notices on a bulletin board, in the company newsletter, through memos, or by some other means. At one point in time, these methods were done manually, but now the approach is electronic. An electronic newsletter, computer blog, email blast to all employees, etc.

Case Study

Ellen thinks she deserves a promotion. Who should she talk to? What should she do at her job to prepare for a promotion?

- **Talk to Your Supervisor**   Tell your supervisor you are interested in a promotion. Supervisors usually know where the vacancies are in the company. Your supervisor can also provide guidance about the skills and experience that are normally needed to move into another job. Also, if you have a good work history, your supervisor should be willing to give you a positive recommendation.
- **Notify the Human Resources Department**   Let the human resources department know you want a promotion. They will ask your supervisor about your job performance and keep you in mind when openings occur. In some organizations, you should notify your supervisor before contacting the human resources department. Find out the proper process for your organization.
- **Create a Network**   "Networking" refers to building friendships with coworkers in other departments. Secretaries and administrative assistants are excellent people to include in your network because they have access to a great deal of information. Ask people in your network to notify you when they hear of possible job openings. For a network to work well, you must be willing to share information and help others in the network.
- **Develop a Good Reputation**   Be a dependable, reliable employee and work hard. Get along with your coworkers. Become highly skilled in your job assignment. Supervisors and managers will notice and remember you when a promotional opportunity arises.

Journal Activity

Use this prompt: "I should be promoted because I . . ."

- **Create Your Own Job** It's possible to create a job for your own promotion. Look for ways to improve the organization. Make suggestions for accomplishing those improvements. Management might reward your creative thinking by placing you in a new job to carry out your suggestions.

Networking

Networking has proven to be one of the most effective job-hunting techniques. You should include business acquaintances, social friends, and family in your network.[4] The network grows as you ask each member of the network to suggest others who could aid in helping you find a job.

Networking is also a helpful technique when you are seeking a different position within your organization. To form a network, you need to build relationships with your coworkers. Don't limit yourself to those working in your department. Workers in other parts of the company may have access to information such as an upcoming retirement, an employee move, or a soon-to-be promotion that may mean a possible job for you.

Not all networking is face to face. LinkedIn and other online professional social networks can be used to maintain contact with business associates anywhere in the world. LinkedIn has job postings as well as information about business opportunities, and it offers facts about other companies. Members list their work skills and interests.

Remember that networking is about sharing information. You are a source of information and support to others in your networking group. You have an obligation to them as well.

One final suggestion: Keep in contact with the people in your network. Even if you move to a different department or a new company, you may need their input later in your career.

When Promotions Occur

Promotions occur only when an organization has a job vacancy or the money to create a new job. You need to be patient about getting a promotion. However, when someone with less seniority than you receives a promotion, you should ask why. Discuss with your supervisor the difference between you and the other worker. Ask for suggestions to improve your performance. Take your supervisor's advice. It will help you compete for the next promotion.

Sometimes it is important to consider office politics to get ahead. Office politics could be a reason to be turned down for a promotion. For example, managers often promote people who they like. It is important to understand that being part of the in-group with your manager or supervisor increases the probability that you will receive a promotion. The way to become part of the in-group is to help the manager whenever there is extra work or new projects. Volunteer when a request is made. In addition, take advantage of invitations to lunch or social events that the manager provides.

1. List the skills and behaviors a worker needs to use to get a promotion.

_____

_____

_____

2. Which skills or behaviors do you feel are most important? Explain your answer.

_____

_____

_____

How Job Savvy Are You?

Ramon has been a carpet layer at the Carpet Emporium for two years. He is dependable and gets along well with the other workers. He is very creative and often suggests timesaving methods for carpeting homes. Ramon often criticizes and argues with the supervisor, but he always gets the job done.

Li Wei has worked at the Emporium for 16 months as a carpet layer. He also is dependable and gets along well with other workers. Li Wei took some classes in supervision at the local community college. He goes out of his way to help the supervisor and gets along well with him.

Business at the Carpet Emporium has been good. Management has decided to form an additional work crew to lay carpet. The department manager can't decide whether to promote Ramon or Li Wei to supervise the new crew.

1. Who would you promote to the new supervisor's position?

_____

2. Explain the reasons for your selection.

_____

_____

_____

_____

_____

Carlos has been a secretary at Happy Acres Real Estate Agency for more than two years and is currently taking a real estate course at the local junior college. He will complete the course in time to take the real estate license test next month. He learned through the office grapevine that one of the agents plans to retire within three months. Carlos talked to the manager about a promotion to an agent's position.

Damita came to work for the agency six months ago. She has her real estate license, but because the agency wasn't hiring agents at that time, she took a position administering the deeds and titles in the office.

Carlos's information is correct. The agency is looking for another agent to replace the one who is retiring. The agency manager plans to promote from within the company rather than hire someone new. Carlos and Damita are the candidates.

1. Who would you promote to the agent's position?

_____

Continues

2. Why did you choose to promote this person?

_____

_____

_____

_____

_____

For the past two years, Tamiko has worked part-time for the Golden Years Home, a residential healthcare center. Tamiko first started working in the home as a volunteer when she was a junior high school student. During high school, she worked as a kitchen aide. Tamiko is studying to be a licensed practical nurse while working weekends at the healthcare center. The staff members know they can depend on Tamiko to be flexible. She has recently expressed an interest in working full-time.

Teresa has been a volunteer at the home for two years and is a recent high school graduate. After graduation, she applied for a full-time position at the home and was hired as a nurse's aide. As a volunteer, Teresa worked with the activities director during social times for the residents and helped plan many social events. Last summer, Teresa traveled with the group to the Senior Citizens' Olympics, held in the state capital. The residents consider Teresa an adopted grandchild.

Because of an increase in the number of residents, the healthcare administrator has decided to create a new staff position—assistant activities director. Both Tamiko and Teresa are being considered for the position.

1. Who would you promote or hire for this position?

_____

2. Why did you choose this person?

_____

_____

_____

_____

_____

Charlene has been a waitress at a French restaurant, Monsieur Jacques, for one year. Charlene is known for excellent service, and customers often ask to be seated at her tables. She receives very good tips because of how quickly she serves customers, but she is impatient with the kitchen workers and those bussing tables when their work slows down her service. Charlene likes to work the business lunch crowd and usually refuses to work at other times. She knows many of the lunch customers by name and greets them as they are seated.

Alex has worked at Monsieur Jacques for two years. He is dependable and serves customers satisfactorily. Alex rarely visits with the customers, but he is always polite. He gets along well with coworkers and is willing to adjust to new work hours when needed. He even helps clear tables during rush hour. Last week the chef shared one of his secret recipes with Alex. No one in the restaurant has known the chef to do this before.

Due to an increase in business, the restaurant manager has decided to add a maitre d' during the lunch hour. This person would be responsible for greeting and seating customers and honoring reservations. Charlene and Alex are both being considered for the promotion.

Continues

1. Who would you choose as the maitre d'?

   _____

2. Why did you choose this person?

   _____

   _____

   _____

   _____

   _____

Career Development

The term **career development** refers to the process of reaching your personal goals in work and in life. Career development may not seem important during the first few years of your work experience, but you should understand the process early in your career and use it to achieve your highest possible level of success. Here are 10 ways you can take action to develop your career within an organization:

Journal Activity

Develop and record your career plan.

1. **Explore job possibilities.** Find out what kinds of jobs are available in your organization. Most organizations have a variety of jobs. Discover the types of jobs available by asking coworkers about their jobs. The federal government provides a website O*NET OnLine at https://www.onetonline.org with detailed information about many jobs. You can discover more information about jobs than you might obtain from your employer. Even more data can be found using the Occupational Outlook Handbook at https://www.bls.gov/ooh/.

2. **Identify your skills and abilities.** Get to know yourself. Identify what you do best. Match your skills with jobs in the organization that require those skills.

3. **Know your values.** Know what you want from your career. People define success in various ways. You may define success by your career achievements, or your job may be secondary to family, friends, and free time. How much time and energy do you want to give to your job? What do you need to accomplish in your career to support your values? These are important questions to answer before setting a career goal within the company.

4. **Set a goal.** Decide on your ultimate job goal within the organization. Make sure this goal is realistic. If you want to be president of the company, are you willing to devote the time and effort required to do it? It may take months or even years before you know the organization well enough to set your career goal.

5. **Develop a career path.** What is the best way to advance to the position you want? You should ask yourself several questions about the job you want:

- What special qualifications are needed for the job? How much experience is required? Is a license or certification necessary for the job?
- What kind of education is needed for the job? What major area of study corresponds with the job requirements? Is a college degree necessary?
- How did other people get this job? What jobs did they have before they were promoted to the job you want?
- What type of classroom or on-the-job training is needed?

6. **Write your plan.** Use the information collected from this list so far to create a career plan, showing the progress you want to make in the organization. Put the plan in writing to motivate yourself to reach your goal. Include a timetable in your plan to keep you on track to reach each job goal within your timeframe.

7. **Find a mentor.** A **mentor** is someone who takes a professional interest in you and advises you about your job. A mentor should be someone who is recognized and respected in the organization. Develop a mentor relationship by asking this person for help on a project or for advice on a situation. Another approach is to ask someone whether they are willing to mentor you.[5] When you approach the potential mentor, know why you think they can help you. Also, be able to tell the person why you think they will make a good mentor and how you hope they can help you.

8. **Keep a record of your accomplishments.** This is sometimes referred to as a "portfolio." The human resources department or your supervisor probably keeps records of your work, but don't expect either of them to keep a detailed record of your accomplishments. You should do this yourself. Keep a list of any special skills you acquire, classes you attend, projects you complete, or ideas you suggest. When you apply for promotions, use this record to help prove your qualifications.

9. **Review your plan.** Look over your plan every six months, and review your progress. If you are pleased with your rate of progress, chances are you'll be motivated to continue to work hard to reach your goal. If you are unhappy about your progress, the review can help show what you need to do to make better progress.

10. **Change your plan when necessary.** Most plans aren't perfect. You will change, and so will your goals. When this happens, develop a new plan. If the organization changes, you will have to change your plan. You may even have to leave your current job and go to another organization to meet your goals.

You must take responsibility for your own career development. Companies won't do it for you, so you must take charge.

Reflected Best Self

Email five people (family, friends, peers, subordinates, managers, professional associates, customers/clients, teachers, and so on) using this explanation:

> The work experience course that I'm taking requires me to complete an exercise called "Reflected Best Self." I would appreciate your help in completing this activity.
>
> Think about the times you have seen me at my best. What did I do that was meaningful to you, to people around you, or to an organization to which we belonged? What did I accomplish? What strength do you think I exhibited in achieving this accomplishment?
>
> It isn't necessary to spend a great deal of time writing a response. Just one or two paragraphs will be sufficient. Please respond to this email within the next two weeks. Thanks for your cooperation and support.

Analyze the responses. After that, reflect on the common themes that you find. Then write a self-portrait on the lines that follow. The self-portrait is a composition of what you learned about yourself. Write it in prose. The process is easier if you begin with one of the following phrases:

I am at my best when . . .

When I am at my best . . .

People see me at my best when . . .

_____

_____

_____

_____

_____

_____

_____

_____

_____

_____

_____

_____

_____

_____

_____

_____

_____

Building a Portfolio

Artists and writers have long used portfolios to demonstrate their skills. An artist's portfolio consists of drawings, designs, paintings, and other works of art that show past accomplishments. Your **portfolio** should consist of examples that demonstrate your skills. The portfolio becomes a tool that you can use in an interview for a promotion or a job with a new employer. Discuss with coworkers and your supervisor what you can use to demonstrate your value to the organization. The following list shows some items that should be in everyone's portfolio:

- **Résumé** The résumé should contain your name, address, phone number, and email address. It should list and describe the jobs that you have held—including the dates when you worked for the employer. Also be sure to feature your most impressive accomplishments. List all schools you attended and the year you received a diploma, certificate, or degree.

- **Letters of Reference** Identify influential people in your life who would be willing to write a letter of reference. These letters should refer to specific examples of accomplishments. These letters might come from teachers, employers, volunteer service directors, community leaders, and religious leaders.

- **Transcripts** Schools do not provide official transcripts to a graduate. However, they usually will give you an unofficial copy that you can include in your portfolio.

- **Continuing-education Documents** Include certificates from courses or training that you've completed. If you don't get a certificate, ask for a letter or some other form that documents your attendance. In addition, keep a copy of the class agenda or outline, which you can use to document the skills you learned in the class. Many online training programs provide badges to verify skills you acquired when taking the courses.

- **Conference and Association Materials** Keep a copy of all programs from conferences that you attend. Include membership certificates for professional associations, unions, and other work-related organizations.

- **Awards and Honors** Include awards and honors that you receive. These might come from schools, employers, or community organizations. Include a document that explains how these items demonstrate skills that an employer might need.

- **Work Output** Your portfolio should include evidence that demonstrates specific skills. Examples of items that can be included in a portfolio are research papers, software programs, spreadsheets, electronic presentations, and photos of completed projects. You can also include specific products that you helped create, design, or build, such as books, clothes, mechanical items, or surveys. Be sure to obtain permission from an employer to include an item that might be considered confidential information.

You can also use a portfolio to assess your skills and plan for further education. Some colleges use portfolios to evaluate the experience and skills of potential students and to award college credit supported by the portfolio. In addition, having a portfolio to look at will help build your self-confidence.

With the increased use of electronic information storage, digital or electronic portfolios are being used to document work skills and job history. The information is basically the same, but the format is different. Software programs are available that make creating your own document simple.

Leaving a Job

Workers leave their jobs for many reasons, which can be summed up in these general categories:

Group Activity

Discuss reasons for leaving a job. How do you tell your employer or supervisor that you are leaving? Why is it important to leave a job with a good relationship intact?

- **Job Dissatisfaction**   Over time, you can become unhappy with a job because of personality conflicts or new management policies. Or your career development plan may not work out with your current employer. You will know you are not satisfied if you dread going to work every day.
- **New Opportunities**   Even when you're happy in your job, you might be offered another job that pays more or provides more opportunities for promotion or better benefits. It can be difficult to decide whether to stay at a job or make a job change.
- **Avoiding Disaster**   You may want to leave a job because something bad is about to happen. The business may close, leaving you unemployed. The company may lay you off, and you can't afford to wait for a recall. Maybe you know the supervisor is unhappy with your work and is going to fire you. You may decide to leave the job before one of these events happens.

The average person changes jobs 12 times between the ages of 18 and 48.[6] Chances are you will leave several jobs. You should understand how to change a career right from the start. Don't make a hasty decision to leave a job that you'll regret later. The following list offers some suggestions that can prepare you to leave a job:

- **Have Another Job Waiting**   Normally, you should not leave a job without having another one lined up. The best time to look for a new job is when you are employed. Leaving a job to look for a job puts you at a great disadvantage. Even when you find a job, it will be harder to bargain for better pay or position if you are desperate for a paycheck.
- **Give Reasonable Notice**   The typical resignation notice is two weeks. Your employer may require a little more or less time than this. Find out from HR the required amount of time.
- **Submit a Letter of Resignation**   You may be asked to submit a letter of resignation. The only information required is stating that you are resigning and when you will be leaving. If you want to thank your employer and coworkers, write briefly. The reason for leaving is not required.
- **Be Tactful**   Don't resign in anger. You may be unhappy, but it isn't a good idea to tell your supervisor what you think is wrong with the organization. You need your employer for a reference and might even want to work for that person again someday. Tell the supervisor the main reason you are leaving and that you aren't angry about the situation.

- **Know the Expectations**   Ask your supervisor what is expected during your remaining time on the job. There may be forms to fill out. The human resources department might conduct an exit interview to find out why you are leaving. Equipment, tools, uniforms, keys, or other items that belong to the organization must be returned. Be sure to get a written receipt showing that you have returned the materials.
- **Don't Be Disruptive**   Coworkers will wonder why you're leaving. Don't complain about your current employer to them. Let them know you've enjoyed working with them and hope to keep in touch. Leaving a job can be sad because you often leave behind friends. If you want to be remembered as a good worker and friend, act accordingly on your last days on the job. You might need a reference or other help from leaders and coworkers in the future.
- **Leave Immediately when Asked**   Some companies require that employees leave immediately upon submitting a resignation. This occurs more frequently when an employee has access to computer-based information that the organization wants to protect. Don't take it personally.

The most important thing about leaving a job is to be fair to both your employer and yourself. Following the guidelines just discussed helps maintain a good relationship with an employer. Your employer will be happy to give you a good reference and may even rehire you in the future if you treat everyone fairly.

How Job Savvy Are You?

Tamara has been a clerk in the post office for five years. She recently completed a four-year degree in accounting and was offered a position with a public accounting firm. The firm wants her to start work in two weeks. Tamara must decide how to resign from her job at the post office.

1.   What steps should Tamara follow to resign from her current job?

_____

_____

_____

Eric is unhappy with his job. The supervisor has been giving him all the "dirty work." He has talked with his supervisor about the problem, but it hasn't helped. Eric found another job that pays better. The new employer wants him to start work immediately. Eric knows that his current employer expects at least two weeks' notice. However, Eric is so mad at his supervisor that he plans to call him on the phone to say he won't be at work anymore.

1.   Do you think Eric should do this?

_____

_____

_____

Continues

Job Savvy: How to Be a Success at Work

> 2. Explain the reasons for your answer.
>
> _____
>
> _____
>
> _____

Finding a New Job

There are times when the best opportunity to advance in your career comes from a new employer. That is why 60%–70% of turnover in jobs is voluntary.[7] When searching for a new job, the best practices for getting promotions described earlier in this chapter will help you. The best strategy for getting a job is networking. At all times, keep the tools that are most useful for a job search up to date. Specifically, keep your résumé updated and maintain a portfolio of your accomplishments. This will provide you with some key resources needed for a job search.

Tools for a Job Search

In this short section of a book on job success, it is impossible to provide the complete discussion needed to help you find a job, so we'll cover the basics here.

Before you begin your **job search**, start with the right tools. Résumés are one tool, but not for the reason many people think. A common misconception is that sending your résumé to lots of HR departments, posting it at many job boards, and giving it to network contacts is the best way to get a job. However, the primary use of a résumé is to give it to people who request it (and, of course, an employer who hires you will need it for their records). A person also needs to maintain a portfolio of job achievements. There is no reason to share a portfolio with someone until you are speaking to an employer in an interview.

Another tool to help you prepare for the job search is the **JIST card** that was originated by Mike Farr and the JIST staff in the 1970s (see Figure 13.1 on the next page). It is a tool to help people find a job. The purpose of the card is to help you network, and networking is the most successful strategy for finding a new job.

The essential data in a JIST card includes (1) your name, (2) contact information, (3) job objective (be specific), (4) summary of your experience and education/training, (5) summary of three to four major accomplishments, (6) special conditions of employment, and (7) list of your greatest strengths or skills. This information should fit on an index card (3" × 5") and be given to everyone you contact while networking for a job. The advantage of an index card is that it sticks out. Many people lay it on their desk. Every so often when they come across the card it reminds them that you are looking for a job. You could also put this information on a business card using both the front and back of the card.

Figure 13.1 JIST Card Example

Maribel Batista, MS

Phone: 888-555-6849
Cell: 888-555-6848
Fax: 888-555-6877
URL: www.linkedin.com/in/maribel-
batista-9692a2113
Email: maribelbatista@JIST.com

Career Summary or Job Objective:
Social Media Strategist, Digital Content Strategist, Digital Content Creator

Skills:
Community Building, Organized and Efficient, Adaptive, Copy Writing, Sales and Customer Service, Strategic, Decisive, Analytical, SEO-driven, Creative, Sense of Humor, Highly Motivated

Accomplishments:
Launched brand business pages and accounts. Grew Facebook Page "likes" to over 5,000, and Twitter followers to 2,200 within one quarter. Distributed product samples to "boat bloggers" community for written and video reviews as well as giveaways. Increased inbound links from blogs and Youtube by 60% from 2018 to 2020.

Outstanding Qualities:
Resourcefulness, Integrity, Adventure, Innovation, Precision, Teamwork, Vision

---

Understanding How the Job Market Works

No matter how high the unemployment rate gets, there are always millions of jobs available. Most people are not taught about how the job market really works. The key facts you need to know about the job market are explained below. These facts will help you understand how to find a job more quickly.

- **Fact 1**   There are always millions of job openings each month. When this book was written in July 2018, there were an average of 6.4 million job openings a month. Even during the height of the great recession in 2009, there were an average of 2.4 million job openings a month.[8] These openings come from existing jobs because employees voluntarily quit their jobs, retire, are no longer able to work, or are fired. In addition, a few hundred thousand new jobs are created each month.

  What does this mean for you? Never get discouraged when looking for a job because there are always millions of openings. The turnover of jobs is lively, and it is only a matter of time before you find one of those job openings that is right for you. Employers are always hiring—even during holiday periods.

  The key to finding a job in less time is spending an average of 20 to 30 hours a week on your job search if you are unemployed and 5 to 10 hours per week when you are employed. The average time per week that people spend on their job search is 11 hours, so beat your competition by spending more time searching for your next job.[9] The length of time it takes to find a job is related to the number of hours you spend seeking a job using the techniques described here.

- **Fact 2**   Most jobs are part of the "hidden" job market. This means almost 80% of all jobs are never advertised. They are not posted on job boards. They are not posted in employment listings for government and private employment. They are filled before advertising is needed. People find out about these openings by family members, friends, or network contacts.

What does this mean for you? Identify people in your network and seek their help finding a job. Write down the names of friends, relatives, neighbors, members of groups you belong to, and people you have worked with in the past. LinkedIn provides an online app to help you identify people in your network and contact them. Touch base with people in your network by phone, email, or social media. Let them know what type of job you are looking for and why you are qualified for the job.

A good way to express this information is by using the JIST card to create an **elevator pitch**. An elevator pitch is a speech that lasts about 30 seconds and is meant to persuade someone to give you a job referral or interview. When it is done in person, you should conclude by giving your JIST card to your contact. There are several websites on the Internet that provide you with hints about how to create an elevator pitch for a job. A search using the words "elevator job pitch" will reveal several sources to help create your own pitch. Table 13.1 shows the best places to find quality talent according to hiring managers.[10]

Table 13.1 How Managers Say the Highest-Quality Employees Are Found

Source of Employee Hires	Percent*
Employee Referrals	41
Promoted Employees	40
Social and Professional Networks	22
Job Boards	11
Direct Applications	7
Recruitment Agencies	7

*The numbers do not add to 100% because some hires were found through more than one source.

- **Fact 3**   Employees who work in small businesses total 48% of all workers (57 million). When looking for a job, consider opportunities that are provided by small businesses because they created 63% of all net new jobs from 1992 to 2013.[11] You might also want to consider working in a nonprofit or government job. The number of nonprofit jobs increased by 14% between 2007 and 2012, providing 11.4 million jobs.[12] There are also 22.3 million jobs in local, state, and federal governments.[13] The point is that you should look for jobs in places you might not have thought about in the past. Don't limit your possibilities.

What does this mean for you? You may have worked in a large business all your life and tend to focus your job search on large businesses. Break this habit and consider other opportunities. Since almost half of all business-related jobs are in small businesses, divide your time equally with small, medium, and large business opportunities.

Likewise, spend a reasonable amount of time seeking jobs with non-profits and the government. Also, don't assume because of the size of a business or type of organization that the pay and benefits will be much less than what is offered by a large business. Check out job openings of all employers. You can always turn down a job that doesn't fit your requirements for pay and benefits.

Steps to Finding a New Job

Getting a new job is not as difficult as it seems. The key facts about the job market you just read support this view. The best way to find a job is to follow the best advice from experts who are successful in helping people find jobs. The following actions are used by this author to help thousands of people successfully find jobs. Use them and you, too, will be successful.

- **Have a Clear Job Objective**   You need to have a clear goal in mind about the job you want. It is important because a clear objective becomes the basis for all planning, actions, and communications during a job search.
- **Identify Your Most Valuable Skills**   The skills you identified in Chapter 7, Knowing Yourself, are a great place to start. Be able to describe your top three skills and top three character strengths.
- **Identify Your Best Achievements**   Find examples that can be used to verify your strengths and skills when communicating with employers. Turn these examples into stories that weave in statistics and facts. Employers, like all people, will remember these stories and facts better than general statements.
- **Create Basic Job Search Tools**   Use your job objective, skills, and strengths to develop a résumé, portfolio, JIST card, and elevator speech.
- **Google Your Name**   This book has offered warnings about social media misuse. One of the pioneers in modern job search techniques is Richard Bolles, who suggests that a job search should begin with a google search of the potential employee's name.[14] Delete texts, photos, website registrations, and anything negative you might find about yourself. If you don't own the content, then you will need to request that the owner delete it. If that doesn't work, you may request that Google prohibit it from showing up in searches.
- **Set a Schedule for Your Job Search**   Plan on spending at least 10 hours each week on the job search. (Spend closer to 25 to 30 hours if you are currently unemployed). Spend at least 70% of your time each week contacting people in your network. Spend about 10% of your time each week signing up for job boards, 10% filling out online applications for specific employers, and 10% with employment agencies.
- **Make Each Contact Count**   Ask each network contact to talk with you for 10 minutes by phone or preferably a videoconference service such as Skype or Zoom before you apply. A free online communications service that lets you easily display documents from your portfolio is ideal. Begin the conversation with your 30-second elevator speech. Finish the script by asking if they'd be interested in interviewing you

for a job. If a person doesn't want to interview you, ask them for one or two names and contact information for someone who might be interested in interviewing you. Follow up conversations with your contacts by sending them an email thanking them for their time and include a pdf of your JIST card. If you have their mail address, you will stand out among competitors by sending a handwritten thank you and JIST card.

- **Focus on the Goal of Getting Job Interviews** Sending résumés, filling out applications (including online applications), and talking with network contacts almost never result in job offers. Employers make hiring decisions after interviewing potential employees. That is why you should end the job script by expressing your interest in the job and asking when the person is available to interview you. Simply say at the end of the script, "When may I have an interview with you?"

- **Keep Improving Your Job Search Skills** Most people only seek a new job every few years, so their job search skills are limited or outdated. Seek help from a career coach to improve your job search skills. There are many low-cost or free job search services available if you are unable to pay for this service.

- **Never Give Up** Many times people give up on their job search because they think it is taking them too long. Everyone eventually finds a good job fit. It is a matter of making enough contacts and getting enough interviews. The more contacts and interviews you have, the more likely you are to reach your job objective. Remember, each no from an employer is one step closer to a yes.

This section on getting a job is a very brief guide for job seekers. There are many free resources, including library books and YouTube videos, that you can use to find more information about job searches. Never feel stuck in a job where you are unappreciated or not receiving the opportunities you want. On the other hand, the old saying that the grass is always greener on the other side is somewhat true. If you are considering whether to seek a new job, think through the decision carefully and get advice from other people before making a serious move like quitting.

A Useful Skill: Negotiation

Negotiation is the ability to bring together others and try to reconcile differences. In some instances this skill is applied to highly emotional situations that require reaching an agreement between employers and employees on a large scale.

This skill is also useful to you as an individual. When you want a raise or a promotion, you will need to negotiate with your supervisor. If your coworker disagrees with the way you are doing a task, you may need to come to a compromise. If a customer wants a refund and doesn't have the receipt, negotiation may occur.

To learn to negotiate, you will need to overcome shyness, control your emotions, state facts, and listen to others. Mastering the skill of negotiating will make your job easier and more rewarding. Negotiating to solve issues you have with your job before resigning is a good option to consider.

Summing Up

A job provides you with many opportunities, including pay raises, promotions, challenges, satisfaction, recognition, friendships, and a career. It's up to you to take advantage of these opportunities. When opportunities seem limited at your job, you may find your career will be better served by finding another job. By following the suggestions in this chapter, you can reach the career goals you set for yourself. Good luck on your journey!

Review and Assessment

Take the Review Quiz. See your instructor or reference your student files in the ebook for additional resources.

In Closing

You have an exciting future ahead. Your job is an important part of that future. It can provide you with the money you need to support a family and have the lifestyle you want, including perhaps a home and car in addition to pursuing the recreational activities you like. Success in the jobs you work at throughout your lifetime also leads to a fulfilling career and meaningful life.

You have the ability to control your success by putting these skills into practice:

- Know what your employer expects from you and do your best to meet those expectations.
- Be a dependable employee who is punctual and works whenever scheduled.
- Have a pleasant appearance and manners. Be the person others like to be around.
- Learn to do your job well. Take advantage of opportunities to improve your skills whenever training is offered. Be a lifelong learner.
- Believe in yourself and in your abilities. Know your skills and apply them. Know your character strengths and work to improve them.
- Recognize the important role leaders play in your job success. Listen, complete assigned tasks, and go beyond what is required. Make yourself an important part of the team. Be a courageous follower.
- Cooperate and be friendly with coworkers. Success is not just personal advancement but knowing you contributed to other people's success along the way.
- Participate in problem solving at work. Look for problems that you can help solve. Work with your supervisor and coworkers to solve problems.
- Be an honest employee. Your employer should be able to rely on your ethical behavior and integrity.
- Know what success on the job means for you. Plan your career and know how your current job fits into your career plans. If you want pay raises and promotions, know what your employer expects you to do to get them.
- Recognize when it is time to move on and find another job. Learn new skills and improve old ones so you will always be competitive and never be afraid to leave a job.

Follow these practical, simple guidelines. Then say to yourself, "Look out, world! Here I come!"

Endnotes

Chapter 1 Endnotes

1. "24 percent of employed people did some or all of their work at home in 2015," *The Economics Daily*, US Department of Labor Bureau of Labor Statistics, July 8, 2016, https://www.bls.gov /opub/ted/2016/24-percent-of-employed-people-did-some-or-all-of-their-work-at-home-in -2015.htm (accessed February 1, 2018).

2. T. Alan Lacey, Mitra Toossi, Kevin S. Dubina, and Andrea B. Gensler, "Projections overview and highlights, 2016–26," *Monthly Labor Review*, US Department of Labor Bureau of Labor Statistics, October 2017, https://doi.org/10.21916/mlr.2017.29.

3. "Characteristics of minimum wage workers, 2017," News Release, US Department of Labor Bureau of Labor Statistics, https://www.bls.gov/opub/reports/minimum-wage/2017/pdf/home.pdf (last updated March 2018).

4. Note: The Bureau of Labor Statistics totals for percentages do not necessarily add to 100 because of rounding. The precise percentages here are whites 58%, Hispanic 20.6%, black, 12.7%, Asians 7.2%, and all other 3.9%, which totals 102.4%. This is the case for all statistics that BLS produces and applies to all statistics in this book.

5. "Employment projections, 2016–2026," News Release, US Department of Labor Bureau of Labor Statistics, October 24, 2017, https://www.bls.gov/news.release/pdf/ecopro.pdf (accessed March 14, 2018).

6. "National business employment dynamics data by firm size class, Table F Distribution of private sector employment by firm size class: 1993/Q1 through 2017/Q1, not seasonally adjusted," US Department of Labor Bureau of Labor Statistics, https://www.bls.gov/bdm/bdmfirmsize.htm (accessed March 16, 2018).

7. Audrey L. Watson, "Employment Trends by Typical Entry-Level Education Requirement," *Monthly Labor Review*, US Department of Labor Bureau of Labor Statistics, September 2017, https://doi.org/10.21916/mlr.2017.22.

8. "Unemployment rates and earnings by educational attainment," Employment Projections, US Department of Labor Bureau of Labor Statistics, https://www.bls.gov/emp/ep_table_001.htm (accessed May 1, 2018).

9. Lawrence F. Katz, and Alan B. Krueger, "The rise and nature of alternative work arrangements in the United States, 1995–2015," National Bureau of Economic Research, September 2016, http://www.nber.org/papers/w22667.

10. Elka Torpey and Andrew Hogan, "Working in a gig economy," *Career Outlook*, US Department of Labor Bureau of Labor Statistics, May 2016, https://www.bls.gov/careeroutlook/2016/article/what -is-the-gig-economy.htm (accessed March 14, 2018).

11. *Learning a Living: A Blueprint for High Performance, a SCANS Report for America 2000*, US Department of Labor, Secretary's Commission on Achieving Necessary Skills (Washington, DC: Government Printing Office, 1992).

12. *Bridging the Skills Gap: How the Skills Shortage Threatens Growth and Competitiveness . . . and What to Do About It*, White Paper, American Society for Training and Development (Alexandria, VA: ASTD Press, 2006).

13. "AMA 2010 Critical Skills Survey: Executive Summary," American Management Association, www.amanet.org/PDF/Critical-Skills-Survey.pdf.

14. "AMA 2010 Critical Skills Survey: Executive Summary," 13.

15. The Carnegie Foundation for the Advancement of Teaching, *A Study of Engineering Education* by Charles Ribogg Mann, *Bulletin Number Eleven*, Prepared for the Joint Committee on Engineering Education of the National Engineering Societies, New York City 576 Fifth Avenue (Boston: DB Updike, The Merrymount Press).

16. Marcel Schwantes, "Why Google's Managers Are So Wildly Successful Comes Down to These 8 Behaviors," *Inc.*, July 27, 2017, https://www.inc.com/marcel-schwantes/the-8-biggest-things-that -google-managers-do-to-su.html.

17. Laura H. Lippman, Renee Ryberg, Rachel Carney, and Kristin A. Moore, "Key 'Soft Skills' That Foster Youth Workforce Success: Toward a Consensus Across Fields," *Workforce Connections*, Child Trends, June 2015, https://www.childtrends.org/wp-content/uploads/2015/06/2015 -24AWFCSoftSkillsExecSum.pdf.

18. Christina Lee, project leader, "Employee Job Satisfaction and Engagement: The Doors of Opportunity are Open," Society for Human Resource Management, Executive Summary, 2017, https://www.shrm.org/hr-today/trends-and-forecasting/research-and-surveys/Documents/2017 -Employee-Job-Satisfaction-and-Engagement-Executive-Summary.pdf.

Chapter 2 Endnotes

1. Klein, Howard J., Beth Polin, and Kyra Leigh Sutton, "Specific onboarding practices for the socialization of new employees," *International Journal of Selection and Assessment*, 23, no. 3 (2015): 263-83, https://doi.org/10.1111/ijsa.12113.

2. "National Compensation Survey: Employee Benefits in the United States," US Department of Labor Bureau of Labor Statistics, 2017 Bulletin (2787), https://www.bls.gov/ncs/ebs /benefits/2017/ebbl0061.pdf.

3. John F. Kelly, "Addiction In The Workplace: What You Need to Know," *Psychology Today*, June 14, 2017, https://www.psychologytoday.com/us/blog/addiction-recovery-101/201706/addiction-in -the-workplace-what-you-need-know.

4. "IRS Withholding Calculator," IRS, https://www.irs.gov/individuals/irs-withholding-calculator (last modified March 7, 2018).

5. Small Business Committee, "Cafeteria Plans: A Menu of Non-Options for Small Business Owners," https://smallbusiness.house.gov/news/documentsingle.aspx?DocumentID=399779 (last modified March 16, 2017).

6. "National Compensation Survey: Employee Benefits in the United States," US Department of Labor Bureau of Labor Statistics, 2017 Bulletin (2787), https://www.bls.gov/ncs/ebs /benefits/2017/ownership/civilian/table02a.pdf.

7. "Employee Benefits in the United States—March 2017," News Release, US Department of Labor Bureau of Labor Statistics, https://www.bls.gov/news.release/pdf/ebs2.pdf (last modified July 21, 2017).

8. Marsha Ludden, *Effective Workplace Communication*, Third Edition (Indianapolis: JIST Publishing, 2007), 23.

Chapter 3 Endnotes

1. Thomas C. Mann, and Melissa J. Ferguson, "Can we undo our first impressions? The role of reinterpretation in reversing implicit evaluations," *Journal of Personality and Social Psychology*, 108, no. 6 (2015): 823–849, https://doi.org/10.1037/pspa0000021.

2. Robert Half, "Just How Casual Is the Dress Code Becoming for Accountants?," June 19, 2017, https://www.roberthalf.com/blog/salaries-and-skills/just-how-casual-is-the-dress-code-becoming -for-accountants.

3. Society for Human Resource Management, "Managing Employee Dress and Appearance," https://www.shrm.org (last updated October 25, 2016).

4. Liz Ryan, "Ten Things Never, Ever To Wear To Work," *Forbes*, October 30, 2017, https://www .forbes.com/sites/lizryan/2017/10/30/ten-things-never-ever-to-wear-to-work/#15b738a84d9b.

5. "Recommended Practices for Safety and Health Programs," US Department of Labor Occupational Safety and Health Administration, www.osha.gov/shpguidelines (accessed June 8, 2018).

6. "Religious Garb and Grooming in the Workplace: Rights and Responsibilities," US Equal Employment Opportunity Commission, https://www.eeoc.gov/eeoc/publications/qa_religious _garb_grooming.cfm (accessed April 9, 2018).

7. Jessica Sussman, "Grooming Policy," XpertHR, https://www.xperthr.com/policies-and-documents/grooming-policy/5955/ (accessed April 10, 2018).

8. Josh Lowe, "Cellphones: Texting While Walking is Causing People to Hurt Themselves," *Newsweek*, http://www.newsweek.com/cellphones-scientists-walking-traffic-630558 (last updated June 30, 2017).

9. "Employers Reveal the Top Factors Preventing Workers' Chance of Promotion in New CareerBuilder Survey," CareerBuilder, July 2, 2015, https://www.careerbuilder.com/share/aboutus/pressreleasesdetail.aspx?sd=7/2/2015&id=pr901&ed=12/31/2015.

Chapter 4 Endnotes

1. CDC Foundation, "Worker Illness and Injury Costs US Employers $225.8 Billion Annually," January 28, 2015, https://www.cdcfoundation.org/pr/2015/worker-illness-and-injury-costs-us-employers-225-billion-annually.

2. Chad Brooks, "Choosing a Time and Attendance System," *Business News Daily*, April 10, 2018, https://www.businessnewsdaily.com/6763-choosing-time-and-attendance-systems.html.

3. Tracy Volkmann, "Paychex Small Business Snapshot: Survey Shows Most Preferred Method of Tracking Time Worked is Online," Paychex, May 16, 2017, http://media.paychex.com/time-attendance-apa-2017.

4. "CareerBuilder Survey Reveals This Year's Most Outrageous Employee Excuses for Being Late," CareerBuilder, https://www.careerbuilder.com/share/aboutus/pressreleasesdetail.aspx?id=pr985&sd=1/26/2017&ed=01/26/2017 (last modified January 26, 2017).

5. Anonymous, "17th Annual Unscheduled Absence Survey," *Medical Benefits*, December 15, 2007, Volume 24 Issue 23: 1–2.

6. John H. Ostdick, "11 Strategies for Managing Stress," *Success*, February 22, 2017, https://www.success.com/article/11-strategies-for-managing-stress.

7. Marco Hafner, Martin Stepanek, Jirka Taylor, Wendy M. Troxel, and Christian Van Stolk, *Why sleep matters–The Economic Costs of Insufficient Sleep: A Cross-Country Comparative Analysis* (Santa Monica, CA: RAND Corporation, 2016), https://.doi.org/10.7249/RR1791.

8. Frank Newport, "For First Time, Majority in US Supports Public Smoking Ban," Gallup, July 15, 2011, http://www.gallup.com/poll/148514/first-time-majority-supports-public-smoking-ban.aspx.

9. Linda Richter, "What is Vaping?," The National Center on Addiction and Substance Abuse, December 2016, https://www.centeronaddiction.org/e-cigarettes/recreational-vaping/what-vaping.

10. Scott Mautz, "Psychology and Neuroscience Blow-Up the Myth of Effective Multitasking," *Inc.*, May 11, 2017, https://www.inc.com/scott-mautz/psychology-and-neuroscience-blow-up-the-myth-of-effective-multitasking.html.

Chapter 5 Endnotes

1. Hart Research Associates, "Falling Short? College Learning and Career Success," Association of American Colleges and Universities, 2015, https://aacu.org/sites/default/files/files/LEAP/2015employerstudentsurvey.pdf.

2. Iring Koch, Edita Poljac, Hermann Müller, and Andrea Kiesel, "Cognitive structure, flexibility, and plasticity in human multitasking—an integrative review of dual-task and task-switching research," *Psychological Bulletin*, 144, no. 6 (2018): 557.

3. Mike Elgan, "With smartphones like these, why do we need laptops?" *Computerworld*, https://www.computerworld.com/article/3241233/smartphones/with-smartphones-like-these-why-do-we-need-laptops.html (last modified Dec 9, 2017).

4. Silvia Bonaccio, Jane O'Reilly, Sharon L. O'Sullivan, and François Chiocchio, "Nonverbal behavior and communication in the workplace: a review and an agenda for research," *Journal of Management*, 42, no. 5 (2016): 1044.

5. Editors and Writers, "Top 8 Differences in Nonverbal Communication Across Cultures," *Silver Sage Magazine*, July 6, 2017, https://www.silversagemag.com/top-8-differences-nonverbal-communication-across-cultures.

6. Foreign Service Institute, "Communication 101: The Basic Elements of Communication," *So You're an American? A Guide to Answering Difficult Questions,* US Department of State, https://www.state.gov/m/fsi/tc/answeringdifficultquestions/html/app.htm?p=module3_p2.htm (accessed May 18, 2018).

7. Georgia Wells and Robert McMillan, "Facebook Fires Employee Who Bragged on Tinder About His Access to User Data," *Wall Street Journal,* May 2, 2018, https://www.wsj.com/articles /facebook-fires-employee-who-bragged-on-tinder-about-his-access-to-user-data-1525294488.

8. Jamie Herzlich, "Email still king for workplace communication, but IM's booming," *Newsday,* July 2, 2017, https://www.newsday.com/business/columnists/jamie-herzlich/email-still-king-for -workplace-communication-but-im-s-booming-1.13773982.

9. "New CareerBuilder Survey Reveals How Much Smartphones Are Sapping Productivity at Work," CareerBuilder, https://www.careerbuilder.com/share/aboutus/pressreleasesdetail.aspx?sd=6%2f9 %2f2016&siteid=cbpr&sc_cmp1=cb_pr954_&id=pr954&ed=12%2f31%2f2016 (last modified June 9, 2016).

10. Randy Hines and Joseph Basso, "Do communication students have the 'write stuff?' Practitioners evaluate writing skills of entry-level workers," *Journal of Promotion Management,* 14, no. 3-4: 293.

Chapter 6 Endnotes

1. Camille L. Ryan and Kurt Bauman, "Educational Attainment in the United States: 2015," US Census Bureau, March 2016, https://www.census.gov/content/dam/Census/library /publications/2016/demo/p20-578.pdf.

2. Malcolm S. Knowles, Elwood F. Holton, and Richard A. Swanson, *The Adult Learner: The Definitive Classic in Adult Education and Human Resource Development, 8th Edition* (New York, NY: Routledge, 2015).

3. Malcolm Gladwell, *Outliers: The Story of Success* (New York, NY: Little Brown and Company, 2008).

4. OECD (2016), "Indicator C6 How Many Adults Participate in Education and Learning?," in *Education at a Glance 2016: OECD Indicators* (Paris, France: OECD Publishing).

5. Matthew Franke, "Your 2018 Guide to College Tuition Tax Breaks," The Motley Fool, LLC, https://www.fool.com/investing/2018/03/17/your-2018-guide-to-college-tuition-tax-breaks.aspx.

6. Peter Senge, *The Fifth Discipline: The Art & Practice of the Learning Organization* (New York, NY: Doubleday, 2006, p. 3).

7. John Naisbitt and Patricia Aburdene, *Re-inventing the corporation* (New York: Warner Books, 1985, p. 141).

Chapter 7 Endnotes

1. Nathan A. Bowling, Kevin J. Eschleman, Qiang Wang, Cristina Kirkendall, and Gene Alarcon, "A meta-analysis of the predictors and consequences of organization-based self-esteem," *Journal of Occupational and Organizational Psychology,* 83, no. 3 (2010): 601–626.

2. Mayo Clinic Staff, "Self-esteem check: Too low or just right?," Healthy Lifestyle: Adult Health, Mayo Clinic, https://www.mayoclinic.org/healthy-lifestyle/adult-health/in-depth/self-esteem/art -20047976 (accessed June 4, 2018).

3. Christopher Peterson, *Pursuing the Good Life: 100 Reflections on Positive Psychology* (New York, NY: Oxford University Press, 2013), 3.

4. Patrick L. Hill and Nicholas A. Turiano, "Purpose in life as a predictor of mortality across adulthood," *Psychological Science,* 25, no. 7 (2014): 1482–1486.

5. Amy Wrzeniewski, *Oxford University Handbook of Positive Organizational Scholarship,* eds. Kim S. Cameron and Gretchen M. Spreitzer (New York, NY: Oxford University Press, 2012), 45.

6. Benjamin M. Galvin, Amy E. Randel, Brian J. Collins, and Russell E. Johnson, "Changing the focus of locus (of control): a targeted review of the locus of control literature and agenda for future research," *Journal of Organizational Behavior,* March 23 (2018): 1-14, https://doi.org/10.1002 /job.2275.

7. Ryan T. Sauers, *Would You Buy From You?,* KMB Publishing Group Worldwide, 2015.

8. Nansook Park and Christopher Peterson, "Character strengths: research and practice," *Journal of College and Character*, 10, no. 4 (2009): 1–10.

9. Chris Argyris, "Good communication that blocks learning," *Harvard Business Review*, 72, no. 4 (1994): 77–85.

Chapter 8 Endnotes

1. Robert D. Ramsey, "The Art of Delegation," *Supervision*, 77, no. 2 (2016): 7–9.

2. Peter G. Northouse, *Leadership Theory and Practice* (Los Angeles, CA: Sage Publications, 2016), 144.

3. Phillip S. Meilinger, "The Ten Rules of Good Followership," *AU Concepts for Air Force Leadership*, 2001: 99–101, www.au.af.mil/au/awc/awcgate/au-24/meilinger.pdf.

4. Alan C. Mikkelson, Joy A. York, and Joshua Arritola, "Communication Competence, Leadership Behaviors, and Employee Outcomes in Supervisor-Employee Relationships," *Business and Professional Communication Quarterly*, 78, no. 3 (2015): 336–354.

5. LaVerne L. Ludden and Tom Capozzoli, *Supervisor Savvy: How to Retain and Develop Entry-Level Workers* (Indianapolis, IN: JIST Publishing, 2000).

6. Liz Ryan, "How to Prepare for Your Performance Review—and Rock It," *Forbes*, December 31, 2015, https://www.forbes.com/sites/lizryan/2015/12/31/how-to-prepare-for-your-performance -review-and-rock-it/#626581a626a5.

7. Ira Chaleff, *Intelligent Disobedience: Doing Right When What You're Told to Do Is Wrong* (Oakland, CA: Berrett-Koehler Publishers, Inc., 2015), 186.

8. Richard E. Boyatzis, "Competencies in the 21st century," *Journal of Management Development*, 7, no. 1 (2008): 5–12.

Chapter 9 Endnotes

1. Jeff Schwartz, Udo Bohdal-Spiegelhoff, Michael Gretczko, and Nathan Sloan, *Global Human Capital Trends 2016, The new organization: Different by design* (Deloitte University Press, 2016).

2. Chad A. Schulenburg, "Perceptions of Wisdom by Organizational Leaders," (PhD dissertation, Department of Leadership Studies, Indiana: Wesleyan University, 2017). Publication number 10642871, https://pqdtopen.proquest.com/doc/1972562183.html?FMT=ABS.

   Also Scott A. Peterson, "An Understanding of Wisdom Within CCCU Presidents" (EdD dissertation, Division of Graduate Studies in Leadership, Indiana Wesleyan University, 2016). Publication number 10286617, https://0-search-proquest-com.oak.indwes.edu/docview/19146769 42?accountid=6363.

   Also Scott R. Livingston, "Perceptions of Executive Coaches About Wisdom in Organizational Leaders" (EdD dissertation, Division of Graduate Studies in Leadership, Indiana Wesleyan University, 2012). Publication number 3509698, https://pqdtopen.proquest.com /doc/1020617202.html?FMT=ABS.

3. Lisa M. Leslie, "A Status-Based Multilevel Model of Ethnic Diversity and Work Unit Performance," *Journal of Management*, 43, no. 2 (2017): 426–454.

4. Stephen Robbins and Timothy A. Judge, *Organizational Behavior*, 14th ed. (Englewood Cliffs, NJ: Prentice Hall Higher Education, 2010).

5. David Keirsey, *Please Understand Me, II* (Del Mar, CA: Prometheus Nemesis Books, 1998).

6. "Employment projections, 2016–2026," US Department of Labor Bureau of Labor Statistics, https://www.bls.gov/news.release/pdf/ecopro.pdf (accessed March 14, 2018).

7. "Employment Projections: Civilian Labor Force by Age, Sex, Race, and Ethnicity," US Department of Labor Bureau of Labor Statistics, https://www.bls.gov/emp/tables/civilian-labor -force-detail.htm (accessed June 7, 2018).

8. Suzanne T. Bell, Shanique G. Brown, Anthony Colaneri, and Neal Outland, "Team Composition and the ABCs of Teamwork," *American Psychologist*, 73, no. 4 (2018): 349–362.

9. Eleanor Cummins, "Why Do We Still Have Fax Machines? Just the Fax, Please," *Popular Science*, May 3, 2018, https://www.popsci.com/why-fax-machines-still-exist#page-2.

10. Lyndsey Matthews, "20 Office Etiquette Rules Every Person Should Follow," *Town & Country*, July 10, 2017, https://www.townandcountrymag.com/society/a10276858/office-etiquette.

11. "Occupational Violence," Centers for Disease Control and Prevention, The National Institute for Occupational Safety and Health (NIOSH), https://www.cdc.gov/niosh/topics/violence/fastfacts .html (last updated March 28, 2018).

12. Thomas Capozzoli and R. Steve McVey, *Managing Violence in the Workplace* (Delray Beach, FL: St. Lucie Press, 1996).

13. Mayo Clinic, "Mental illness," https://www.mayoclinic.org/diseases-conditions/mental-illness /symptoms-causes/syc-20374968 (accessed June 19, 2018).

Chapter 10 Endnotes

1. "#WellActually, Americans Say Customer Service is Better Than Ever," American Express Press Release, December 15, 2017, https://about.americanexpress.com/press-release/wellactually -americans-say-customer-service-better-ever.

2. "4 Best Practices to Retain Your Current Customers While Growing Your Agency," Pagewiz, September 1, 2016, https://www.pagewiz.com/blog/online-marketing/retain-customers-growing -agency.

3. "#WellActually, Americans Say Customer Service is Better Than Ever," 1.

4. Sling Team, "The 20 Most Important Customer Service Skills You Need to Have," Sling, August 11, 2017, https://getsling.com/blog/customer-service-skills.

5. Michael Roennevig, "Top 10 Ways to Handle Verbally Abusive Customers." Small Business, Chron.com, http://smallbusiness.chron.com/top-10-ways-handle-verbally-abusive -customers-23714.html (accessed 15 August 2018).

6. Fred Jandt, *The Customer Is Usually Wrong!* (Indianapolis, IN: Park Avenue Productions, 1995).

7. Karen Leland and Keith Bailey, *Customer Service for Dummies*, 3rd ed. (Hoboken, NJ: John Wiley and Sons, Inc., 2006).

Chapter 11 Endnotes

1. Nathan Bennett and G. James Lemoine, "What VUCA Really Means for You," *Harvard Business Review*, 92, no. 1–2 (2014): p. 27.

2. Danica Bakotić and Andrijana Rogošić, "Employee involvement as a key determinant of core quality management practices," *Total Quality Management & Business Excellence*, 28, no. 11–12 (2017): 1209–1226.

3. Wendall Williams, "Employee Competencies for the Future," *Journal of Corporate Recruiting Leadership*, 6, no. 4 (May 2011): 15–17.

4. Ingrid J. Guerra-López, *Performance Evaluation: Proven Approaches for Improving Program and Organizational Performance* (San Francisco, CA: Jossey-Bass, 2008) 168–171.

5. Bill Murphy, Jr., "How to Solve Any Problem by Asking 5 Questions, *Inc.* magazine, March 11, 2016, https://www.inc.com/bill-murphy-jr/how-to-solve-any-problem-by-asking-5-questions.html.

6. Daniel Kahneman, *Thinking, Fast and Slow* (New York, NY: Farrar, Straus and Giroux, 2011).

Chapter 12 Endnotes

1. Madeline Boehmer, "25 Jaw Dropping Stats About Employee Fraud," Business 2 Community, June 7, 2016, https://www.business2community.com/human-resources/25-jaw-dropping-stats -employee-fraud-01561237.

2. "Software Management: Security Imperative, Business Opportunity," BSA Global Software Survey, BSA The Software Alliance, June 2018, https://gss.bsa.org/wp-content/uploads/2018/05/2018 _BSA_GSS_Report_en.pdf.

3. Valerie Bolden-Barrett, "HBR: Internal Cyber Threats Account for 39% of Breaches," HR Dive, December 6, 2017, https://www.hrdive.com/news/hbr-internal-cyber-threats-account-for-39-of -breaches/512343/.

4. Phillip Perry, "Workplace Drug Abuse: Reducing the Risk of Impaired Workers," *National Oil and Lube News,* July 31, 2017, https://noln.net/2017/07/31/workplace-drug-abuse-reducing-risk -impaired-workers/.

5. Kenneth Blanchard and Norman Vincent Peale, *The Power of Ethical Management* (New York, NY: Morrow, 1988), 47.

6. Ira Chaleff, *The Courageous Follower: Standing up to and for Our Leaders* (San Francisco, CA: Berrett-Koehler, 2009).

7. Immanuel Kant, *The Moral Law: Groundwork of the Metaphysics of Morals* (New York, NY: Routledge, 2005).

8. Peter Gasca, "With Data Theft by Employees on the Rise, Don't Look at Cybersecurity as a Mission Impossible," *Entrepreneur,* https://www.entrepreneur.com/article/272319 (last updated on March 14, 2016).

9. BSA The Software Alliance, 2.

10. "Summary of the HIPAA Security Rule," US Department of Health & Human Services, Health Information Privacy, https://www.hhs.gov/hipaa/for-professionals/security/laws-regulations/index .html (accessed June 12, 2018).

11. "Family Educational Rights and Privacy Act (FERPA)," US Department of Education, Laws & Guidance/General, https://www2.ed.gov/policy/gen/guid/fpco/ferpa/index.html (last updated March 1, 2018).

Chapter 13 Endnotes

1. "Revelations from Workforce Turnover," ADP Research Institute, 2018, https://www.adp .com/tools-and-resources/adp-research-institute/research-and-trends/research-item-detail. aspx?id=D7376F79-6113-4294-BC2D-A698ACC0ED8B.

2. Christina Lee, "2017 Employee Job Satisfaction and Engagement: The Doors of Opportunity Are Open," Society for Human Resource Management, April 24, 2017, https://www.shrm.org /hr-today/trends-and-forecasting/research-and-surveys/pages/2017-job-satisfaction-and -engagement-doors-of-opportunity-are-open.aspx.

3. Jari J. Hakanen, Maria C. W. Peeters, and Wilmar B. Schaufeli, "Different types of employee well being across time and their relationships with job crafting," *Journal of Occupational Health Psychology,* 23, no. 2 (2018): 289–301.

4. Matt Slinger, "2018 Job Seeker Nation Study Researching the Candidate-Recruiter," *Jobvite,* April 24, 2018, https://www.jobvite.com/jobvite-news-and-reports/job-seeker-nation-2018-the -candidate-recruiter-relationship.

5. Marissa Levin, "Chasing Down a Mentor to Help You Grow? Be Ready to Answer These 4 Questions," *Inc.,* March 19, 2018, https://www.inc.com/marissa-levin/4-questions-to-answer -before-you-ask-someone-to-be-your-mentor.html.

6. "Number of Jobs, Labor Market Experience, and Earnings Growth Among Americans at 50: Results From a Longitudinal Survey," News Release, US Department of Labor Bureau of Labor Statistics, August 24, 2017, https://www.bls.gov/news.release/pdf/nlsoy.pdf.

7. "Revelations from Workforce Turnover," 1.

8. "Databases, Tables & Calculators by Subject: Job Openings and Labor Turnover Survey," US Department of Labor Bureau of Labor Statistics, July 31, 2018, https://data.bls.gov/timeseries /JTS00000000JOL.

9. "New CareerBuilder Study Unveils Surprising Must Knows for Job Seekers and Companies Looking to Hire," CareerBuilder, June 1, 2016, http://www.careerbuilder.com/share/aboutus /pressreleasesdetail.aspx?ed=12%2F31%2F2016&id=pr951&sd=6%2F1%2F2016.

10. "Deal-Breakers, Biases, and Best Practices: Everything That Goes Into Evaluating the Perfect Hire," 2017 Recruiter Nation Report, Jobvite, https://www.jobvite.com/wp-content /uploads/2017/09/Jobvite_2017_Recruiter_Nation_Report.pdf (accessed July 3, 2018).

11. "Frequently Asked Questions About Small Business," US Small Business Administration Office of Advocacy, June 2016, https://www.sba.gov/sites/default/files/advocacy/SB-FAQ-2016_WEB.pdf.

12. Erik Friesenhahn, "Nonprofits in America: New Research Data on Employment, Wages, and Establishments," *Monthly Labor Review,* US Department of Labor Bureau of Labor Statistics, February 2016, https://www.bls.gov/opub/mlr/2016/article/nonprofits-in-america.htm.

13. "The Employment Situation—MAY 2018," News Release, United States Department of Labor Bureau of Labor Statistics, June 1, 2018, https://www.bls.gov/news.release/pdf/empsit.pdf.

14. Richard N. Bolles, *What Color is Your Parachute?: A Practical Manual for Job-Hunters and Career-Changers* (New York, NY: Ten Speed Press, 2018).

Glossary

Terms are marked with location references. For example, 2/42 is Chapter 2, page 42.

A

Active listener A person who pays careful attention to what is being said by others—particularly leaders and training personnel—and who may record the information being shared. 2/42

Analyze Study in detail the parts or characteristics of something (e.g., a problem) to better understand its nature and how its parts are related. 11/171

B

Benefits Non-monetary compensation for work an employee does, in addition to wages that are earned. Examples of common benefits are health insurance, life insurance, vacation days, and paid holidays. 2/19

Brainstorming A meeting where employees share creative ideas without criticism or debate. 11/172

Business attire Clothes an employee wears that are appropriate for the workplace and the job. 3/44

C

Career development The lifelong process of managing the activities needed to reach your personal goals in work and in life. 13/207

Character strengths Individual traits that have a moral, virtuous, or ethical aspect; e.g., courage, wisdom, and humility. 7/104

Classroom instruction Employer-provided training for several employees at the same time. It uses many methods, including lectures, digital media, discussion, role-playing, case studies, games, and learning exercises. 6/88

Coaching Communication from a supervisor to employees about their job performance, with the goal of helping employees do the best job possible. A good supervisor can help employees improve work performance. 8/124

Confidentiality Keeping data, information, and knowledge private (i.e., not sharing it with anyone unless they are authorized by organization leaders). 12/193

Conflict resolution The act of resolving a conflict between employees or between employees and managers by discovering the reasons for the conflict and finding solutions to the conflict. 8/132

Courageous followership The ability to question an order when it doesn't seem legal, ethical, or in accordance with company policies. This approach might result in refusing to carry out a supervisor's order as a last resort. 8/131

Courteous Treating people in a respectful, polite, civil, and caring manner. 10/156

Coworkers People who you work with at an organization. They typically include other employees who perform similar work and are at a similar level within the workplace. 9/138

Creativity The expression of ideas or actions that are original, new, inspirational, or inventive. 11/174

Critical thinking The application of an orderly thinking process that compiles accurate facts, makes assumptions, follows a logical process, makes conclusions, and settles on a correct belief or action. 1/14

Customer An individual who purchases a service or product from an organization (also *clients*, *patrons*, and *shoppers*). 10/153

Customer service Positive treatment of customers that results in customer satisfaction with a product or service and that encourages customers to buy services or products and return to the organization to make more purchases. 10/153

Cyber loafing Using the Internet for personal use during working hours; e.g., playing games, shopping, and chatting with friends. 12/190

D

Decision-making A process, either formal or informal, that a person uses to make a decision. 1/14

Deductions The money withheld from an employee's pay to reimburse the employer for benefits an employee pays to receive. It also includes money an employee elects to withhold for donations to charities, such as United Way. 2/27

Dependability The characteristic or skill of being on time and at work every day as scheduled or notifying your supervisor when you are unable to be at work as planned. 1/1

Direct deposit A method for paying employees that involves transferring payment for work from an organization's bank account directly to the employee's back account. 2/28

Disciplinary action An option taken by a supervisor to discipline employees when their job performance is poor and not improving. Actions can include oral and written warnings, suspension, or termination. 8/133

Diversity Differences between individual employees including preferences (values), temperaments, and individual characteristics (such as gender, ethnicity, and age). Diversity is considered a positive team attribute in the workplace. 9/140

E

Ecommunication Communicating with another person using the Internet to transfer information; e.g., email, videoconference, and chat apps. 5/77

Education A formal process in which professional teachers plan and assist students in learning about a subject. Education institutions include elementary, junior/middle, and high schools; colleges; community programs; and universities. 1/4

Elevator speech In a job search context, a speech (or *pitch*) that lasts about 30 seconds and is meant to persuade someone to give you a job referral or interview. 13/215

Emotional intelligence The capacity individuals have to be aware of, control, and express their own emotions and those emotional responses of other people as a way to handle relationships judiciously and empathetically. 8/132

Employability The position of having the necessary education, training, technical skills, and soft skills to gain new employment. 1/4

Employee absenteeism An employee's absence from work on the date and time they are scheduled to work, sometimes resulting in the workplace's need to find another employee to work. 4/56

Employee involvement A process used by leaders in an organization to involve employees in solving problems, providing new ideas about work processes, and developing policies and procedures. 11/170

Ethical dilemma A situation in which a person is confronted with an action to which there is ethical uncertainty. 12/183

Ethics Principles or standards that a majority of people in society believe should govern behavior. These principles apply to all situations, but in this book, it applies specifically to work situations. 12/185

Ethnic group A category of people with a common place of origin, language, culture, religion, or other common set of traits. 1/3

Etiquette The behaviors a person is expected to display for acceptance by a group in certain situations (also *good manners*). Often this applies to meal times, clothing selections, work meetings, and special occasions (e.g., weddings). 9/149

G

Geolocation The geographic location of an employee determined by an electronic device (often a computer or cell phone). 4/57

Gig economy A labor market in which people provide the labor for one task and are immediately paid when the task is finished. People are not employed but provide a service to whoever is willing to pay for it; e.g., Lyft drivers. 1/8

Grievance procedure A formal procedure created by some workplaces to provide employees a method for appealing a decision by a manager. Specific steps for the procedure are written in personnel policies. 8/133

H

Harassment The act of repeatedly treating people in a manner that offends them or in a way they do not want to be treated—often because of a person's characteristics; e.g., appearance, race, or gender. 9/149

Hardworking An employee who takes personal responsibility to complete a job in an energetic and timely manner. 1/14

Human Resources (HR) A department of an organizational that provides the services to recruit, hire, train, retain, protect, evaluate, and dismiss employees. 2/19

Human relations The behavior and psychology of working with other people (particularly coworkers and leaders) to accomplish a task or achieve a goal. 9/145

I

In-group A group of followers who are willing to go above and beyond the job requirements. Members work well with their leaders and typically receive preferred treatment, more access to the leader, and richer feedback. 8/120

Integrity Being honest, truthful, ethical, and following moral principles in one's actions. 1/11

Initiative The independent actions employees take without being prompted by a leader but can reasonably be expected to result in the approval of leaders. 8/127

J

Jargon The unique terms, acronyms, and phrases developed and used within an organization. 8/122

JIST card An index card-sized paper that contains your job objective, key accomplishments, skills, qualities, and contact information for employers or people in your network. 13/213

Job crafting The process of independently making changes in your job tasks and interactions with coworkers so the job better fits your abilities, preferences, or career goals. 13/199

Job description A written form of communication an employer provides to employees that describes the tasks, responsibilities, and working conditions for each specific job performed in the organization. 6/87

Job-related skills These are precise skills required for a specific job. They may be learned with the help of education, training, or experience; e.g., a firefighter must know how to attach a hose to a fire hydrant. 7/113

Job search The process or series of activities a person uses to find a job. 13/204

L

Labor force All people who are available and want to work. Anyone who is looking for a job or working at a job is a member of the labor force. 1/2

Learning organization An organization that encourages employees to learn and think about their job in new ways and then collectively share this learning in a way that allows all employees to learn from the experience of others. 6/84

Learning style Unique ways each person prefers to learn something new as demonstrated by how well and quickly the person learns. 6/92

Lifelong learning A type of learning that takes place throughout a person's lifetime. It includes formal learning in schools and colleges, and work-related training, on-the-job learning, and informal learning (like reading). 6/83

Locus of control The degree to which people feel they control events and outcomes in their lives. They either feel they control their own lives or that other people and conditions control them. 7/102

M

Mannerism Something a person does repetitively out of habit (often without realizing it), such as specific gestures, movements, voice styles, or facial expressions. 3/51

Meaning in work When an individual finds a job fulfilling to his or her purpose in life. 7/100

Mentor A person who takes a professional interest in advising you on your career goals, such as how to perform well on the job and in your workplace. 13/208

N

Netiquette The behaviors a person is expected to display for acceptance by a group when using electronic communications—particularly when sending work-related communications (email or messaging). 5/80

Networking Becoming acquainted with people's career goals and strengthening relationships with business acquaintances, friends, and family to establish contacts who can help you reach your own career goals or with a job search. 13/204

Nonverbal communication Expressing or enhancing verbal messages through body movement, eye movement, voice qualities, touch, appearance, and even smell. 5/75

O

Orientation The process of introducing new employees to an organization, taking care of necessary paperwork, reviewing policies, and selecting benefits that are offered by an employer. 2/19

Onboarding A series of ongoing activities provided by an organization to help new employees learn to do their job well and feel as though they are part of an organization. 2/19

Online learning Content offered through the Internet that helps people learn, sometimes organized as small amounts of knowledge or skills—sometimes called "modules"—or large amounts of learning that include college courses or degrees. 6/89

On-the-Job Training One-on-one training where a supervisor or coworker explains how to perform a task, shows you how to do it, watches while you practice, and then tells you how well you did in practice. 6/88

Out-group A group of followers who insist on doing only the work required by their job descriptions. 8/120

Organization A group of people organized to accomplish a common purpose or mission. It is a general term that includes corporations, businesses, nonprofit groups, associations, societies, and institutions. 1/1

P

Paralanguage The manner in which words are spoken. It encompasses the tone of the voice, inflection, loudness, speed, and pitch that is used when one is speaking. 5/76

Paycheck A method for paying employees that involves issuing a check in payment for work. 2/27

Payroll card A method for paying employees that involves transferring payment for work from an organization's bank account directly to a card in an employee's possession that can be used like a debit card. 2/28

Performance appraisal A written report that a supervisor makes about an employee's job performance. It typically uses a rating system to evaluate various aspects of an employee's responsibilities. 8/125

Persuasion The ability to convince others to accept your ideas or change their minds or behavior. 9/144

Portfolio A collection of a person's résumé, objects, documents, reports, and other items that demonstrate the individual's work skills and accomplishments. 13/210

Positive attitude A mindset that is optimistic about being able to accomplish tasks and achieve goals by working in harmony with coworkers and leaders. 1/14

Positive psychology A field of psychology that focuses on helping people flourish and become happier. It typically considers how to help people build on their strengths rather than identifying and fixing weaknesses. 7/99

Preferences The values we attach to ideas, things, or people. Parents, friends, teachers, religious and political leaders, significant events, media, and our community influence the development of preferences. 9/141

Problem-solving A process or system used by individuals to discover a solution to problems. 1/14

Probation A period of time, usually a few months, when an employee's performance is monitored to determine if the person can do an adequate job. The person can usually be fired without warning or cause during this time. 13/199

Profit The amount of money an organization has left after selling its products or services and subtracting all the money paid to run the organization. Profit is what owners earn from their business. 1/16

Promotion Advancing to a job that requires more skills or responsibility and usually results in a raise in pay. 13/202

Proxemics Nonverbal communication based on the physical space between people. The closer or further one person stands from another affects the message being communicated. The distance can cause comfort or stress. 5/76

R

Responsibility Successfully completing an assignment, reporting this information to your supervisor, and then looking for other tasks to do. 1/11

S

Safety equipment The items worn to protect your body from being harmed by a job hazard. 3/46

Salary A flat payment per week or month, regardless of hours worked. 13/200

Self-concept The mental image or set of beliefs we have about ourselves. 1/14

Self-control The ability to restrain our thoughts and emotions so we are able to behave in a manner that is consistent with our ideals and beliefs. It can be thought of as willpower or personal discipline. 1/1

Self-esteem How you feel about your abilities and limitations. Your overall opinion of yourself. Healthy self-esteem is feeling good about yourself and believing you deserve the respect of others. 7/99

Self-management skills These skills reflect the control you have over your life: how you plan, implement, change, and evaluate the activities in your life. 7/106

Self-motivation The ability to personally initiate and complete tasks without having other people monitor or encourage the behavior. 1/14

Service economy An economy primarily based on providing services rather than goods. 1/4

Service orientation A skill that involves actively looking for ways to help customers. Workers with this skill listen to customers to learn their wants and needs. 10/167

Social media Websites and applications that allow the sharing of communications and information with other people using computer-based equipment; e.g., Facebook, LinkedIn, Twitter. 5/77

Social skills The personal abilities needed to relate and get along well with individuals and groups of people. 1/14

Soft skills The abilities a person needs to do a job well in addition to the technical skills required for the job; e.g., communication and social skills a plumber needs to work well with customers. 1/1

Software piracy An illegal act of copying or distributing computer software applications without purchasing the applications or having a license to use them. The legal term is called "software copyright infringement." 12/192

Synergy The extra energy and capability that results from a combined group effort to accomplish an objective that goes beyond the combination of people working individually to achieve the same objective. 9/139

T

Tardiness A situation in which an employee fails to arrive at the workplace at a time specified in the person's work schedule. 4/57

Teams A term commonly used in organizations for a group of employees who are established to achieve common tasks and objectives. 9/137

Teamwork Actions and work done by a group of employees to work effectively and accomplish tasks and objectives. 1/12

Temperament The distinctive way you think, feel, and react to the world. Everyone has a unique temperament. 9/142

Time management A skill that consists of organizing and maximizing the productivity of an employee's time at work. It consists of a variety of techniques to use time on a task as efficiently as possible. 4/65

Training The process of teaching a person the knowledge and skills needed to accomplish workrelated tasks. 1/4

Transferable skills These are skills that can be used in many different jobs rather than a specific job; e.g. budget, research, care for people, instruct, operate copiers/printers, write, assemble, and repair. 7/108

V

VUCA An abbreviation that describes the composition of challenges, issues, and problems today's organizations typically encounter—volatility, uncertainty, complexity, and ambiguity. 11/169

W

Wage A specific amount of money earned for each hour worked. 13/200

Whole-part-whole method A method of training where the entire task is demonstrated, then all parts of the task are individually shown, and finally the entire task is presented again. 6/86

Workforce A term used synonymously with labor force but sometimes is used to describe only those people actively employed. 1/2

Index

A

absenteeism
  cost of, 55–56
  excuses for, 58–59
  tips for avoiding, 61–64
Aburdene, Patricia, 91
acne problems, 51
acronyms, 122
active learning, 97. *See also* learning
active listening, 42, 68–70
adaptability, 127
  as basic work skill, 11
adoption leave, 33
adult learners, characteristics of, 85
age of labor force, 144
agricultural industries, percentage of labor force, 4
alarm clocks, 64
alcohol usage, 59, 192
allowances on tax withholding, 27
American Society for Training and Development (ASTD), 11
analysis of data, 171
andragogy, 85
angry customers, 165
appearance, 48–51
Argyris, Chris, 106
asking questions, 123
assertive communication, 72
association, as memorization technique, 86
attendance systems, 57
attire for work, 20–21, 44–48
Automatic Data Processing (ADP) Research Institute, 197
awards in portfolios, 210

B

Bailey, Keith, 160
basic skills, 10–12
bathing, 49

believing in yourself, 101
benefits, 30–36
  cafeteria plans, 30–31, 32
  employee services, 35
  overview of, 30–32
  paid time off, 32–33
  required benefits, 34
  voluntary deductions, 34–35
Benefits and Deductions You Want worksheet, 33
bereavement leave, 33
Blanchard, Ken, 186
blogs, 78
body language, 75–76
Bolles, Richard, 216
bosses. *See* supervisors
brainstorming, 172
breaks
  extending, 126
  policies for, 40
building security, learning on first day, 39–40
business casual attire, 45
business formal attire, 44
business professional attire, 44
business talk versus small talk, 71

C

cafeteria plans, 30–31, 32
calendars for work schedules, 62
calling in sick, 63
Capozzoli, Thomas, 151
career development, 207–209
casual business attire, 45
casual street attire, 45
cell phone policies, 38, 74–75
Chaleff, Ira, 131
character strengths, 104–105
Character Strengths Assessment worksheet, 105
charity donations, 34
cheating employers out of time worked, 190
checklists. *See* worksheets

Check the Benefits Your Employer Provides worksheet, 36
Check Your Verbal Communication Skills worksheet, 71
chewing gum, 51
child support deductions, 34
choosing solutions to problems, 173
citizenship verification, 23
classroom instruction offered by employers, 88
coaching, 124–125
collaboration, 137
communication skills, 53
  active listening, 68–70
  electronic communication, 77–80
  electronic etiquette, 147–148
  importance of, 68
  nonverbal communication, 75–76
  telephone communication, 73–75
  verbal communication, 71–72
  written communication, 76–77
communication systems, learning on first day, 37–38
communication with supervisor, 121–125
  asking questions, 123
  coaching, 124–125
  courageous followership, 130–131
  following instructions, 121–122
  performance appraisals, 129–130
  reporting results, 123–124
companies. *See* organizations
complaints
  from customers, 164–165
  filing, 135
complex problem-solving skills, 179

socialization with coworkers, 60
social media usage, 77–78, 148
Social Security number, 23
Social Security tax, 27
Society for Human Resource
    Management, 17, 197
soft skills, 1
    importance of, 13–14
software piracy, 192
solutions to problems
    in creative thinking, 180
    developing, 171–172
    evaluating, 172–173
    implementing, 174
    selecting, 173
speaking skills, 53
starting conversations, 72
state employment laws, 134
state income tax, 27
status reports to supervisor,
    123–124
stealing from company, 191
stock options, 35
strengths
    building on character
        strengths, 104–105
    evaluating, 116–117
substance abuse, 192
supervisors
    calling when late or absent, 63
    communication with, 121–
        125
        asking questions, 123
        coaching, 124–125
        courageous followership,
            130–131
        following instructions,
            121–122
        performance appraisals,
            129–130
        reporting results, 123–124
    ethical conflicts with, 184
    expectations of, 126–128
    leader-member exchange
        (LMX), 119
    learning job responsibilities
        from, 87
    overview of, 119
    problems with, 132–135
        conflict resolution, 132–133
        disciplinary actions, 133–134
        grievance procedures, 133

        resolving employee rights
            issues, 134–135
    as team leaders, 120–121
supplies and equipment
    learning on first day, 37
    stealing, 191
suspension, 134
synergy, 139
systems skills, 11

T

tardiness, 57
    excuses for, 58–59
    tips for avoiding, 64
tattoos, 50
taxes, withholding, 27
team leaders, supervisors as,
    120–121
team members. *See* coworkers
teamwork
    importance of, 137
    management through, 170
    synergy, 139
teamwork, problem solving via,
    170
technology skills, 11
telephone communication skills,
    73–75
telephone customer service,
    160–162
telephone policies and operation,
    37–38
temperaments, 142–143
temporary workers, 7
texting, 51
thinking about problems, 176
Thinking About Your Education
    worksheet, 6
Thinking Outside the Box work-
    sheet, 175
thinking skills, 11
360-degree feedback, 130
time management, 65–66
time wasting on the job, 190
tools needed on first day, 22
traditionalist preferences, 141
training, offered by employers,
    4, 5
training offered by employers, 88
transcripts in portfolios, 210
transferable skills, 108–113

Transferable Skills Checklist,
    109–113
transferring telephone calls, 162
transportation, tips for, 61
trends, monitoring, 198–199
21st-century skills
    basic skills, 10–12
    best jobs for, 13–14
    how benefit employer, 15–16
    public's view of, 12–13
    skills most needed, 12

U

uncertainty about expectations,
    183
unemployment insurance, 34
unethical behavior
    cost of, 182
    knowledge of others' behavior,
        194
uniforms, 20–21, 45, 46
union contracts, 135
union dues, 34
United States Agency
    for International
    Development (USAID)
    Education, 14
USCIS number, 23

V

vacation leave, 32
values, 141–142
verbal communication skills,
    71–72
viewpoints, considering in prob-
    lem solving, 175–176
violating
    company policies, 194
    confidentiality, 193
violence in workplace, 151–152
visitor entrances, 39
voluntary deductions, 34–35
VUCA (volatility, uncertainty,
    complexity, ambiguity),
    169

W

W-4 (2012) form, 29–30
wages, 200
weaknesses, evaluating, 116–117
weapons restrictions, 39